PARKWAY BYWAYS

**Explore the charming countryside close to
The Blue Ridge Parkway
The Shenandoah National Park
The Great Smoky Mountains National Park**

by

James R. Hinkel

Creative Travel Writing from the Creekhouse

Parkway Publishers, INC.
P. O. Box 3678 • Boone, NC 28607

1998

Library of Congress Cataloging-in-Publication Data
Hinkel, James R.
    Parkway byways: explore the charming countryside close to the Blue Ridge Parkway, the
Shenandoah National Park, and the Great Smoky Mountains National Park / by James R. Hinkel
        p.   cm.
    "Creative travel writing from the Creekhouse."
    Includes bibliographical references and index.
    ISBN 1-887905-07-3
    1. Blue Ridge Parkway Region (N.C. and Va.)--Tours. 2. Automobile travel--Blue Ridge
Parkway Region (N.C. and Va.) 3. Shenandoah National Park Region (Va.)--Tours. 4. Great
Smoky Mountains
National Park Region (N.C. and Tenn.)--Tours   I. Title.
F217.B6H56 1998   97-42177
917.5504'43--dc21   CIP

For my friend, Jim Rhodes

TABLE OF CONTENTS

ACKNOWLEDGMENTS

I gratefully acknowledge and express my profound appreciation to the following people who have helped with this book. Without them, my work would have been much more difficult and would have taken a great deal longer.

Managers and workers at dozens of Welcome Centers, Chambers of Commerce, and Tourist Development Authorities provided extensive information about their communities. These fine people were consistently friendly, helpful, and enthusiastic about my project, and many sent me pictures, which now grace the pages of the book.

Dr. Jim Rhodes, Sandra and Dallas Lassen, and other members of the **Blue Ridge Writer's Group** frequently supplied encouragement, practical advice, and critical appraisal of my writing in general and about the content and organization of *Parkways Byways* in particular.

Jim and Sue Hinkel, my son and daughter-in-law, made many helpful suggestions about the design of the routes and the choice of attractions. They have driven these roads frequently over the years and have a fine appreciation of how to have fun on a weekend or vacation. Many of my explorations occurred before and after visits to their homes in Virginia and Tennessee from my residence in North Carolina.

Rao Aluri and Mary Reichel, owners of Parkway Publishers, were especially helpful in every phase of this work from the beginning. They were both supportive and imaginative in their contributions. I consider them two of my very best friends as well as my publishers. **Patty Wheeler,** editor for Parkway Publishers, made a number of essential corrections in my manuscript and contributed substantially to its quality. **Julie Shissler** frequently helped with editorial assistance and advice. **Lucy Brashear** read an early version of the book and made several useful suggestions.

Bert Dollar, a great photographer, tire dealer, automotive expert, and all-around great fellow, shot the beautiful cover picture of my home town, Jefferson, North Carolina, from the summit of Mount Jefferson. He also contributed several other photographs and, along with **Barbara Farmer** and **Dale and Kathy Osborne** helped me get the pictures ready for publication.

Beth Ball, Dennis Fournier, and Danny Witherspoon, of Bootin' Up Computer, all dear friends and computer wizards of the highest order, offered tons of brilliant advice and kept my computer running perfectly.

Bill May, owner of Stellar Graphics, designed the impressive book cover. Bill is a real genius in the field of computer graphics.

Jo Green, Joanne Kemp, and the rest of the staff at Ashe County Public Library frequently and tirelessly helped me with research information, ideas, and assistance.

Steven J. Peskaitis, President, Chicago Map Corporation, made a significant contribution by providing the computer mapping software that I used, with his generous permission, to generate all of the maps used in the book. Chicago Map Corporation develops, manufactures, and markets mapping software for consumer and business solutions. I found this company's software easy to use, quite versatile, and of the highest quality.

INTRODUCTION

Millions of people visit the Shenandoah National Park, Blue Ridge Parkway, and Great Smoky Mountains National Park every year — the area is a national treasure of scenic beauty. However, many of these visitors, and even local residents, are not aware of the great variety and diversity of byways, towns, and attractions in the surrounding countryside. This book describes nineteen loop trips through this beautiful area, each starting and ending at the Blue Ridge Parkway.

In writing this book, I explored over 200,000 miles of mountain highways in five states: Virginia, West Virginia, North Carolina, Tennessee, and Georgia. Each of these states has designated sections of their highways as unusually scenic. The nineteen loops include and connect portions of these scenic highways with the Blue Ridge Parkway. All of the routes were designed to provide a diverse and contrasting experience of mountains and valleys, open fields and wooded spaces, as well as towns and rural areas. I designed the loops to highlight the scenic, cultural and historical heritage of the mountain regions of southern Appalachia, "heritage tourism" at its best.

All of the places listed are owned or managed by non-profit organizations, government agencies, or are natural wonders. A few places charge a small admission or maintenance fee but most are free. This book will help you plan economical, family-oriented trips and vacations that include a maximum of scenic beauty, education, history, and just plain fun at the lowest possible cost.

The following information is included to help you understand and use this book:

The book is written from a first person, "editorial" point and expresses my opinion about which byways to take, which is the most scenic, and what attractions are worth visiting. You will surely discover many other byways, towns, and attractions of equal interest.

Many travel resources are available at Welcome Centers, Chambers of Commerce, and Forest Service Ranger offices. These are listed first for every town and I urge you to visit them, especially if you plan to spend some time there or stay overnight.

Although the byways are quite different, several towns and attractions are listed more than once. Descriptions of attractions are duplicated in each chapter for your convenience.

Chapter numbers and route numbers are the same. Odd-numbered routes are primarily located on the southeast side of the Parkway and even-numbered routes are on the northwest side. In order to maintain this pattern, I chose not to use a chapter/route 13.

Odd-numbered routes are presented in a clockwise direction and even-numbered routes run counterclockwise. This is not intended to suggest that one direction is better that the other. All of the routes are quite scenic — and quite different — in both directions; you will "double your pleasure" by traveling both ways.

Times to drive each route are not given because this will vary so much with the traveler. An average of 40 miles per hour plus time for stops is a reasonable figure to use.

Since they change so frequently, hours of operation and phone numbers are not listed, except for visitors' centers, where you can quickly get up-to-date information. Many attractions maintain standard "business hours."

Mileage figures used are as accurate as I could make them but depend on where you start and stop. Sources for mileage information frequently disagree: distances quoted in brochures provided by attractions, data on official county and state maps, figures used by computer mapping programs, and my own speedometer often gave different numbers. In general, I used even miles except where tenths of a mile seemed necessary and used the word "about" when the degree of uncertainty was most significant.

Be very careful when exploring the waterfalls listed in the book. A fall could cause a serious or fatal injury.

Some of the towns don't have listed attractions but are especially picturesque, scenic, or historic, and I have included them for that reason.

Parkway Byways contains thousands of details, many of which are in a state of change or transition. Please send me corrections, suggestions, and ideas for improvement to be used in subsequent editions. Anything you send will be greatly appreciated and will be of great service to future readers.

Please send your corrections, suggestions, and comments to:

James R. Hinkel
c/o Parkway Publishers, Inc.
P. O. Box 3678
Boone, NC 28607

CHAPTER 1 - ROUTE 1

Skyline Drive, VA
Front Royal, VA
Charlottesville, VA

ROUTE 1

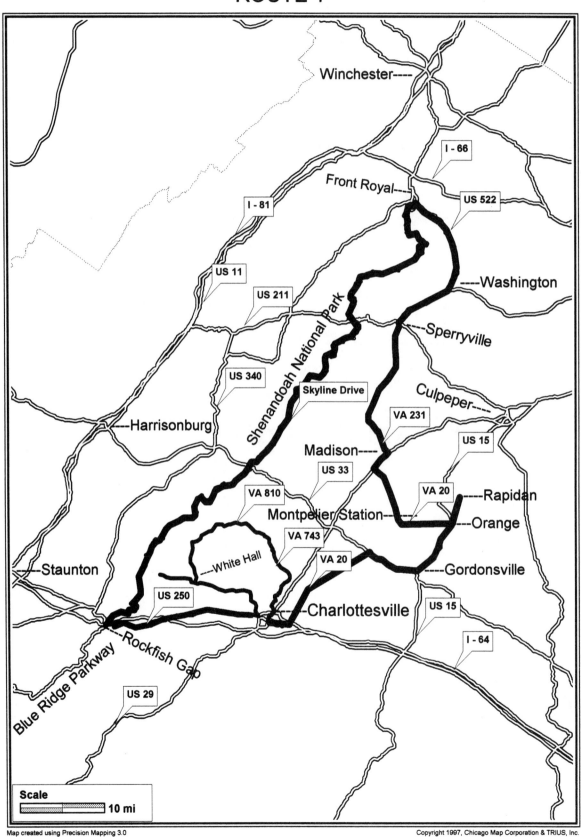

The Skyline Drive - Front Royal - Charlottesville Route tours the Shenandoah National Park and the Virginia counties of Warren, Rappahannock, Madison, Orange, and Albemarle. It is about 330 miles long. Although the byways traveled are quite different, the attractions listed for Charlottesville, Orange, Rapidan, and Gordonsville may also be visited on Route 3. This trip begins and ends at Rockfish Gap, Milepost 0, on the Blue Ridge Parkway and is presented in a clockwise arrangement with the Skyline Drive first.

THE BYWAYS —

This trip starts from Rockfish Gap and continues north on the Skyline Drive across the Shenandoah National Park. The Skyline Drive is a national treasure, similar in many ways to the Blue Ridge Parkway. There are impressive views of the Shenandoah Valley to the west, the Virginia Piedmont to the east, and of the mountains themselves. Many scenic overlooks provide places to park and enjoy the views. The pace is leisurely.

The next section of the trip, from Front Royal to Charlottesville, is through the foothills of the Blue Ridge Mountains and the Piedmont region of north-central Virginia. Almost all of this part of the trip is on scenic Virginia Byways. VA 231, beginning at Sperryville, was described as "One of America's Ten Most Outstanding Scenic Byways" by the organization, *ScenicAmerica*. Fine homes and lavish, well cared for estates are everywhere you look. The classic architecture and landscaping are most impressive.

After you have visited Charlottesville, a very special drive is included next on Route 1. This is a loop through some of the most beautiful part of Albemarle County, a rural area of imposing country homes and farms, backed by panoramic views of the Blue Ridge Mountains.

Many more views of the Piedmont are available as you travel back up the mountains to Rockfish Gap.

THE TOWNS —

All of the towns from Front Royal to Charlottesville are located in an area rich in history and culture. Three American presidents, Thomas Jefferson, James Monroe, and James Madison had homes in the area. All three of them were on the first board of the University of Virginia which was founded and designed by Jefferson. Charlottesville property values are among the highest in the Eastern United States reflecting the great charm, prosperity, and ambience of the area.

The smaller Virginia towns include Front Royal, which is only 66 miles from Washington, D.C.; Orange, the birthplace of Zachary Taylor; and Washington, which was surveyed by George Washington in 1749.

Allow time to drive and/or walk around these interesting old towns. Visit the shops and talk to the friendly people.

THE ATTRACTIONS —

Rockfish Gap, Virginia

1. The Regional Visitors Center is at the junction of the Blue Ridge Parkway, the Skyline Drive, Interstate 64, and US 250. 540-943-5187 or 800-471-3109.

Go 0.2 miles north on the Skyline Drive to:

Skyline Drive & Shenandoah National Park, Virginia

2. Rockfish Gap Entrance Station is at the southern entrance to the Skyline Drive. The Rangers here will give you a great map of the Drive which contains useful information for your trip. Study it carefully; it provides many details about the park such as the history of its formation, a description of the park's geology, and an introduction to the park's animal inhabitants.

The Shenandoah National Park is located along the Blue Ridge Mountains for about 105 miles between Rockfish Gap and Front Royal. The park covers approximately 300 square miles. There are hundreds of miles of hiking trails including 101 miles of the Appalachian Trail. Scenic overlooks are frequent and exciting views of the mountains and valleys occur at every turn.

Park Visitor Centers are located at Mileposts 4.6 and 51 where exhibits, information, and educational programs are provided. The Shenandoah National History Association sells books, slides, maps, postcards, etc.

Family campgrounds are located at Mileposts 51 and 79.5 but hookups for sewage, water, and electricity are not supplied. Back country camping is available and free but requires a permit which you can get at a Visitor Center.

There are seven picnic areas at Mileposts 4.6, 24.1, 36.7, 51, 57.5, 62.8, and 79.5. Each is equipped with tables, drinking water, fireplaces, and restrooms.

Overnight lodging is available at Mileposts 41.7, 51.2, and 57.5 and there are restaurants at Mileposts 41.2 and 51.2. Horseback riding is available at Milepost 41.2.

3. Front Royal Entrance Station is at the northern entrance to the Skyline Drive. This is your last chance to get answers from the Rangers to any questions you have about the park.

Drive 1 mile north on US 340 to:

Front Royal, Virginia

The Virginia Mushroom and Wine Festival in mid-May and the Festival of Leaves in mid-October are special occasions for residents and visitors to Front Royal.

4. The Visitors' Center is at 414 East Main Street in the old Southern Railroad Station. 540-635-3185 or 800-338-2576.

5. The Historic Central Business District is located along Main and Chester Streets. This area has been renovated so that it is now a fine place to walk around and enjoy the old town. Residents are especially proud of the village clock, gazebo, and several nearby historic houses.

6. The Warren County Courthouse is in the Central Business District. Note the historic monuments on the lawn. One is the Confederate Monument which was dedicated on July 4, 1911; the other is the Monument Commemorating Korea and Vietnam.

7. Belle Boyd Cottage is at 101 Chester Street. Belle Boyd lived here while serving as a spy for the Confederate army. The Warren Heritage Society offers tours of the building that feature the story of this famous woman.

8. The Warren Rifles Confederate Museum is on Chester Street next to the Belle Boyd Cottage. It contains weapons, flags, uniforms, and pictures of Civil War soldiers and other noteworthy people. It is operated by the Warren Rifles Chapter of the Daughters of the Confederacy.

9. The Prospect Hill Cemetery on Prospect Street contains the **Mosby Monument** constructed in memory of seven Confederate soldiers who were executed on orders of General Grant. Stonewall Jackson used a hill in this cemetery to direct the battle of Front Royal on May 23, 1862.

Go 19 miles south on US 522 to:

Washington, Virginia

10. Middle Street Gallery, on the corner of Gay and Middle Streets, is a nonprofit cooperative of painters, sculptors, and photographers. Exhibits are changed monthly.

11. First Washington's Museum is on Main Street south of Porter Street. Artifacts are exhibited here that relate to the history of the town of Washington and Rappahannock County. Pick up a copy of the "Visit Historic Washington Virginia" brochure which contains information about the county. For example, the streets still have the same layout designed by the surveyor, later to become President George Washington. The Courthouse and County Jail were both built in 1833.

Drive 7 miles south on US 522 to VA 231, then go 20 miles south on VA 231 to:

1-1 Madison County Courthouse — Photo courtesy of the Madison Chamber of Commerce and Martha Cornwell

Madison, Virginia

Two of Madison's annual festivals are the Taste of the Mountains Main Street Festival in late August - early September and the Madison Harvest Festival in October.

12. The Arcade Visitor Center is on Main Street between Washington and Church Streets, in the Madison Arcade, built in 1790. It is a registered National and Virginia Landmark. Get information about the Walking Tour and other Madison attractions and services. **The Madison County Courthouse**, across the street from the Arcade, is also a registered Historic Landmark.. 540-948-4455

Go 13 miles south on VA 231 to VA 20, then travel 3 miles east on VA 20 to:

13. Montpelier, the home of James Madison, author of the Constitution, and fourth President of the United States. He lived here with his wife Dolley in a house later enlarged by the Dupont family into a 55-room mansion. The oldest part of the house was built when Madison was a child. The estate contains 2,700 acres, a National Landmark Forest, and restored nineteenth-century formal gardens. It is now a National Trust Historic Site.

Drive 4 miles east on VA 20 to:

Orange, Virginia

Orange holds three festivals of note during the year: the Montpelier Wine Festival in early May, the Street Festival in early September, and the Fall Fiber Festival in early October.

14. The Orange County Visitor Center is at 154 Madison Road. 540-672-1653.

15. The James Madison Museum, at 129 Caroline Street, maintains four permanent exhibits that portray Madison's life and times. Special exhibits are also conducted regularly, along with a Hall of Agricultural Progress that displays farm implements and tools. Also known for innovative farming, Thomas Jefferson called his friend Madison, "the best farmer in the world."

16. The Orange County Historical Society is across the street from the Madison Museum at 130 Caroline Street. You may want to pick up a copy of their interesting brochure, "A Brief History of Orange County, Virginia."

17. St. Thomas Episcopal Church is at 119 Caroline Street. Thomas Jefferson designed only one church which was later destroyed. This building, a copy of Jefferson's, was built in 1833-34. Louis Comfort Tiffany designed one of its stained glass windows. Call 540-672-3761 for an appointment to tour the church.

Go 7 miles north on VA 615 to:

Rapidan, Virginia

Here's an interesting story about Rapidan: This village is located on both sides of the Rapidan River. According to a local legend, Civil War soldiers of both armies would fight during the day and then swim the river at night to trade things. The town changed hands fifteen times during the Civil War. No one knows how often the personal possessions changed hands.

18. The Train Station is a noteworthy landmark in this charming town.

19. The Waddell Memorial Church, at 7133 Rapidan Road, is worth visiting for its great architecture. It is considered one of the finest Gothic buildings in Virginia. To tour the church, call 540-672-0334.

Go 16 miles south on VA 615 and US 15 to:

Gordonsville, Virginia

20. The Exchange Hotel and Civil War Museum is at 400 South Main Street. Medical and military exhibits are featured here. Built as a large hotel, it originally served passengers on the Virginia Central Railway. During the Civil War, it became the Gordonsville Receiving Hospital, treating soldiers from both the Confederate and Union armies. Over 70,000 were treated and more than 700 are buried on the grounds.

Drive 6 miles west on US 33 to VA 20, then go 18 miles southwest on VA 20 to:

Charlottesville, Virginia

Among many annual festivals, two are especially noteworthy. The Virginia Festival of the Book, an experience of great interest to writers and readers alike, occurs in mid-March. This important four-day event features lectures, signings, discussions, and fairs. The Crozet Arts and Crafts Festival is in mid-October.

21. The Monticello Visitors Center, at 600 College Drive, is south of Exit 121 — Interstate 64 on VA 20. This Center has an extensive exhibit relating to Thomas Jefferson and his home. More than 400 artifacts are displayed, some discovered recently. A film, *Thomas Jefferson: The Pursuit of Liberty,* is presented in its theater. Ask them for brochures which describe walking tours at the University of Virginia and downtown Charlottesville and for the best places to park around the UVA campus. 804-977-1783.

22. The campus of the University of Virginia, west of downtown Charlottesville, should be a primary destination for any visit. Thomas Jefferson planned the layout and designed the older buildings for this most beautiful and historic place. Some of the buildings and gardens around the central lawn are especially noteworthy. They were originally the homes of the professors and students. This arrangement provided an academic community where social and educational activities were combined. "Serpentine" brick walls enclose gardens behind the buildings. The domed Rotunda, at one end of the original campus, was designed to resemble the Roman Parthenon. The University of Virginia was ranked number one among "Public National Universities" in the September 1, 1997 issue of *U.S. News & World Report* indicating its continuing prominence in the world of education.

23. The Virginia Museum of Natural History, in Clark Hall on the University campus, features permanent exhibits on minerals and fossils and occasional exhibits on natural history and ecology. It is a branch of the Martinsville, Virginia Museum of Natural History.

24. The Virginia Discovery Museum, at 524 East Main Street, provides art and science exhibits for younger children. Opportunities for hands-on involvement, demonstrations, classes, and workshops are available.

Charlottesville, Virginia

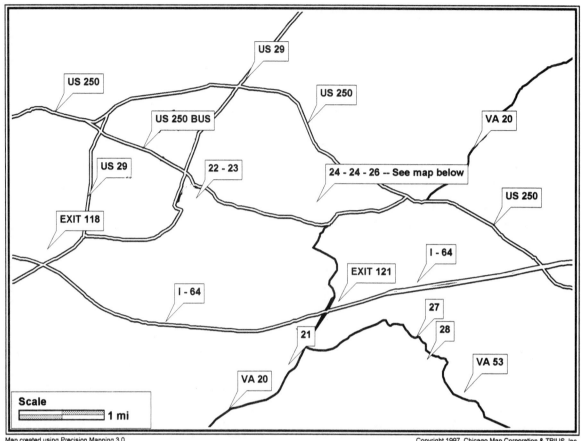

Map created using Precision Mapping 3.0

Charlottesville -- Downtown

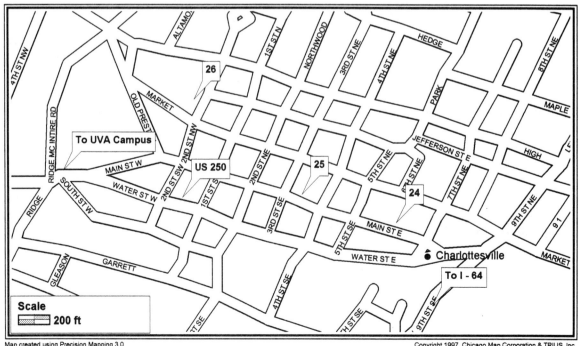

Map created using Precision Mapping 3.0

1-2 Ash Lawn - Highland — Photo courtesy of Ash Lawn - Highland

25.   Historic Court Square, the Downtown Historic District, and the Downtown Mall are special treats for Charlottesville's guests.   Walk where Jefferson, Madison, and Monroe once strolled together and enjoy the wonderful ambience. This friendly place features the brick-paved, automobile-free former Main Street where residents and visitors now shop, eat, and talk.

26.   The McGuffy Art Center, at 201 Second Street NW, is a cooperative of artists, some of whom may be working when you visit.   Their studios are in a building originally used as a school.

27. Monticello is about two miles southeast on VA 53.   Monticello was the home of Thomas Jefferson and is one of the most prestigious historic homes in the United States.   No trip to the Charlottesville area would be complete without a visit here.   The estate   has   magnificent   architecture, extensive landscaping, and an enormous

· (80 by 1000 feet) garden containing over 250 varieties of vegetables and herbs from Jefferson's time.   The house was started in 1768, completely redesigned in 1796, and more-or-less finished and furnished by 1809. Complete guided tours of the house and grounds are included with your admission.

28. Ash Lawn — Highland, the former home of President James Monroe, is near Monticello on VA 795. Consider adding this historic home to your itinerary as a complement to President's Jefferson's masterpiece.

Here is the special scenic drive through rural Albemarle County mentioned in the introduction section above on byways. See the Albemarle County, Virginia map.

Drive 0.4 miles   north of the US 250 Bypass on US 29 to VA 743 (Hydraulic Road). Turn west and follow VA 743 north past   the   Charlottesville   Airport   to

Albemarle County, Virginia

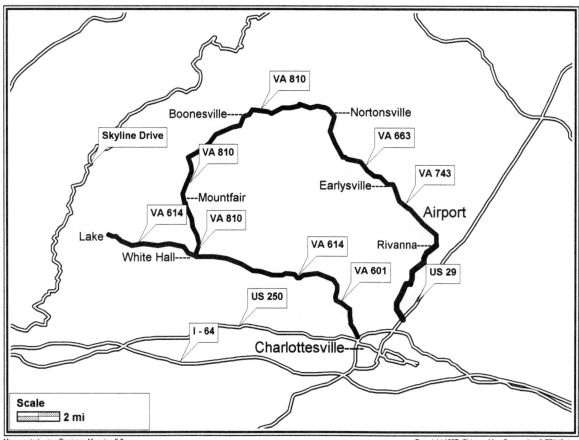

Map created using Precision Mapping 3.0   Copyright 1997, Chicago Map Corporation & TRIUS, Inc.

Earlysville and VA 663. Continue on VA 663 to Nortonsville and VA 810. Turn west on VA 810 and go through Boonesville and Montfair to White Hall and VA 614. Turn west on VA 614 and go along the Moorman River to the Sugar Hollow Reservoir, which serves as the water supply for Charlottesville.

Return to White Hall and continue east on VA 614 and VA 601 to Charlottesville and US 250.

Complete Route 1 by driving 20 miles west on US 250 to the Blue Ridge Parkway — Milepost 0.

Staunton, VA
Cass, WV Scenic Railroad
Goshen Pass, VA

ROUTE 2

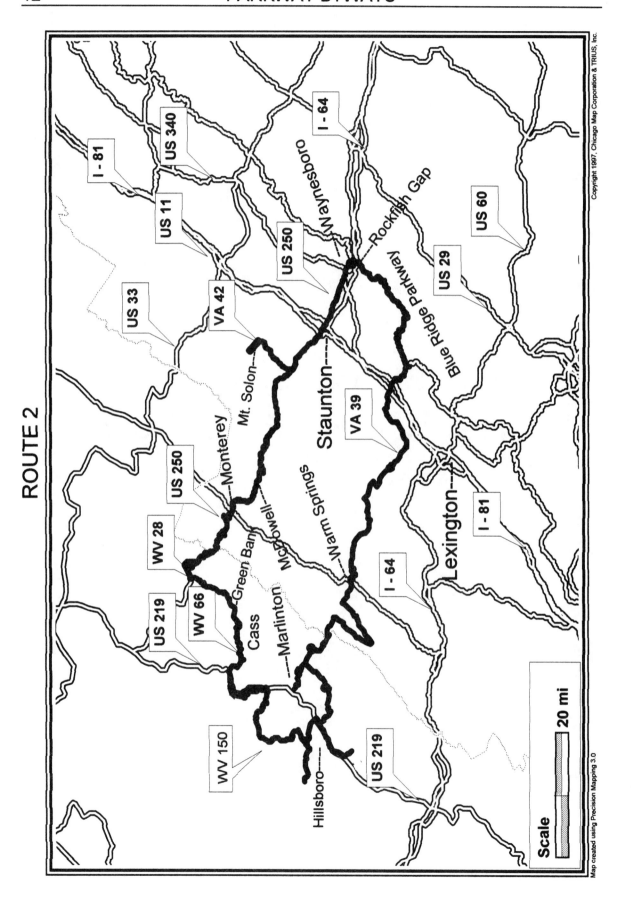

I - 81

US 340

I - 64

Waynesboro

US 11

Rockfish Gap

US 250

US 60

US 33

VA 42

Blue Ridge Parkway

US 29

Mt. Solon

Staunton

Monterey

VA 39

Warm Springs

US 250

McDowell

WV 28

I - 64

Lexington

I - 81

US 219

WV 66

Green Bank

Cass

Marlinton

WV 150

US 219

Hillsboro

Scale

20 mi

T he Staunton - Cass - Goshen Pass Route tours the Virginia counties of Augusta, Highland, Bath, and Rockbridge plus the West Virginia county of Pocahontas. It is about 420 miles long. Ideally, you need to take at least two and perhaps as many as four days to really explore this large area. Route 2 begins at Rockfish Gap, Milepost 0, on the Blue Ridge Parkway and continues in a counterclockwise direction to Milepost 27.2 on the Parkway.

THE BYWAYS —

This trip starts on US 250, crosses the beautiful Shenandoah Valley, and then crosses a series of parallel mountain ranges into West Virginia. These ranges run from southwest to northeast. As the highway runs east to west, the route is a succession of views of dramatic mountains from the valleys followed by sights of peaceful valleys from the mountains. The overall effect is a spectacular scenic experience. The whole area is quite prosperous looking. Three rivers in the area have the unusual names of Cowpasture, Bullpasture, and Calfpasture. US 250 is a scenic Virginia Byway from VA 42 to the West Virginia line.

Pocahontas County, West Virginia roads all run through charming countryside but one section is outstanding. This is the Highland Scenic Highway, a National Forest Scenic Byway. The 22-mile Parkway section, from US 219 to the Cranberry Mountain Visitor Center, goes through an uninhabited mountain area at elevations of 2325 feet to over 4500 feet. It is very much like the Blue Ridge Parkway and Skyline Drive with four overlooks of grand vistas, many trails, public restrooms, etc. This road is limited to recreational traffic.

Most of the rest of Route 2, after you re-enter Virginia, is on a Virginia Byway, VA 39. The trip is back over the same series of mountain ranges you encountered on the way to West Virginia. The Goshen Pass is a special scenic surprise, where VA 39 and a breathtaking section of the wild Maury River wind through a narrow gorge. . It is not only something to see, however. There are plenty of places to park, picnic, and get in the river to swim, tube, and climb over the gigantic rocks. You could spend a whole day here, there are so many fun things to do.

THE TOWNS —

All of the towns in this area are interesting in their own right but a few stand out. The Augusta County towns of Waynesboro and Staunton are both over 200 years old. Waynesboro is the smaller of the two and is known for its neat neighborhoods, great parks and interest in the arts. The Battle of Waynesboro in 1865 ended the control of the South in the Shenandoah Valley.

Staunton, founded in 1747, is noteworthy for its five National Historic Districts, many museums, and fine architecture. It is one of the most unique towns covered in this book.

Staunton, Virginia

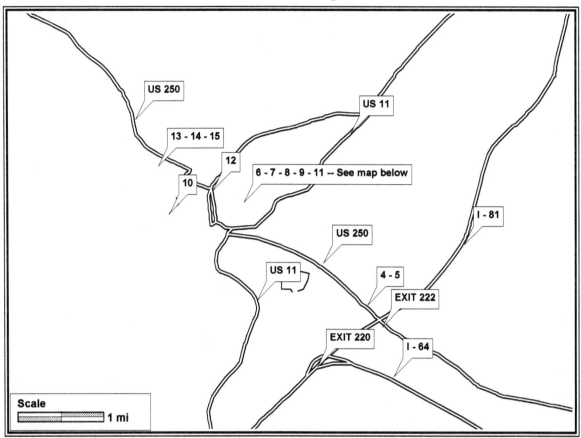

Scale 1 mi

Staunton -- Downtown

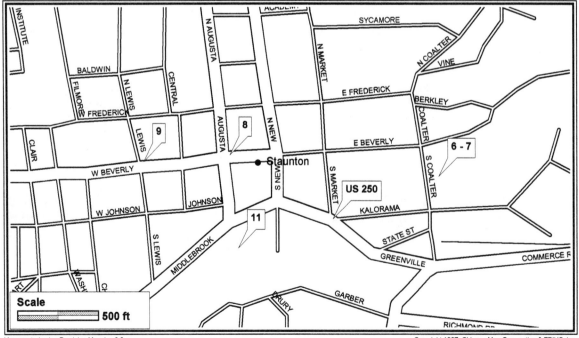

Scale 500 ft

You will want to spend a lot of time here, especially in the downtown area, in order to capture its essence.

Monterey and surrounding Highland County, Virginia is also a special place because of its picturesque and remote beauty. The 3,000 county residents are very friendly and are glad to tell visitors about their community. Monterey is about 50 miles from a city of any size and in a county with the highest mean elevation of any county east of the Mississippi River. Linger awhile and talk to some people about local places like Seldom Seen Road, Possum Trot, the Devil's Backbone, and anything concerning maple syrup. If you have a little extra time, drive awhile on the local country roads. Park your car and stroll up and down Main Street. You will store up some great memories and will probably plan to return as soon as you can.

Marlinton, in the West Virginia County of Pocahontas, is the cultural and business center for a large and remote area. It was founded as Marlin's Bottom in 1747 and was the first settlement west of the Allegheny Mountains. It is located along the banks of the scenic Greenbrier River. You will enjoy walking and driving around this great little town.

THE ATTRACTIONS —

Rockfish Gap, Virginia

1. The Regional Visitors Center is at the junction of the Blue Ridge Parkway, the Skyline Drive, Interstate 64, and US 250. 540-943-5187 or 800-471-3109.

Drive 4 miles west on US 250 to:

Waynesboro, Virginia

Visit Waynesboro in July for the Summer Extravaganza and early in October for the annual Fall Foliage Festival.

2. The Association of Virginia Artisans Fine Craft Gallery is at 327 West Main Street. This is the state headquarters of the Association. Art works of the members are on display at the Gallery. Objects made of clay, fiber, glass, metal, paper, and wood are included. A section of the Gallery is set aside monthly to feature a particular artisan.

3. The Shenandoah Valley Art Center, at 600 West Main Street, is a place for local and regional artists to display their works. The Center also presents music and dramatic programs and conducts art classes and workshops for adults and children. Several of the artists have studios at the center. The Shenandoah Valley Art Center is associated with the Virginia Museum of Fine Arts.

Go 12 miles west on US 250 to:

Staunton, Virginia

The Frontier Festival, held on the first weekend in September, is a craft show with music, a food fair, and a dance festival.

Staunton's African American Heritage Festival features both African American and traditional African history, music, dance, food, jewelry, paintings, and clothing. This celebration takes place in Staunton's Wharf area on the third weekend in September.

4. The Staunton-Augusta Visitors Center is just west of Exit 222 — Interstate 81 at the Museum of American Frontier Culture. 540-332-3972 or 800-332-5219.

5. The Museum of American Frontier Culture is also located just west of Exit 222 on US 250. This unique museum consists of reconstructions of four historic working farms — three from Europe and one from Botetourt County, Virginia. Of the European farms, one is from England, one is from Germany, and one is from Northern Ireland. All three present the cultures and lifestyles of people who settled the Shenandoah Valley many years ago. The American farm is a composite of the European influences as modified by the American environment. All four farms include authentic buildings, furnishings, animals, crops, gardens, fences, etc. — all explained and interpreted by guides in period costumes. Demonstrations of skills and crafts such as butchering, spinning, baking, candle making, hearth cooking, quilting, and many others are frequently presented. If a picture is worth a thousand words, the sights, sounds, and smells on these farms are worth a thousand volumes.

6. The Staunton Welcome Center is at the Woodrow Wilson Birthplace and Museum at 18-24 Coalter Street, just off Beverly Street. Staunton has — believe it or not — five National Historic Districts. Get walking tour maps of these wonderful areas at this Welcome Center. Here's a chance to get some exercise and see one of Virginia's finest towns up close. 540-332-3971.

7. The Woodrow Wilson Birthplace and Museum is also at 18-24 North Coalter Street. Celebrating its 150th anniversary, this was the home of our 28th President. It has been restored to look as it did during the Civil War, and portrays the lifestyle of that period. Interpreters will guide you through the home and grounds. The museum is the

2-1 Woodrow Wilson Birthplace — Photo courtesy of
Staunton Convention and Visitors Center

only one exhibiting Mr. Wilson's memorabilia on a permanent basis. Check out the Pierce-Arrow limousine he used while at the White House.

8. The Museum of Bank History. This museum is located in the Crestar Bank at Beverly and Augusta Streets. A special feature is the ornate lobby. A brochure, available from any teller, gives you more information about this unusual place.

9. The Trinity Episcopal Church, at Beverly and Lewis Streets, is noted for its distinctive architecture and stained glass windows designed by Louis Comfort Tiffany.

10. The Thornrose Cemetery is on Beverly Street just west of the historic downtown area. There is an interesting Civil War Memorial here in addition to the special ambience of a very old cemetery.

11. The Restored C&O Train Station is at South Augusta and Middlebrook Streets. It not only serves as the Amtrak station but is an important landmark in its own right. The architecture and furnishings of this historic building will take you back to another era.

12. The Jumbo Antique Fire Engine, exhibited at 500 North Augusta, is a fun thing to see. The restored 1911 Robinson Pumper is displayed here for the delight of the young and the young at heart. It's the last one around anywhere.

13. The Statler Brothers maintain an office and museum at 501 Thornrose Ave. Visit here to see items collected during the Statler Brothers' long career as popular musicians. You may even see them in person as they hurry about their work.

14. Gypsy Hill Park on US 250 West and Thornrose Avenue is an extremely large and interesting place to picnic, swim, play golf, attend a band concert or art show, or just relax and take it easy. This is a fantastic city park, exceptional in every way!

15. The Staunton-Augusta Art Center is located near the entrance to Gypsy Hill Park in a former pump house. This is a setting where local artists give and take classes in various art techniques and exhibit their work. Others come for lectures or music. A major art show is a special attraction each year in May.

Go 8 miles west on US 250 to:

Churchville, Virginia

Turn right here and travel 8 miles north on VA 42 to VA 731, then drive 2 miles north on VA 731 to:

Mt. Solon, Virginia

16. Natural Chimneys Regional Park is located 0.5 miles north of Mt. Solon on VA 731. The outstanding feature here is a group of enormous rock formations rising from the ground like giant chimneys. They are the result of the forces of nature operating in what was once a great ocean. The Park also has a 136-site campground with hookups, a swimming pool, camp store, laundry facilities, playgrounds, and hot showers. There are places to hike, bike, and picnic.

From the Natural Chimneys Park, go north on VA 731 for 0.5 miles. Turn west on VA 730, then go 3 miles to the Stokesville junction. Turn northwest on VA 718 and go 1 mile to FDR 95. Take FDR 95 west for 2 miles to the Todd Lake turn-off.

17. Todd Lake Recreation Area is a USDA Forest Service facility that has 20 campsites (tent pad, grill, and picnic table only) a lake for swimming and boating, a picnic area, and several good trails. Drinking water, flush toilets, and warm showers are available. A dump station is located near the entrance.

Go 4.6 miles southwest past the Todd Lake turn-off on FDR 95 (gravel) to FDR 95B, then go 1 mile southeast on FDR 95B to:

18. North River Campground. This is a primitive USDA Forest Service facility with a hand water pump and pit toilets. It is located on the banks of the North River and provides an opportunity for fishing, hiking, and observing wildlife.

Return to FDR 95. If you are interested in boating or fishing (no gasoline motors), turn southwest on FDR 95, cross a ridge, and continue about 2 miles to:

19. Elkhorn Lake, where you may use your boat or fish from the platform provided.

Return to Mt. Solon, then drive 10 miles south on VA 731 and VA 42 to US 250. Turn northwest and go 6 miles on US 250 to VA 715. Turn north on VA 715 and then west on FDR 348.1. Follow the signs about 0.5 miles to:

20. Braley Pond, a USDA Forest Service picnic area with opportunities for hiking and fishing in the 5-acre pond. There are picnic tables, grills, drinking water, and toilets.

Return to US 250, then drive 5 miles northwest to:

21. Mountain House, a picnic and day use area managed by the USDA Forest Service. You can park here and hike or fish for trout in the nearby Ramseys Draft Wilderness Area.

Go 2 miles northwest on US 250 to:

22. The Confederate Breastworks, a historic site from the Civil War period. Confederate soldiers built fortifications here to protect their position on Shenandoah Mountain. There is a great view of the Cowpasture River Valley from an observation point.

Drive 12 miles northwest on US 250 to:

McDowell, Virginia

23. The McDowell Battlefield, near McDowell, was the site of Stonewall Jackson's first victory in the 1862 Valley Campaign.

Travel 10 miles northwest on US 250 to:

Monterey, Virginia

The Highland County Maple Festival attracts about 70,000 people to Monterey every year. Visitors enjoy watching the production of the delicious syrup, a large craft show, and a variety of good food in an atmosphere of beautiful sights and pleasant people. The **Little Highland Maple Museum**, highlighting artifacts relating to syrup making, is open during the festival and throughout the year.

Go 17 miles northwest on US 250, **crossing into West Virginia,** to:

24. Old House Run Recreation Area. This USDA Forest Service picnic area also offers fishing.

2-2 View of Blue Grass Valley near Monterey, Virginia
Photo courtesy Highland County Chamber of Commerce and Irene Chapman

Drive 6 miles northwest on US 250 to WV 28/WV 92, then go 9 miles southwest on WV 28/WV 92 to:

Green Bank, West Virginia

25.   The National Radio Astronomy Observatory is a leading center for study of the science of radio astronomy.   It is operated by Associated Universities for the National Science Foundation.   It is the largest steerable radio telescope in the world at more than 300 feet across and cost over 75 million dollars. Visitors are welcome and tours are provided.

Drive 2 miles southwest on WV 28/ WV 92 to WV 66, then go 5 miles west on WV 66 to:

Cass, West Virginia

26. The Cass Scenic Railroad State Park is the site of an excursion train and small town which make up a most unusual State Park. Antique Shay steam locomotives pull the train to a viewing area over 4,000 feet high, the second highest spot in the state. These trains once served the logging industry.   The town of Cass has been restored and the park provides places to stay in the old houses. These cottages, which feature fully equipped kitchens, bathrooms, and linens, are rented by the day. No pets are allowed.   For reservations or more information, call 1-800-CALL WVA.

Cass Scenic Railroad State Park is one of the most exciting and interesting attractions in this book. Allow plenty of time to enjoy it to the fullest.

Go 11 miles west on WV 66 to US 219, then drive 14 miles southwest on US 219 to:

27. WV 150 — The Highland Scenic Highway, a National Forest Scenic Byway. The 22-mile Parkway section, from US 219 to the Cranberry Mountain Visitor Center, goes through an uninhabited mountain area at elevations of 2325 feet to over 4500 feet. It is very much like the Blue Ridge Parkway and Skyline Drive with four overlooks of grand vistas, many trails, public restrooms, etc. This road is limited to recreational traffic.

Go 21 miles northwest, then south on WV 150 to:

28. Cranberry Glades Botanical Area. This is West Virginia's largest area of bogs, which are unusual wetlands found normally in the northern United States and Canada. Since the ground is wet and spongy, the plants growing here are uncommon in the mountains. A boardwalk is provided for visitors so the fragile area will not be damaged.

Drive 1 mile south on WV 150 to:

29. Cranberry Mountain Visitor Center, which is at the junction of WV 150 and WV 39. This Center is operated by the USDA Forest Service and is a part of Monongahela National Forest. An exhibit hall and audio visual programs present information about the forest ecosystem, wildlife, and local history. Books, post cards, maps, and other items relating to the area are for sale.

Travel 6 miles west on WV 39 to:

30. Falls of Hills Creek Scenic Area, just off WV 39. Three waterfalls drop 25, 45, and 63 feet, the latter being the second highest waterfall in West Virginia. A 3/4 mile trail leads from the parking area to viewing platforms. WV 39, from Cranberry Mountain to the Falls of Hills Creek, is also part of the Highland Scenic Highway.

Return to Cranberry Mountain Visitor Center, then go 6.6 miles southeast on WV 39 to US 219. Drive 2.5 miles southwest on US 219 to:

Hillsboro, West Virginia

31. The Pearl S. Buck Birthplace is on US 219. The house was built in 1892 and contains a museum, furniture, and other possessions of Pearl S. Buck and her family. Her book, *The Good Earth,* won the Pulitzer Prize for Literature in 1932. She also won the Nobel Prize for Literature in 1938. She is the only American woman to receive both awards.

Travel 2 miles southwest on US 219 to WV 20, then go 3 miles south on WV 20 (Locust Creek Road) to:

32. The Locust Creek Bridge, the only covered bridge remaining in Pocahontas County. It is also one of the very few covered bridges around anywhere.

Return to US 219, then drive 2 miles southwest to:

33. Droop Mountain Battlefield State Park, site of West Virginia's largest Civil War battle which occurred on November 6, 1863. The battle was fought between 1,700 Confederate soldiers under the command of General J. Echols and 3,500 Union troops under the command of General W. W. Averell. Confederate earth works, exhibits, and a museum are available for visitors. You may also want to walk on some of the many trails to see the field of battle up close. Get a map and trail guide at the park office.

Go 3.5 miles south on US 219 to a Beartown State Park sign, then drive about 1 mile east on Beartown Road to:

34. Beartown State Park. This 107-acre natural area features some of the most unusual rock formations I have ever seen. Deep crevasses in the rocks look as if giant creatures had walked here for millions of millions of years. The effect is startling, to say the least. An added bonus is hundreds of feet of boardwalks over and through the "canyons." The park also features a picnic area and restrooms.

Return to Hillsboro on US 219, drive 1.3 miles northeast to the Watoga State Park sign, then go about 9 miles southeast on WV 27/WV 21 to:

35. Watoga State Park, which covers more than 10,000 acres. This is West Virginia's largest State Park and has just about every possible recreational feature including campgrounds (some sites with electrical hookups), picnic tables, central bathhouses, and coin-operated laundry

equipment. The Park also offers a restaurant, a commissary, a lake, and rental cabins (call 1-800-CALL WVA for reservations) along with horses for adults, ponies for children, paddleboats, rowboats, and miles and miles of hiking trails.

Drive northeast on WV 21 to WV 39 at Hunterville. (Mileage will depend on where you start in the park — about 11 miles). Go 6.5 miles northwest on WV 39 to:

Marlinton, West Virginia

The Pioneer Days Festival, held in mid-July, celebrates Marlinton's heritage with parades, woodchopping contests, bluegrass music, clogging, crafts, a liars contest, wagon rides, and other fun things for the whole family. Late September brings the Roadkill Cook-off and the Autumn Harvest Festival.

2-3 The Former C&O Railroad Station — Photo courtesy of the Pocahontas County Tourist Commission and Stephen J. Shaluta, Jr.

36. The Pocahontas County Tourist Commission is on WV 39 in the former C&O Railroad Station. If you want to know more about the Marlinton area, you can obtain a copy of the "Southern Pocahontas County Historical Audio Tour," a cassette tape available at the Tourist Commission. 800-336-7009.

This is a good place to decide whether you want to explore:

37. The Greenbrier River Trail, which runs past the Tourist Commission building. This is a rail-to-trail conversion starting at Cass and continuing along the Greenbrier River for 75 miles south to the White Sulphur Springs area. Although the trail runs through the mountains, it is quite level and suitable for family hiking, biking, and cross country skiing. You can get more information on the trail at the Tourist Commission.

This trail is a unique opportunity to see some beautiful West Virginia countryside up close. You experience the River and see the mountains at the same time. Plan to spend a day or two on the trail if you can.

38. The Pocahontas County Historical Museum is in a house on US 219 just south of WV 39. It is operated by the Pocahontas County Historical Society and contains displays of local memorabilia from Indian days to the present.

39. The Marlinton Ranger District, USDA Forest Service, is just off WV 39 on Cemetery Road at the eastern edge of Marlinton. If you are a Civil War buff, get a copy of the "Monongahela National Forest Civil War Auto Tour" here. Several sites listed are in Pocahontas County.

Drive 20 miles southeast on WV 39, **crossing back into Virginia,** to VA 600. Continue 7 miles southwest on VA 600 to:

40. Lake Moomaw Recreation Area, which includes Bolar Flat Marina, three picnic areas, Bolar Mountain Beach, and two campgrounds. Drinking water, flush toilets, and a trailer dump station are also available.

Go 6 miles northeast on VA 603 to VA 687. (VA 603 runs along a beautiful section of Lake Moomaw but is gravel and narrow in places. You can also return to VA 39 on VA 600.) Travel 3 miles northeast on VA 687 to VA 39, then go 3 miles southeast on VA 39 to US 220. Drive 4 miles southwest on US 220 to:

Hot Springs, Virginia

Hot Springs celebrates the Fourth of July with an arts and crafts festival called Bath Sellabration.

41. The Bath County Chamber of Commerce is in the Virginia Building on US 220 in downtown Hot Springs. Get information here on walking tours and bathing in the warm water pools that Bath County is famous for. 540-839-5409 or 800-628-8092.

Travel 4 miles northeast on US 220 to:

Warm Springs, Virginia

42. The Bath County Historical Museum is on the Courthouse Square. Artifacts of Bath County are displayed with a focus on the Civil War and Indians. A genealogy library attracts those interested in former residents of this part of Virginia.

Drive 27 miles southeast on VA 39 to:

43. Goshen Pass, a special scenic surprise, where VA 39 and a breathtaking section of the wild Maury River wind through a narrow gorge. It is not only something to see, however. There are plenty of places to park, picnic, and get in the river to swim, tube, and climb over the gigantic rocks. You could spend a whole day here, there are so many fun things to do.

Go 6 miles southeast through Rockbridge Baths to VA 252, then travel 7 miles northeast to VA 606. Drive 5 miles east on VA 606 to:

44. The Cyrus McCormick Farm, where Cyrus McCormick first demonstrated his invention, the mechanical reaper, in 1831. McCormick later moved to Chicago where he started the International Harvester Co. The farm is now a research station for Virginia Tech and is open to the public. A restored blacksmith shop, museum, and gristmill are featured.

Drive 6 miles southeast on VA 606, then VA 56 to the Blue Ridge Parkway — Milepost 27.2.

2-4 The Cyrus McCormick Farm — Photo courtesy of
Lexington/Rockbridge County Tourism

CHAPTER 3 - ROUTE 3

Charlottesville, VA
Scottsville, VA
Crabtree Falls, VA

ROUTE 3

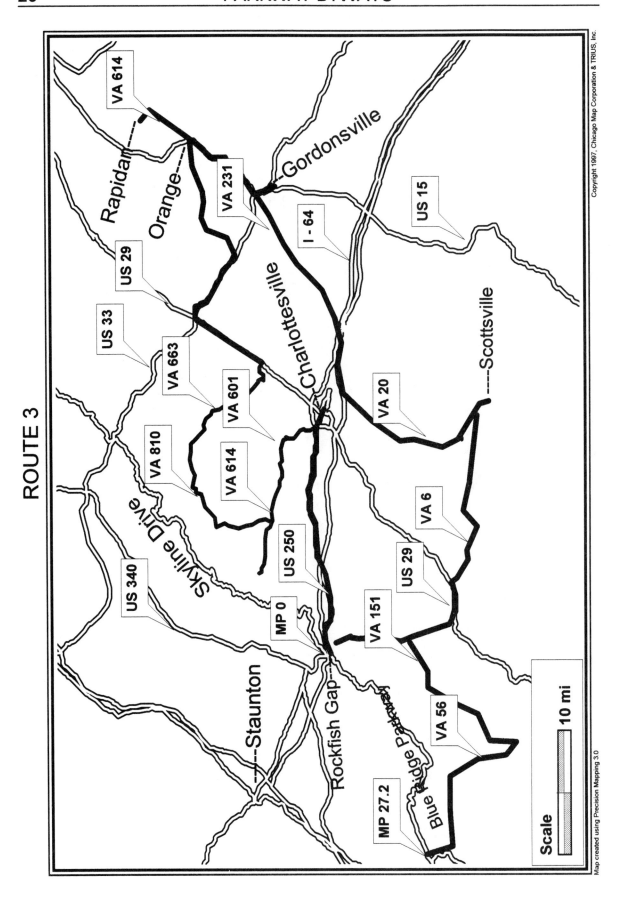

Scale

10 mi

The Charlottesville - Scottsville - Crabtree Falls Route tours the Virginia counties of Albemarle, Orange, and Nelson. It is about 360 miles long. Although the byways traveled are quite different, the attractions listed for Charlottesville, Orange, Rapidan, and Gordonsville may also be visited on Route 1. This trip begins at Rockfish Gap, Milepost 0, on the Blue Ridge Parkway and continues in a clockwise direction to Milepost 27.2 on the Parkway.

THE BYWAYS —

This trip starts on US 250 and travels east toward Charlottesville. You start at a mountain pass and go steadily downhill through the foothills to the Virginia Piedmont far below. There are frequent long range views extending to Richmond on a clear day. This section of US 250 is a scenic Virginia Byway.

After you have explored Charlottesville, you have a special treat in store. The route travels for miles through some of the most impressive rural scenery covered in this book. These are not just farms, they are estates with grand houses, landscaped grounds, manicured fields, fine horses — and there are hundreds of them. All are different and many are outstanding examples of gracious country living. The Blue Ridge Mountains rising in the west provide a perfect backdrop. Several sections of these roads are designated Scenic Roads.

South of Charlottesville, the route runs through the Piedmont and then back up into the mountains. These mountain to valley (and valley to mountain) transition areas provide some of the most dramatic scenic views, perhaps for the same reason that takeoffs and landings are the most interesting experiences in flying.

The trip continues with two more of these "transitions". All the rest of Route 3, starting at Charlottesville and ending at Milepost 27.2 on the Parkway, is on Virginia Byways.

Here is some local Nelson County history. These roads run through an area that has an unusual claim to fame. Hurricane Camille dropped a world record 46 inches of rain during a six hour period in 1969. Entire mountains were washed into the valleys, property damage was severe, and more than 100 people died as a result of the storm. You will see little if any evidence of this disaster now, reflecting the difficult and tireless efforts of local residents in rebuilding their homes and farms.

THE TOWNS —

Charlottesville is the most prominent town on this route and provides the largest selection of things to see and do. It has an outstanding collection of historical, cultural, educational, business, and recreational opportunities — all in a setting of great beauty and prosperity. It is the ideal "college town."

Charlottesville, Virginia

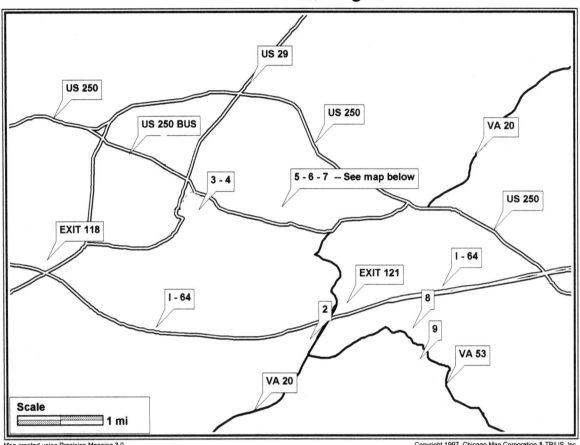

Charlottesville -- Downtown

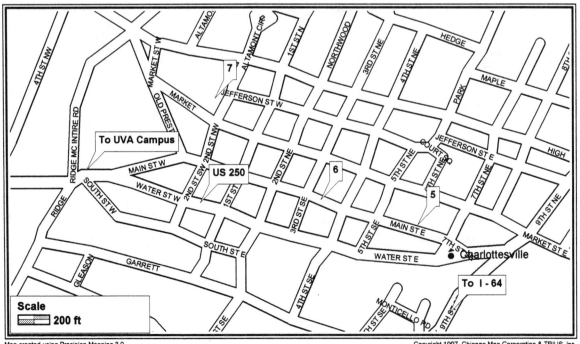

The smaller towns of Orange, Gordonsville, Scottsville, and even smaller villages are pleasant places to visit. Walk and drive around, shop, talk to the friendly people, and soak up the wonderful small town atmosphere.

THE ATTRACTIONS —

Rockfish Gap, Virginia

1. The Regional Visitors Center is at the junction of the Blue Ridge Parkway, the Skyline Drive, Interstate 64, and US 250. 540- 943-5187 or 800-471-3109.

Drive 21 miles east on US 250 to:

Charlottesville, Virginia

Among the many annual festivals in Charlottesville, two are especially noteworthy. The Virginia Festival of the Book, an experience of great interest to writers and readers alike, occurs in mid-March. This important four-day event features lectures, signings, discussions, and fairs. The Crozet Arts and Crafts Festival is in mid-October.

2. The Monticello Visitors Center, at 600 College Drive, is south of Exit 121 — Interstate 64 on VA 20. This Center has an extensive exhibit relating to Thomas Jefferson and his home. More than 400 artifacts are displayed, some discovered recently. A film, *Thomas Jefferson: The Pursuit of Liberty,* is presented in its theater. Ask them for brochures which describe walking tours at the University of Virginia and downtown Charlottesville and for the best places to park around the UVA campus. 804-977-1783.

3-1 The Rotunda - University of Virginia Campus — Photo courtesy of the Charlottesville/Albemarle Convention and Visitors Bureau

3.   The campus of the University of Virginia, west of downtown Charlottesville, should be a primary destination for any visit. Thomas Jefferson planned the layout and designed the older buildings for this most beautiful and historic place. Some of the buildings and gardens around the central lawn are especially noteworthy. They were originally the homes of the professors and students. This arrangement provided an academic community where social and educational activities were combined. "Serpentine" brick walls enclose gardens behind the buildings. The domed Rotunda, at one end of the original campus, was designed to resemble the Roman Parthenon. The University of Virginia was ranked number one among "Public National Universities" in the September 1, 1997 issue of *U.S. News & World Report* indicating its continuing prominence in the world of education.

4.   The Virginia Museum of Natural History, in Clark Hall on the University Campus, features contains permanent exhibits on minerals and fossils and occasional exhibits on natural history and ecology. It is a branch of the Martinsville, Virginia Museum of Natural History.

5.   The Virginia Discovery Museum, at 524 East Main Street, provides art and science exhibits for younger children. Opportunities for hands-on involvement, demonstrations, classes, and workshops are available.

6.   Historic Court Square, the Downtown Historic District, and the Downtown Mall are special treats for Charlottesville's guests. Walk where Jefferson, Madison, and Monroe once strolled together and enjoy the wonderful ambience. This friendly place features the brick-paved, automobile-free former Main Street where residents and visitors now shop, eat, and talk.

7.   The McGuffy Art Center, at 201 Second Street NW, is a cooperative of artists, some of whom may be working when you visit. Their studios are in a building originally used as a school.

8. Monticello is about two miles southeast on VA 53. Monticello was the home of Thomas Jefferson and is one of the most prestigious historic homes in the United States. No trip to the Charlottesville area would be complete without a visit here. The estate has great architecture, extensive landscaping, and an enormous (80 by 1000 feet) garden. This garden contains over 250 varieties of vegetables and herbs from Jefferson's time. The house was started in 1768, completely redesigned in 1796, and more-or-less finished and furnished by 1809. Complete guided tours of the house and grounds are included with your admission.

9.   Ash Lawn -- Highland, the former home of President James Monroe, is near Monticello on VA 795. Consider adding this historic home to your itinerary as a complement to Mr. Jefferson's masterpiece.

Now for the special drive I promised in the section on byways above. This is a trip through the rural area of northern Albemarle and western Orange Counties. There are hundreds of fine farms and country estates located along scenic roads with a mountain backdrop.

The Albemarle County map shows the first portion of this route, a loop starting and ending on US 29, which is about 44 miles long. Start at the junction of US 250, US 29, and VA 601 in northwest Charlottesville. Drive north on VA 601, then west on VA 614 to the village of White Hall. Continue west on VA 614 along the Moorman River to the Sugar Hollow Reservoir which serves as the water supply

Albemarle County, Virginia

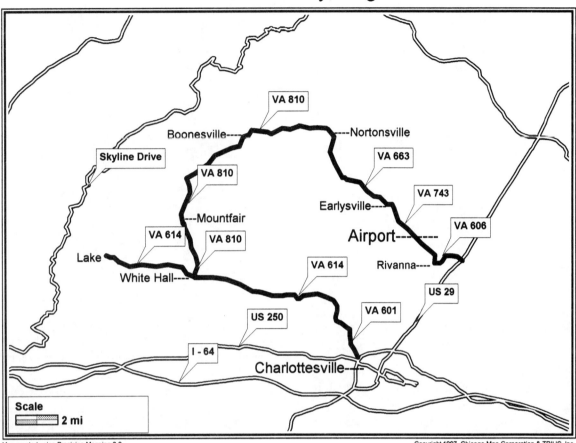

Map created using Precision Mapping 3.0

for the city of Charlottesville. There is a good place to picnic along the lake. Return to White Hall, then go northeast on VA 810 through Mountfair, Boonesville, and Nortonsville. Turn southeast on VA 663, to Earlysville. Continue on VA 743, VA 606, and VA 649 past the Charlottesville Airport to US 29.

Continuing on Route 1 through the area of beautiful farms and estates, go 8 miles northeast on US 29 to Ruckersville, then drive 7 miles southeast on US 33 to Barboursville and VA 20. Travel 8 miles northeast on VA 20 to:

10.   Montpelier, the home of James Madison, author of the Constitution, and ourth president of the United States. He lived here with his wife Dolley, in a house later enlarged by the Dupont family into a 55-room mansion. The oldest part of the house was built when Madison was a child. The estate contains 2,700 acres, a National Landmark Forest, and restored nineteenth-century formal gardens. It is now a National Trust Historic Site.

Go 4 miles east on VA 20 **to:**

3-2 Montpelier - Photo courtesy of the Orange County Visitors Bureau

Orange, Virginia

Orange holds three festivals of note during the year: the Montpelier Wine Festival in early May, The Street Festival in early September, and the Fall Fiber Festival in early October.

11. The Orange County Visitor Center is at 154 Madison Road. 540-672-1653.

12. The James Madison Museum, at 129 Caroline Street, maintains four permanent exhibits that portray Madison's life and times. Special exhibits are also conducted regularly along with a Hall of Agricultural Progress that displays farm implements and tools. Also known for innovative farming, Thomas Jefferson called his friend Madison, "the best farmer in the world."

13. The Orange County Historical Society is across the street from the Madison Museum at 130 Caroline Street. You may want to pick up a copy of their interesting brochure, "A Brief History of Orange County, Virginia."

14. St. Thomas Episcopal Church is at 119 Caroline Street. Thomas Jefferson designed only one church which was later destroyed. This building, a copy of Jefferson's, was built in 1833-34. Louis Comfort Tiffany designed one of its stained glass windows. Call 540-672-3761 for an appointment to tour the church.

Drive 7 miles north on VA 615 to:

Rapidan, Virginia

Here's an interesting story about Rapidan: This village is located on both sides of the Rapidan River. According to a local legend, Civil War soldiers of both armies would fight during the day and then swim the river at night to trade things. The town changed hands fifteen times during the Civil War. No one knows how often the personal possessions changed hands.

15. The Train Station is a noteworthy landmark in this charming town.

16. The Waddell Memorial Church, at 7133 Rapidan Road, is worth visiting to see

CHARLOTTESVILLE - SCOTTSVILLE - CRABTREE FALLS

CHARLOTTESVILLE - SCOTTSVILLE - CRABTREE FALLS 33

its great architecture. It is considered one of the finest Gothic buildings in Virginia. To tour the church, call 540-672-0334.

Travel 16 miles south on VA 615 and US 15 to:

Gordonsville, Virginia

17. The Exchange Hotel and Civil War Museum is at 400 South Main Street. Medical and military exhibits are featured here. Built as a large hotel, it originally served passengers on the Virginia Central Railway. During the Civil War, it became the Gordonsville Receiving Hospital, treating soldiers from both the Confederate and Union armies. Over 70,000 were treated and more than 700 are buried on the grounds

Drive 15 miles southwest on VA 231 and VA 22 to Shadwell, then go 3 miles west on US 250 to exit 124 on I - 64. Continue 3 miles west on I - 64 to exit 121 and VA 20, then drive 18 miles south on VA 20 to:

Scottsville, Virginia

18. The Scottsville Museum, on Main Street, is the place to learn about this picturesque small town, which was a major James River port in the mid-nineteenth century. Formerly called Scotts Landing, the town got its present name in 1744. The museum, located in a former Disciples of Christ church built in 1846, holds exhibits relating to the James River, the Civil War, and other subjects of local and regional interest.

Go 17 miles west on VA 6 to US 29, then continue 4 miles west on VA 6/US 29 to:

19. The Nelson County Wayside, on VA 6/US 29, a scenic picnic area on the Rockfish River. The Wayside offers picnic tables and barbeque grills.

Drive 12 miles north on VA 6 and VA 151 to the village of Avon and 3 miles north on VA 6 to Afton. Return to Avon and go 22 miles south on VA 6 and VA 151 to VA 56.

This part of Route 3 takes you back into the mountains followed by a return to the valley. More great views of the Piedmont and of the mountains are the result.

Go 11 miles northwest on VA 56 to:

20. Crabtree Falls, the highest U.S. waterfall east of the Mississippi River. There are five major cascades and many smaller ones that together fall 1200 feet. You can park just off VA 56 where there are rest rooms and a beautiful laminated wood bridge over the Tye River. A trail runs along Crabtree Creek to a series of overlooks where you can view the falls. The first overlook is 700 feet from the start of the trail.

This waterfall is a highlight of Route 3, but does require quite a bit of walking to enjoy it fully. I think you will be glad you made the effort.

Travel 3.7 miles west on VA 56 to VA 690, then go 0.5 miles south on VA 690 to:

21. A State Fish Hatchery, where about 150,000 brook, brown, and rainbow trout are hatched and grown to maturity each year. You can see fish of various sizes in cascading pools but are not permitted to fish. Picnic tables and rest rooms are provided.

Return to VA 56, then continue 3.5 miles northwest to the Parkway — Milepost 27.2.

CHAPTER 4 - ROUTE 4

Lexington, VA
Falling Spring Falls, VA
New Castle, VA

ROUTE 4

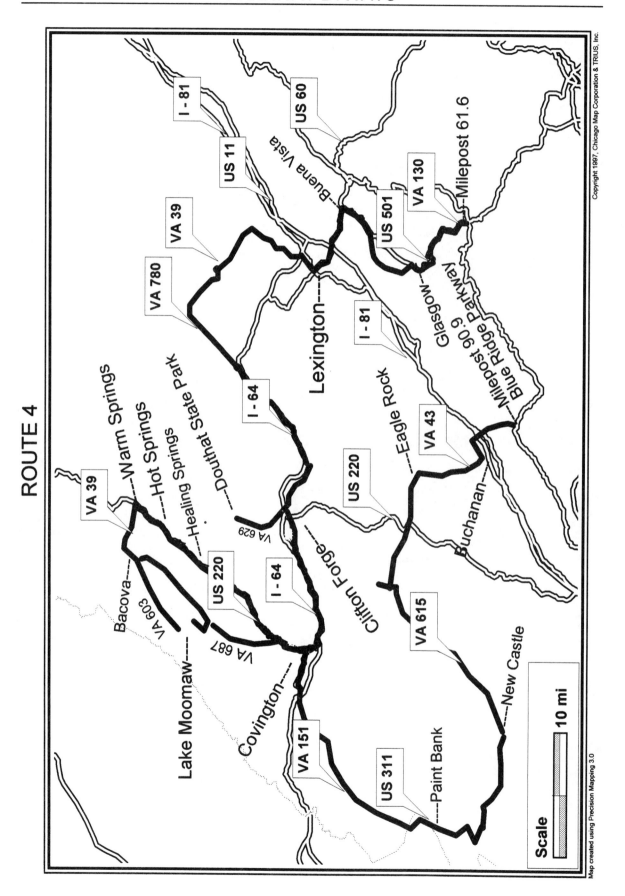

Scale

10 mi

The Lexington - Falling Spring Falls - New Castle Route tours the Virginia counties of Rockbridge, Alleghany, Bath, Craig, and Botetourt. It is about 360 miles long. This trip begins at Milepost 61.6 on the Blue Ridge Parkway and continues in a counterclockwise direction to Milepost 90.9 on the Parkway.

THE BYWAYS —

This trip starts on VA 130, travels down the mountains to the James River, and then on toward Lexington and the Shenandoah Valley. The descent from the Parkway is nothing less than spectacular because of the great views of the river and the valley beyond. Route 4 then goes northwest across the narrow southern part of the Shenandoah Valley and back into the mountains.

A special surprise awaits you before you reach the mountains — Goshen Pass, where VA 39 and a breathtaking section of the wild Maury River wind through a narrow gorge. It is not only something to see, however. There are plenty of places to park, picnic, and get in the river to swim, tube, and climb over the gigantic rocks. You could spend a whole day here, there are so many fun things to do. VA 39 is a Virginia Byway.

A side trip begins at Covington and goes northeast on US 220 through an area famous for healing waters and public bathing facilities. You will also visit Gathright Dam and Lake Moomaw, a project of the US Corps of Engineers. A special feature of this side trip is Falling Spring Falls, a waterfall described by Thomas Jefferson as "The only remarkable cascade in this country." It is clearly visible from US 220. Space to pull off the highway and view the waterfall at your leisure is provided.

Route 4 then returns to Covington, goes past the unusual covered Humpback Bridge, then travels into the Allegheny Mountains. All of the rest of the Route, starting on VA 159, is on Virginia Byways. It's easy to see why they were chosen; the views are exceptional in every direction as you cross a series of mountain ranges and valleys before returning to the Parkway. VA 43 from Eagle Rock south to Springwood is especially noteworthy. It runs parallel to a 16-mile section of the James River which has been designated as a Virginia Scenic River. This part of the river, called the Upper James, is well known for great fishing and canoeing.

THE TOWNS —

The history of Lexington was greatly influenced by four famous generals: George Washington, Robert E. Lee, Stonewall Jackson, and George Marshall. This heritage has been enhanced by efforts of local citizens to restore and maintain the town so that it is now a showplace of fine old buildings, tree lined streets, and the landscaped grounds of two distinguished schools. It's the sort of place where you may lose track of time as you walk around enjoying the charming sites and sights.

Clifton Forge and Covington are large towns that contain a lot of industrial and railroad activities along with several museums and historic buildings. Clifton Forge produced cannons and cannonballs for the Civil War. Covington, settled in 1746, has a gigantic Westvaco paper mill. Visit these towns and look at the quaint houses and other buildings, many of which are very old.

Bath County contains several towns with names taken from the many warm springs in the area such as Healing Springs, Warm Springs, and Hot Springs. This is a retirement and resort area featuring many large houses with landscaped grounds and a world class resort hotel, The Homestead. Although not an attraction in this book — it's definitely for-profit — the "beautifying" effect of The Homestead on Hot Springs and the surrounding countryside is substantial. The resort maintains 15,000 acres, much of it landscaped, and three championship golf courses.

The rest of the towns are small but interesting examples of rural Virginia. All of them are unique and will reward you with a pleasant viewing experience as you walk or drive through them.

THE ATTRACTIONS —

Starting at Milepost 66.1 on the Parkway, go 9 miles northwest on VA 130 and US 501 to:

Glasgow, Virginia

From Glasgow, drive 2 miles northeast on US 501, then turn northwest on VA 663 (River Road). VA 663 is a Virginia Byway that runs along the Maury River. Continue for 7 miles to return to US 501. Go 3 miles northeast on US 501 to:

Buena Vista, Virginia

Labor Day in Buena Vista is celebrated with a major festival in Glen Maury Park.

1. **Glen Maury Park** is west on Tenth Street at the Maury River. The park provides facilities for river fishing, a campground, a swimming pool, tennis courts, playgrounds, picnic shelters, a roller skating rink, hiking trails, ball fields, and sales of ice, firewood, propane, soft drinks, and snacks.

2. **Pedlar Ranger District Office — USDA Forest Service** is at 2424 Magnolia Avenue (US 501). Get information here on the George Washington and Jefferson National Forests.

Drive 3 miles west on US 60 to:

3. **The Ben Salem Lock Wayside Park** is a place to see the ruins of the old lock, enjoy a picnic, and walk along the Maury River.

Go 4 miles west on US 60 to:

Lexington, Virginia

Late August is the time to help Lexington residents celebrate the Rockbridge Community Festival. In early September, visit Lexington for the Rockbridge Food and Wine Festival.

Lexington, Virginia

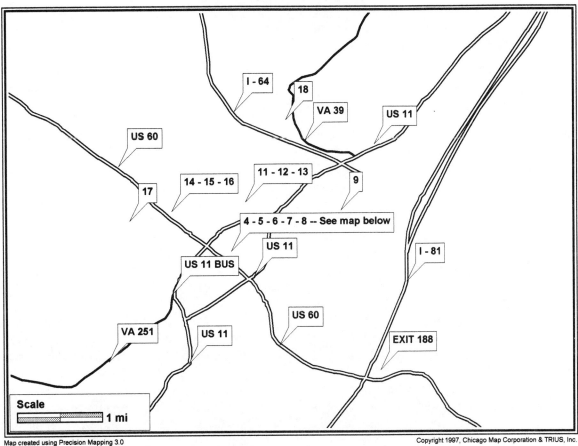

Map created using Precision Mapping 3.0

Copyright 1997, Chicago Map Corporation & TRIUS, Inc.

Lexington -- Downtown

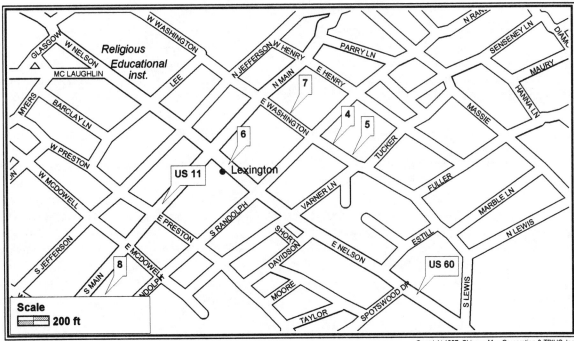

Map created using Precision Mapping 3.0

Copyright 1997, Chicago Map Corporation & TRIUS, Inc.

4. The Lexington Visitor Center, at 106 East Washington Street, provides travel counselors who will help you enjoy your visit to Lexington and Rockbridge County. 540-463-3777.

5. The Rockbridge Historical Society headquarters building is diagonally across the street from the Visitor Center at 103 East Washington Street. The Society maintains a collection of artifacts relating to the history of Lexington and Rockbridge County.

6. Historic Downtown Lexington provides a fine example of people working together to restore and preserve the architecture of a bygone era. Some of the buildings were built in the latter part of the 18th century and many more were added in the 19th century. Preservation efforts started in the 1960's and have been remarkably successful.

7. The Stonewall Jackson House, at 8 East Washington Street, was the home of Thomas Jonathan (Stonewall) Jackson who was a professor of natural philosophy at Virginia Military Institute before he became famous as a Confederate general in the Civil War. His house, restored in 1979 by the Historic Lexington Foundation, and now owned and operated by the Stonewall Jackson Foundation, is open to visitors. Many Jackson artifacts are on display. Guided tours are offered every half hour.

8. The Stonewall Jackson Memorial Cemetery is in the 300 block on South Main Street. Many notable people in addition to General Jackson are buried here including early presidents of Washington College and VMI, two Virginia governors, and Jackson's sister-in-law, who was well known as a poet. A marker at the entrance of the cemetery lists the names of these and other famous people and indicates where their graves are located.

9. The Chessie Nature Trail begins near the north end of the US 11 bridge over the Maury River and follows the former Chesapeake and Ohio railroad for 12 miles to Buena Vista. Pick up a trail map at the Lexington Visitor Center. Traces of the railroad and of a canal that used the Maury River are visible along the way, especially the Reid Lock and Dam which is about 2 miles from Lexington.

10. Woods Creek Park, a two-mile trail and linear park, runs along Woods Creek from near a playground in southwest Lexington to the Maury River in the northwest part of the city. The park contains groves of pines, grassy areas, and cleared forest land.

11. The Virginia Military Institute is located in the northern part of Lexington. Founded in 1839, VMI is the oldest state-supported military college in the United States. It provides about 1,200 students with a four-year college program combined with a daily experience of military training and discipline. Visitors are welcome. The VMI AM radio station (1600) caries information about the college and scheduled events.

12. The Virginia Military Institute Museum is located in the lower level of Jackson Memorial Hall on the VMI campus. It was established in 1856 and contains many military artifacts that have been collected over the years and now make up a large and impressive collection.

13. The George C. Marshall Museum is also on the VMI campus. It was dedicated in 1964 by Presidents Johnson and Eisenhower as a memorial to General Marshall who served with such distinction in World War II and later introduced the Marshall Plan. This museum contains artifacts, murals, and videos that present the story of General Marshall's life from his boyhood in

Uniontown, PA, to life as a cadet at VMI, and later as General of the Army, Secretary of State, and Secretary of Defense.

14. Washington and Lee University is in the western part of Lexington north of US 60. Founded in 1749, it was first known as Augusta Academy. It became Washington and Lee University in 1871 reflecting the financial contribution of George Washington and in honor of Robert E. Lee who was president of the University from 1865 until his death in 1870. The Reeves Center and the Watson Pavilion contain permanent collections of Asian and European ceramics, silver, furniture, and paintings.

15. The Lee Chapel, on the Washington and Lee Campus, was built in 1866 to replace an older chapel room. Lee's former office and the Lee Museum are in the lower level of the chapel. Especially noteworthy

items in the museum are the Charles Wilson Peale portrait of George Washington, the Theodore Pine portrait of Lee, and the recumbent statue of Lee by Edward Valentine.

16.   The Lenfest Center for the Performing Arts, on the Washington and Lee Campus, presents student and professional concerts, plays, and other performances. Call the Lenfest Box Office at 540-463-8000 for information about schedules and tickets.

17. The Theater at Lime Kiln is south of US 60 on Borden Road in the Washington and Lee neighborhood.   This unusual outdoor theater was built in the ruins of a 19th century lime quarry and kiln and now offers professional theatrical and musical productions. The reputation of this theater for developing original plays has resulted in grants from the Rockefeller Foundation and

4-1 Washington and Lee University — Photo courtesy of
Lexington/Rockbridge County Tourism

the Lila Wallace/Readers Digest Fund. Call 540-463-3074 for information about current offerings and tickets.

Drive 2 miles north on US 11 to VA 39, then go 1 mile northwest on VA 39 to:

18.   The Virginia Horse Center was established in 1985 by the Virginia Assembly to provide a place for state, national, and international horse shows and sales. The facilities are extensive including a coliseum seating 4,000, an exhibit area, concessions, meeting rooms and offices. Call 540-463-2194 for information about scheduled events.

Travel 11 miles north on VA 39 to:

19. Goshen Pass, where VA 39 and a breathtaking section of the wild Maury River wind through a narrow gorge.

Linger awhile and enjoy this spectacular place.

Go 8 miles northwest on VA 39 to VA 780, then 9 miles southwest on VA 780 to VA 850. Turn left on VA 850, then quickly right to I - 64. Go 8 miles southwest on I - 64 to Exit 35 and VA 269, then drive 2 miles west on VA 269 to:

20. The Longdale Recreation Area turn-off. Go about 1 mile south to a USDA Forest Service day use facility that offers swimming in a two-acre lake, a bath house with cold water showers, hiking, picnic tables, toilets, and drinking water. Overnight camping is not permitted.

Return to VA 269, then drive 4.5 miles northwest to VA 632. Go 2 miles west on VA 632 to the junction of VA 632, US 60, I - 64 and VA 629 to:

4-2 Goshen Pass — Photo courtesy of Lexington/Rockbridge County Tourism

Clifton Forge, Virginia

Drive 7 miles north on VA 629 to:

21. Douthat State Park, the oldest park in the Virginia system, which is listed on the National Register of Historic Places for its role as an example in the design of state parks throughout the United States. This park offers many visitor services including a 50-acre lake, a restaurant, a swimming beach, a bathhouse, cabins, tent and trailer campgrounds with electrical/water hookups, a trailer dumping station, hiking trails, fishing, groceries, and mountain biking. Some facilities for disabled people and educational and environmental programs are also available.

Return to Clifton Forge on VA 629.

The Fall Festival, on the third weekend in October, is celebrated every year by residents and many visitors.

22. The Alleghany Highlands Chamber of Commerce is at 501 E. Ridgeway Street (US 220/US 60). 540-862-4969.

23. Historic Downtown Clifton Forge is on the National Register of Historic places and is a Virginia "Main Street" community. The Clifton Forge Post Office, built in 1910, is an example of the historic architecture.

24. The Alleghany Highlands Arts & Crafts Center is located at 439 East Ridgeway Street (US 220/US 60). This nonprofit organization maintains galleries that feature and sell fine art works and crafts of local and regional artists. Visit the Center for pottery, stained glass, wood products, jewelry, quilts, paintings, and other graphic arts. Exhibits are changed monthly.

25. The Chesapeake and Ohio Historical Society Archives, at 312 East Ridgeway Street (US 220/US 60), is engaged in preserving and interpreting the history of the C&O and CSX Railroads. Look at the displays of railroad memorabilia and get a copy of the "World Famous Chessie Calendar".

26. The Stonewall Theater, at 510 Main Street (US 220/ US 60), is a performing arts center providing weekly entertainment. It is operated by Appalfolks of America.

27. Iron Gate Gorge is 1 mile south of Clifton Forge on US 220. It was created by the water of the Jackson River over the ages and contains many rock formations of interest to geologists and nature lovers alike.

Travel 12 miles west on US 60, US 220, and I - 64 to:

Covington, Virginia

Major festivals in Covington are Pioneer Day in early May and the Street Scene in mid-August, which features antique cars, street vendors, and lots of good food.

28. The James River Ranger District — USDA Forest Service is at 810 Madison Avenue (US 220/US 60)) very close to Exit 16 on I - 64. It is on the north side of Madison Avenue next to a Texaco station.

29. The Alleghany Highlands Chamber of Commerce is located at 241 West Main Street. 540-962-2178.

30. The Alleghany County Courthouse on Main Street has been restored to reflect the original design used in 1911. It is located in downtown Covington, which is on the National Register of Historic Places.

4-3 Bath County Courthouse — Photo courtesy of the
Bath County Chamber of Commerce

Drive 7 miles north on US 220 to:

31. Falling Spring Falls, a spectacular 200-foot waterfall, can be viewed from a parking area just off US 220. This imposing sight is a highlight of Route 4 and certainly is a "remarkable cascade" as stated by Thomas Jefferson in 1778.

Go 9 miles northeast on US 220 to:

Healing Springs, Virginia

Drive 1 mile northeast on US 220 to:

32. The Warm Springs Ranger District — USDA Forest Service, northeast of Healing Springs on US 220. You can get information here on the facilities available in the George Washington National Forest.

Go 2 miles northeast on US 220 to:

Hot Springs, Virginia

Hot Springs celebrates the Fourth of July with an arts and crafts festival called Bath Sellabration.

33. The Bath County Chamber of Commerce is in the Virginia Building on US 220 in downtown Hot Springs. Get information here on walking tours and bathing in the warm water pools that Bath County is famous for. 800-628-8092.

Travel 4.5 miles northeast on US 220 to:

Warm Springs, Virginia

34. The Bath County Historical Museum is on the Courthouse Square. Artifacts of Bath County are displayed with a focus on the Civil War and Indians. A genealogy library attracts those interested in researching their family history.

35.   The Garth Newel Music Center presents chamber music performances from July to September and concerts throughout the year. Call 540-839-5018 or ask at the Chamber of Commerce in Hot Springs for more information.

Go 3 miles northwest on VA 39 to VA 687, then drive 3 miles southwest on VA 687 to VA 603.

(VA 603 runs along a beautiful section of Lake Moomaw but is gravel and narrow in places. If you prefer, you can continue south on VA 687 — if not see below.)

Drive 6 miles southwest on VA 603 to:

36.   Lake Moomaw Recreation Area, which includes Bolar Flat Marina, three picnic areas, Bolar Mountain Beach, and two campgrounds. Drinking water, flush toilets, and a trailer dump station are available.

Return to VA 687 on VA 603

Travel 12 miles southwest on VA 687 to VA 38. Turn west on VA 638, then go 2 miles on VA 638, VA 666, and VA 605 to:

37. Morris Hill Campground is a USDA Forest Service facility with 55 campsites, 3 bath houses, flush toilets, warm water showers, and a dump station. There are many picnic tables in the vicinity at Morris Hill Picnic Area and at Cole Mountain Picnic Area on Lake Moomaw. Fortney Branch Marina is also located close by on VA 600.

Drive 2 miles northeast on VA 605 to:

38. Gathright Dam and Visitors Center is an US Army Corps of Engineers project. Displays and brochures at the Visitors Center explain how Lake Moomaw was created to provide flood and water quality control on the Jackson and James Rivers.

4-4 Humpback Bridge — Photo courtesy of the
Alleghany Highlands Chamber of Commerce

Completed in 1981, the lake is available for swimming, fishing, and boating and the surrounding land areas can be used for hiking and hunting.   Lake Moomaw is adjacent to the 13,248-acre T. M. Gathright Wildlife Management Area which is managed by Virginia Commission of Game and Inland Fisheries.

Return to VA 687 by way of VA 605, VA 666, and VA 638. Go 12 miles south on VA 687, then US 220 to US 60 in Covington.

Drive 4 miles west on US 60 to:

39.   The Humpback Bridge State Wayside Park which contains the only curved-span, trussed-arch covered bridge in the United States. This bridge is a National Historic Landmark.

Go 1 mile west on US 60 to VA 159, then Drive 12 miles southwest on VA 159 to US 311. Travel 14 miles south on US 311 to:

Paint Bank, Virginia

Go 3.5 miles northeast on VA 18 to:

40.   Steel Bridge Campground, a USDA Forest Service campground on Potts Creek, a cold mountain stream stocked with trout. Facilities include 20 camping units with a picnic table, lantern post, and a tent pad. A hand pump and toilets are also available..

Return to Paint Bank.

41.   Tingler's Mill, built in 1873, is a historic landmark.   Electricity for the community of Paint Bank was produced here.   The mill is presently closed for restoration but should be open soon.

42. Paint Bank Fish Hatchery is on US 311. Stop here to see how fish are grown for stocking in Virginia streams, rivers, and ponds.

Travel 17 miles southeast on US 311 to:

New Castle, Virginia

43.   Downtown New Castle is the location of a historic courthouse built in 1852 with bricks made in the vicinity and featuring a bell cast at the same foundry as the Liberty Bell.   Buildings on the National Register of Historic   Places,   in   addition   to   the courthouse, include the Old Brick Hotel and the Star Saloon housing the Craig County Historical Society and Museum.   There are also many beautiful old houses in the town.

Drive 2 miles northeast on VA 615 to:

44. The New Castle Ranger District — USDA Forest Service, an office of the Jefferson National Forest. 540-864-5195.

Go 10 miles northeast on VA 615 through Oriskany to VA 817. Turn right on VA 817 and right again in 0.5 miles at the Recreation Area sign to:

45.   The Craig Creek Campground and Picnic area. This is an area maintained by the USDA Forest Service for primitive camping.   Hiking, wading in Craig Creek, and picnicking are featured. Vault toilets are provided but there is no drinking water.

Return to VA 615, then go 9 miles northeast to VA 621. Drive 1 mile northwest on VA 621 to:

46.   Roaring Run Furnace and Picnic Area is a nineteenth-century iron furnace used to make iron stoves, ingots, and other iron products. It is now on the National Register of Historic Places. Besides seeing the old furnace, you can picnic along Roaring Run Creek and hike 1.5 miles to Roaring Run Falls.

Return to VA 615, then go 5.4 miles southeast to US 220. Drive 1.4 miles northeast on US 220 to VA 43, then 2 miles south on VA 43 to:

Eagle Rock, Virginia

47. The Upper James River in the Eagle Rock area offers an opportunity to explore old stone locks, dams, and abutments, dating from the time before the Civil War when it was the James River and Kanawha Canal. The James offers the angler great fishing for smallmouth bass, rock bass, bream, muskie, and catfish.

48. The last lock on the James River and Kanawha Canal is just north of Eagle Rock.

There is a place to park and see this historic site.

49. Three historic kilns are located at the northern edge of Eagle Rock. A sign says, "Kiln donated to the Stoner Eagle Rock Garden Club for Historic Preservation in 1991. First kiln was built in 1847." An old railroad caboose is displayed on this same site.

Go 15 miles southeast on VA 43 to:

Buchanan, Virginia

50. A swinging bridge, the only one crossing the James River, rests on supports built 150 years ago. This bridge is open for people to walk across and is adjacent to the highway bridge. Parking is available on the north side of the river at Bridge Street.
Drive 5 miles south on VA 43 to the Parkway, Milepost 90.9.

CHAPTER 5 - ROUTE 5

Appomattox Court House, VA
Lynchburg, VA
Bedford, VA

ROUTE 5

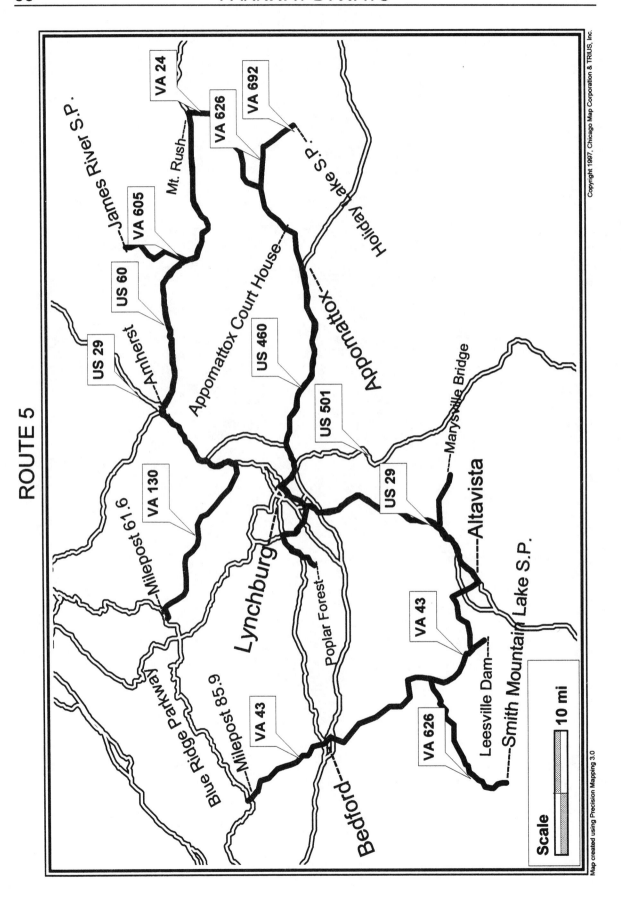

Scale

10 mi

The Appomattox Courthouse - Lynchburg - Bedford Route tours the Virginia counties of Amherst, Buckingham, Appomattox, Campbell, and Bedford. It is about 260 miles long. This trip begins at Milepost 61.6 on the Blue Ridge Parkway and continues in a clockwise direction to Milepost 85.9 on the Parkway at the Peaks of Otter Visitor Center.

THE BYWAYS —

This route starts on VA 130, a Virginia Byway, and travels down the mountains into the Virginia Piedmont. Panoramic views of central and eastern Virginia are presented as the highway descends. Well kept and picturesque farms are numerous as you make the transition from mountains to the lower elevations. US 29 to Amherst and US 60 to Mt. Rush continue in this pattern through rolling hills and past winding streams. You will cross the James River and drive along its eastern banks if you visit the James River State Park.

All of this area is rich in American history and culture. Many of our ancestors lived, worked, and fought here — fought the Indians, the British, and among themselves. The roads you will travel through Appomattox County are the same ones used by those farmers and soldiers whose heritage we can consider as we visit the country where they lived. Parts of VA 24 and US 460 are Virginia Byways.

The streets of Lynchburg will reward you with great views of the architecture of the past. Drive through residential, commercial, and industrial areas; all are unique and quite historic.

VA 43, also a Virginia Byway, completes your trip. It will take you back into the mountains and provide many exciting mountain views in the process.

THE TOWNS —

Lynchburg is the largest and most diverse city on this route. Some of the more famous attractions are identified below, but these are only the tip of the Lynchburg iceberg. There are many, many more. If you're interested in knowing more about this unusual city, get the fascinating 136-page book, *Tour Lynchburg*, edited by Peter W. Houck. It is an absolute treasure-trove of valuable information. The friendly people at the Visitors Center will tell you where to obtain a copy.

Bedford is the other large town and is a little like Lynchburg but with its own special qualities. It is smaller, less hilly, less crowded, and was settled somewhat later because it is well away from the rivers that were the early highways. It has plenty of historic places to visit (218 buildings on the National Register of Historic Places), however, as you walk and drive around.

Amherst, Appomattox, and Altavista are great places to experience small town life at its best. These very old towns also contain many modern homes and business buildings.

THE ATTRACTIONS —

Starting at Milepost 66.1, go 17 miles southeast on VA 130 to US 29, then drive 11 miles northeast on US 29 to:

Amherst, Virginia

Amherst celebrates October in a big way: the Sorghum Festival is held during the first weekend, the Garlic Festival is the second weekend, and the Apple Festival is the third weekend.

1. Amherst County Historical Museum, at 301 South Main, contains exhibits relating to local history and a **Visitors Information Center.** The museum is located in a 1910 Georgian Revival house. 804-946-5595.

Drive 15 miles east on US 60 and cross the James River bridge.

There are three Virginia state parks on this Route. They are all quite different, but you may want to choose only one or two if your time or interest is limited.

If you decide to visit the James River State Park, turn north on VA 605. (If not, continue on US 60.) Go 7 miles north along the river to VA 606. Turn west on VA 606 and drive to:

2. The James River State Park. This park is still under development but visitors can picnic, hike along the river, and fish. Pit toilets are provided.

Return to US 60 and drive 13 miles east to Mt. Rush. Turn southwest on VA 24 and go 11 miles on VA 626, then turn east on VA 626 and drive 3.1 miles to VA 640. Drive 0.3 miles northeast on VA 640 to VA 692, then go 2.7 miles southeast on VA 692 to:

3. Holiday Lake State Park. This park has camping with electrical/water hookups, a dumping station, showers, toilets, picnicking, bridle trails, hiking, mountain biking, swimming, boating on a 150-acre lake (no motorboats), rowboat and paddleboat rentals, a snack bar, a visitors center, and some facilities for the disabled.

Return to VA 24, then drive 6 miles southwest to:

4. Appomattox Court House National Historical Park. General Robert E. Lee surrendered to General Ulysses S. Grant at this place on April 9, 1865, ending the Civil War. Three days later, soldiers of the Army of Northern Virginia laid down their flags and weapons and returned to their homes. The National Park Service maintains this park and provides interpreters to explain the events that happened here. A village of 27 restored buildings is within easy walking distance along old country roads.

Go 3 miles southwest to:

Appomattox, Virginia

A two-day celebration, the Historic Appomattox Railroad Festival, is held in mid-October. Ask at the Visitor Center or call 804-352-8268 for dates and more information.

5. The Appomattox Visitor Information Center is on Main Street in a renovated railroad depot. This building, replacing one that burned in 1923, contains displays that feature local attractions. 804-352-2621.

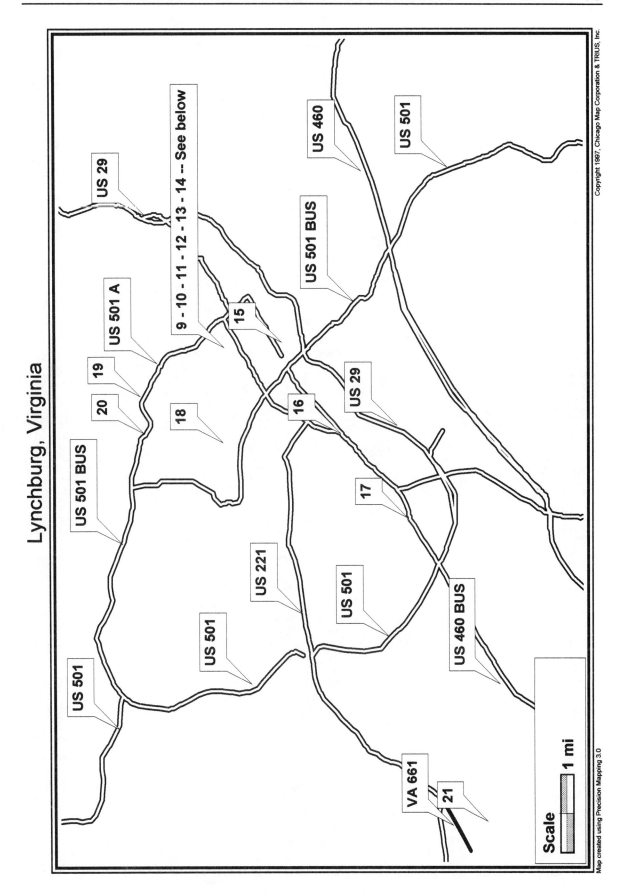

Lynchburg, Virginia

US 29

9 - 10 - 11 - 12 - 13 - 14 -- See below

US 460

US 501

US 501 BUS

US 501 A

19

20

18

15

16

US 29

17

US 501 BUS

US 221

US 501

US 501

US 501

US 460 BUS

VA 661

21

Scale
1 mi

Map created using Precision Mapping 3.0

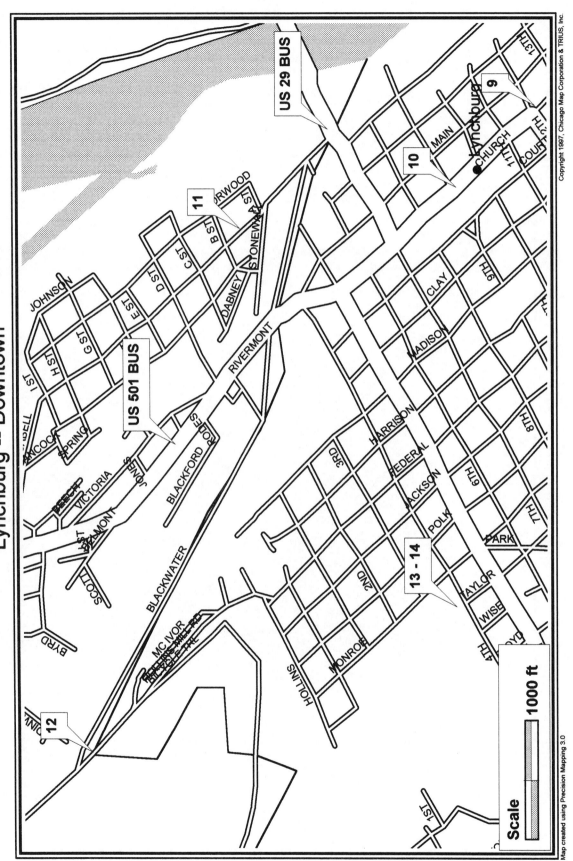

Lynchburg -- Downtown

Scale 1000 ft

6. A Historic Homes Walking Tour, that visits 44 historic Appomattox houses, starts at the Visitor Information Center, where you can obtain a descriptive brochure.

7. The Appomattox County Historical Museum is located on the Court House Square. The museum, formerly used as a jail, was built in 1897, houses a doctor's office, a jail cell, an old school room, and a country store. Many artifacts relating to the area are displayed. The museum also owns and operates the **Cloverhill Village Living History Museum,** a collection of restored buildings on property north of Appomattox. Cloverhill Village is normally open by appointment only; check at the Historical Museum for more information. Also visit the historic **Appomattox County Court House** which is next door to the museum.

8. The Hazel Moon Museum is on Church Street in the Liberty Baptist Church. Dr. Moon was a native of Appomattox who served as a nurse and missionary in Nigeria for over 30 years. Many of her letters, diaries, photographs, and other artifacts are displayed here.

Although not part of a route covered in this book, you may want to take a driving tour called **Lee's Retreat** which runs from Appomattox to Petersburg, Virginia. This tour includes 20 tour stops and retraces the route Lee followed just before his surrender. Call 1-800-6-RETREAT or write to Virginia's Retreat, P. O. Box 2107, Petersburg, Virginia, for a map and brochure.

Drive 23 miles west on US 460 to:

Lynchburg, Virginia

Lynchburg holds several festivals along the James River each June. Other celebrations occur in September. Contact the Visitors Center for details.

5-1 Batteau Festival on the James River — Photo courtesy of the Greater Lynchburg Chamber of Commerce

9.   The Lynchburg Visitors Center is located at Twelfth and Church Streets. 804-847-1811 or 800-732-5821

10. The Lynchburg Museum is in the old Court House at Ninth and Church Streets. Exhibits depicting the history of Lynchburg are displayed in a restored 1855 courthouse.

11. Point of Honor, at 112 Cabell Street, is a renovated mansion once owned by an eminent physician, Dr. George Cabell. Dr. Cabell was Patrick Henry's personal doctor. Built in 1815, this landmark is now operated by the Lynchburg Museum System. High on a bluff overlooking the James River, the house and other buildings, ornate furnishings, gardens and grounds are open for visitors. This is a large and impressive old house, an outstanding example of the Federal style of residential architecture.

12. Blackwater Creek Natural Area is an extensive   park and natural area along Blackwater Creek.   Although there are a number of access points, the most convenient is on Hollins Mill Road. This park has several miles of hiking trails and a paved bike path which is accessible to the handicapped.   There are many places to picnic. Get more information at the Visitors Center.

13.   The Old City Cemetery and the Confederate Cemetery are at Fourth and Taylor Streets.   These cemeteries feature interesting horticulture displays and are described by brochures available at the site.

14. The Pest House Medical Museum is also located at Fourth and Taylor in the City Cemetery. Exhibits here include a restored 1840 medical office, instruments, and other artifacts relating to the practice of medicine in the late nineteenth century. Smallpox patients were quarantined here during the Civil War.

5-2 Point of Honor — Photo courtesy of the
Greater Lynchburg Chamber of Commerce

15.   The Anne Spencer House and Garden is located at 1313 Pierce Street. Tours of the house and garden of the Harlem Renaissance poet are offered.

16.   Fort Early is at the intersection of Memorial Avenue and Fort Avenue (US 460 BUS).   This group of breastworks and trenches relate to the Civil War Battle of Lynchburg that occurred here in June 1864. Plaques at the site and across the street give many of the details.

17.   The Smith River Meeting House, at 5810 Fort Avenue, is a restored meeting house where the history of the Quaker community is featured. Guided tours are available on request.

18.   The Lynchburg Fine Arts Center, at 1815 Thompson Drive, contains two art galleries, a 500-seat theater, and places for classes and workshops in dance, music, art, and drama.   It is affiliated with the Virginia Museum of Fine Arts.

19.   Riverside Park is accessible from the 2200 block of Rivermont Avenue.   In addition to great views of the James River, the park features places to walk and picnic, the historic **Miller-Claytor House,** and a part of the **packet boat Marshall** which carried the body of Stonewall Jackson on the Kanawha Canal to Lexington for burial. You can also see an unusual bridge that was moved here from Old Forest Road.

20.   The Maier Museum of Art is at 1 Quinlan Street on the campus of Randolph-Macon Woman's College at 2500 Rivermont Avenue.   Nineteenth and twentieth century paintings by American artists are featured including works by Georgia O'Keeffe, Winslow Homer, and James McNeill Whistler.

21. Jefferson's Poplar Forest is southwest on US 221 and east on VA 661.   This unusual octagonal house surrounded by magnificent landscaping was built by Thomas Jefferson as a retreat from the frequent visitors and other pressures of his life at Monticello.   Foundations of the house were laid in 1806 and construction continued until Jefferson's death in 1826. It is one of only two houses that he designed and built for his personal use.   In 1812, Jefferson said, "When finished, it will be the best dwelling house in the state, except that of Monticello; perhaps preferable to that, as more proportional to the faculties of a private citizen."   The house, a National Historic Landmark, is open to visitors who can see the restoration of buildings, grounds, and gardens currently in progress.

From downtown Lynchburg, travel 25 miles south on US 29 to Altavista, Virginia or, if you have time, and want to see an old covered bridge:

Go 21 miles south on US 29 to VA 699. Turn east, then go 5.2 miles to VA 696. Drive 0.5 miles south on VA 696 to VA 700, then go 2.3 miles southeast on VA 700 to VA 705.   Turn east and drive 0.8 miles to:

22.   Marysville Bridge, the second-oldest covered bridge still standing in Virginia. Built in 1878, it was recently restored.   It crosses Seneca Creek.

Return to US 29, then drive 4 miles southwest to:

Altavista, Virginia

23.   Avoca Museums and Historical Society are in a Victorian house at 1514 Main Street.   This house was the home of

Colonel Charles Lynch, who settled here around 1755. A prominent soldier and statesman, Lynch lived and is buried here. The museum features several interpretive exhibits relating to the history of the area which include Indian and Civil War artifacts.

24.   The Staunton Riverfront Park is Altavista's town park and features places to hike and picnic.

Go 9 miles west on VA 43 through Leesville to VA 630. Drive 0.4 miles south on VA 630 to VA 718, then go 1.8 miles south on VA 718 to:

25. Leesville Dam and Lake, which is part of a two-lake electricity generating system that also includes Smith Mountain Lake. Water flows through the Smith Mountain Dam into Leesville Lake. When the demand for electricity is lower, some of this water is pumped back into Smith Mountain Lake to restart the process. Electricity is generated when water flows through either dam.

Return to VA 43, then drive 6.5 miles northwest to VA 626. Go 12 miles southwest on VA 626 to:

26.   Smith Mountain Lake State Park. Facilities include primitive camping, a dumping station, cold water showers, pit toilets, boat launching (motor boats permitted), paddleboat rentals, fishing pier, hiking trails, swimming, picnic tables, a snack bar, a visitors center, programs, and some facilities for the disabled.

Return to VA 43, then drive 15 miles northwest to:

Bedford, Virginia

Bedford celebrates an Antique, Classic Car, and Kite Flying Festival in mid-April that sounds like a lot of fun. Late September brings Centerfest, a downtown street festival.

5-3 National Home B-P-O of Elks — Photo courtesy of
the Bedford Area Chamber of Commerce

Bedford, Virginia

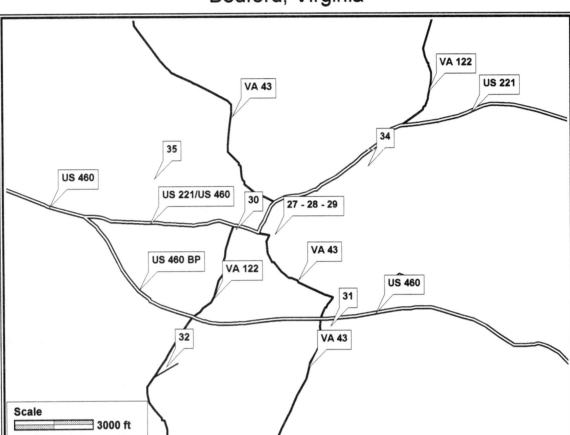

Scale
3000 ft

Map created using Precision Mapping 3.0

27.   The Bedford Area Chamber of Commerce and Visitors Center is at 305 East Main Street. 540-586-9401 or 800-993-9535.

Bedford is in the process of building a major national monument in honor of the veterans of D-Day of World War II. Ask about the location and for more information at the Visitors Center.

28. The Bedford City/County Museum at 201 East Main Street maintains permanent and occasional exhibits portraying the history of Bedford County . Artifacts of the Revolutionary and Civil Wars, Indian relics, weapons, tools, clothing, quilts, flags, and household goods are on display.

29.   The Bedford Downtown Historic District is listed on the National Register of Historic Places and includes 218 buildings. Italianate architecture was used primarily in this area, which was established in 1782, and was formerly known as the town of Liberty.   **Avenel,** a mansion built about 1838 by William Burwell, and now being restored, is a prominent landmark The stately **Bedford County Courthouse**, on Main Street, is also in the Historic District.

30. The Bedford Historic Meeting House, on Main Street, was built in 1838 and served as the first meeting house for Methodists. It was purchased by the Bedford Historical Society in 1970 and has been restored.

31. Poplar Park, located south of US 460 Bypass and east of VA 43, contains the national champion poplar tree which is the largest tree in Virginia and the largest poplar tree in the world. There is a place to park, look at the tree, and have a picnic.

32. Liberty Lake Park is south of US 460 Bypass and just off VA 122. It includes a lake stocked for fishing; picnic shelters; tennis, basketball, and racquetball courts; baseball and softball fields; plus places for walking and roller skating.

33. Holy Land U.S.A. is 3 miles southwest of Bedford on VA 746 (off VA 122). This is a 400-acre tract of land that has been developed into a re-creation of Syria, Israel, and Jordan during the days of Jesus. Their sign says, "A Nature Sanctuary - A Living Memorial to All Who Love God's Creation." There is no charge for admission or self-guided walking tours.

34. The Longwood Cemetery is northeast of the downtown area on VA 122/US 221.This burial site dates from the Revolutionary War period and is Bedford's first cemetery. The earliest marker is dated 1826. Excellent examples of cemetery art and monuments are found here.

35. The Elks National Home, northwest of the downtown area, is the national retirement center for members of the Benevolent and Protective Order of the Elks. The residents create an enormous Christmas lighting display each year which draws more than one hundred thousand visitors.

Drive 11 miles northwest on VA 43 to the Parkway, Milepost 85.9.

CHAPTER 6 - ROUTE 6

Fincastle, VA
Cascade Falls, VA
Salem/Roanoke, VA

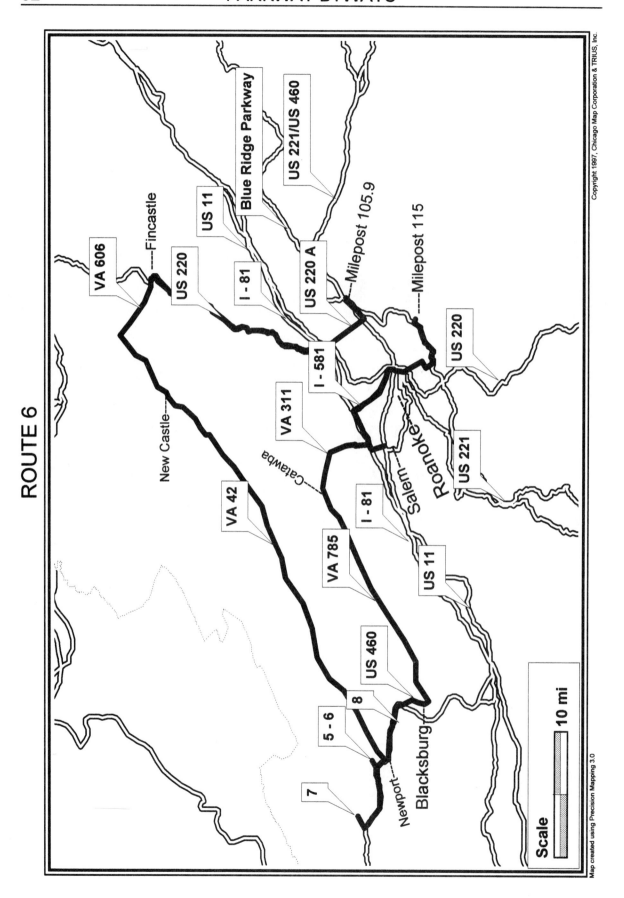

ROUTE 6

Blue Ridge Parkway

US 221/US 460

US 11

Fincastle

VA 606

US 220

I - 81

US 220 A

Milepost 105.9

Milepost 115

I - 581

US 220

VA 311

New Castle

Catawba

US 221

Roanoke

Salem

VA 42

I - 81

VA 785

US 11

US 460

8

5 - 6

7

Newport

Blacksburg

Scale

10 mi

Copyright 1997, Chicago Map Corporation & TRIUS, Inc.

Map created using Precision Mapping 3.0

The New Castle - Cascade Falls - Salem/Roanoke Route tours the Virginia counties of Botetourt, Craig, Montgomery, and Roanoke. It is about 160 miles long. Although the byways traveled are quite different, the attractions listed for Roanoke and Salem can also be visited on Route 7. This trip begins at Milepost 105.9 on the Blue Ridge Parkway and continues in a counterclockwise direction to Milepost 115 on the Parkway at the road to Virginia's Explore Park.

THE BYWAYS —

Route 6 starts on US 460, continues on US 220, then takes you to Fincastle, the first of the interesting towns, and to VA 606, the first of the scenic byways. Most of the remaining roads on this route are designated Virginia Byways. These highways run through a countryside that is quietly and serenely picturesque, characterized by well-kept farms, winding rivers and streams, and neat towns.

Mountains in southwest Virginia frequently run in ranges from southwest to northeast with valleys between the ranges. Most roads on Route 6 travel through these valleys. Since you're closer to the farms and houses, you can observe the lifestyle of people and farm animals more clearly than from high on the ridges. The mountains are always in view as a backdrop to the fields in the foreground.

6-1 A Parkway Byway in Roanoke County, Virginia — Photo courtesy of the Roanoke Valley Convention and Visitors Bureau

THE TOWNS —

Fincastle, Virginia, is described by local residents as a museum of eighteenth-century architecture. In existence for more than 250 years, this fine old town was once the seat of government for a large area of the United States, including parts of West Virginia, Ohio, Indiana, Illinois, and all of Kentucky. It contains many buildings from its long history, from log houses, to a courthouse designed by Thomas Jefferson, to more modern structures. The 400 residents and many other Virginians are deservedly proud of this historic town.

Blacksburg also has many old buildings — some have been there more than 200 years — but also has a very up-to-date atmosphere. The growth of the town has been influenced by the engineers and scientists of Virginia Tech resulting in such additions as a corporate research center and several industries. The overall effect is a richly harmonious blend of history, scenery, and technical sophistication. Roanoke and Salem have an extremely diverse background involving railroads, commerce, manufacturing, and cultural activities. Home to 230,000 people, this is the largest metropolitan area in southwest Virginia. Festivals are very prominent here — Roanoke's Festival in the Park attracts 350,000 people annually and Salem's Fair draws about 200,000. Museums, art exhibits, musical and theatrical performances, and recreational facilities are fully integrated into everyday life. The Center in the Square/Farmer's Market complex in Roanoke is one of the most exciting downtown areas in the United States. Combine these cultural advantages with a great climate, excellent health care, and a low crime rate and you have an outstanding community to visit or a place to live.

THE ATTRACTIONS —

Starting at Milepost 105.9 drive 3 miles southwest on US 460/US 221 to US 220-A. Turn north on US 220-A, then travel 6 miles to US 220. Continue 9 miles north on US 220 to:

Fincastle, Virginia

Visit the Fincastle Fall Festival in late September or early October for crafts, art, music, food, and entertainment.

1. The Botetourt Chamber of Commerce is located in the Old Botetourt County Jail which is near the Courthouse. Ask them for the brochure, "Walking Tour Guide" which was prepared by Historic Fincastle, Inc., an organization dedicated to preservation, restoration, and education. 540-473-8280.

2. The Botetourt County Courthouse, on Court House Square, was designed by Thomas Jefferson, built in 1845, burned in 1970, and was recently restored. It is one of fifteen county sites on the National Register of Historic Places.

Drive 11 miles west on VA 606 to VA 615, then go 5 miles southwest on VA 615 to:

3. The New Castle Ranger District — USDA Forest Service, an office of the Jefferson National Forest, where you can obtain information about Forest Service facilities in the area.

Drive 2 miles southwest on VA 615 to:

New Castle, Virginia

4. Downtown New Castle is the location of a historic courthouse built in 1852 with bricks made in the vicinity and featuring a bell cast at the same foundry as the Liberty Bell. Buildings on the National Register of Historic Places, in addition to the courthouse, include the Old Brick Hotel and the Star Saloon housing the Craig County Historical Society and Museum. There are also many old houses in the town.

Drive 29 miles southwest on VA 42 to US 460, then go 2 miles northwest on US 460 to VA 700. Turn north and go 0.3 miles on VA 700 to:

5. Links Farm Bridge, a 55-foot covered bridge over Sinking Creek. It was built about 1916 and left standing when a new bridge was built in 1963.

Go just past the bridge to VA 604, then drive 1.3 miles east on VA 604 to VA 601. Turn south on VA 601 to:

6. The Sinking Creek Covered Bridge, which was also built about 1916 and left in place for the property owner when a new bridge was built in 1949.

Return to US 460, then drive 8 miles west to Pembroke and VA 623. Go 4 miles north on VA 623 to:

7. Cascades Recreation Area, a USDA Forest Service facility. The area features an impressive 66-foot waterfall which is accessible at the end of a 2-mile trail from the parking lot (4 miles round trip). This facility also provides picnic tables and grills, flush toilets, and water fountains.

Return to US 460, then travel 11 miles southeast to a sign directing you to:

8. Pandapas Pond, a day use area managed by the USDA Forest Service. An easy 1-mile trail and several side trails wind around the 8-acre pond. You can fish or use your canoe in the pond. Camping and the use of bicycles and horses are not permitted.

Go 8 miles southeast on US 460 to:

Blacksburg, Virginia

Blacksburg celebrates an annual festival on the first weekend in August called Steppin' Out. Visit this exciting event for arts, crafts, festival foods, children's activities, live music, and other forms of entertainment. Attendance is usually greater than 25,000 people.

9. The Blacksburg Regional Visitors Center is at 1995 South Main Street, Suite 902. Drive here first to get information about historic buildings located in the Original 16-Block Grid, the Huckleberry Trail, and good places to park when visiting Virginia Tech attractions. 540-552-4503 or 800-288-4061.

10. The Original 16-Block Grid in downtown Blacksburg contains more than a dozen historic buildings dating from 1839 to 1906. Pick up a brochure at the Visitors Center that explains the history of these buildings and indicates their location.

11. The Huckleberry Trail, with an access point at Miller Street and Preston Avenue, near the Public Library, is a downtown walking trail that will provide you with a different view of Blacksburg as well as a little exercise. Get a brochure and map at the Visitors Center for more access points and other details.

Blacksburg -- Downtown

Map created using Precision Mapping 3.0

Copyright 1997, Chicago Map Corporation & TRIUS, Inc.

12. The Price House and Garden Park Museum, at Wharton and Lee Streets, contains exhibits relating to the history of Blacksburg and Montgomery County. Visit the garden in the spring to see the prize winning iris display. This fine old house, circa 1853, is one of the earliest built in Blacksburg.

The following four attractions are on or close to the Virginia Tech campus. Ask at the Blacksburg Regional Visitors Center office for suggestions about the best places to park.

13. The Armory Art Gallery is at 210 Draper Road. This Virginia Tech art Gallery, one of several on campus, features national, regional, and student exhibits. This gallery is in the Old Blacksburg Armory.

14. The Virginia Museum of Natural History, at 428 North Main Street, is a branch of the Martinsville, Virginia, museum. The Blacksburg facility maintains exhibits called *The Age of Reptiles, Our Age of Mammals, The Dan River People: Ancient Virginians and Their Environment,* and *A Closer Look.* Children of all ages will enjoy the *Discovery Corner.*

15. The Virginia Tech Museum of Geological Sciences is at 2062 Derring Hall. This museum contains a full-scale model of an Allosaurus, fossils, gemstones, a seismograph, and the largest display of Virginia minerals in the state.

16. The Smithfield Plantation House, at 1000 Smithfield Plantation Road, is the former home of the Preston family. The restored house and garden is a Virginia Historic Landmark and is the birthplace of two Virginia governors. The **Virginia Tech Duck Pond,** in the same area, is a perfect place for a picnic. Park benches, picnic tables, and a gazebo are provided.

Drive 21 miles northeast on VA 785 (Roanoke Street, Owens Street, and Harding Avenue) to VA 311, then go 10 miles southeast on VA 311 to:

Salem, Virginia

Salem's major festival is the annual Salem Fair. The dates are in early July and the place is the Salem Civic Center. A large antique car show is held annually during Old Salem Days in mid-September.

17. The Salem Visitor's Center, at 1001 Boulevard, is in the Salem Civic Center. Ask for the brochure describing the **Historic Salem Walking Tour.** If you're a baseball fan, the Class A affiliate of the Colorado Rockies, the Salem Avalanche, plays in a stadium close to the Civic Center. 540-375-3004 or 888-827-2536.

18. Lake Spring Park is at the corner of West Main and Green Streets. This downtown park is a place to walk, fish, rest, and get a glimpse of local people and their activities.

19. The Salem Farmers Market, at Main and Broad Streets, will provide a nice change of pace for you. Visitors enjoy a profusion of natural, colorful sights and intriguing smells.

20. Roanoke College, 221 College Lane, operates art galleries that display traditional and contemporary works of both regional and nationally known artists. The campus of this downtown college is characterized by shady lawns and historic buildings, the oldest built in 1847.

21. The Salem Museum is located at 801 East Main Street in Longwood Park. Regional history, Civil War history, education, and early photography are featured in this museum in the Williams-Brown House, circa 1845. A fitness trail and a wide variety of playground equipment are available in the park.

Go 1.5 miles north on VA 311 to I-81, then 4 miles northeast on I-81 to I-581. Turn southeast and go 6.4 miles on I-581 to downtown:

Roanoke, Virginia

The Roanoke Festival in the Park is a fantastic eleven-day event occurring in late May/early June. Involving more than three thousand volunteers, and attracting thousands of visitors, this is a must-visit activity. Concerts, art shows, fireworks, a carnival, foods of all kinds, children's activities, a river race, bike and road races, and a parade are among the many featured adventures. A picture of this celebration would be the perfect illustration for the word festival in any dictionary.

22. The Roanoke Valley Visitor Information Center is at 114 Market Street. Be sure to stop here before you explore the city. There are many festivals, shows, and performances that you won't want to miss and they will know about them all. Ask for information about a walking tour of downtown Roanoke including the fascinating **Farmer's Market.** 540-342-6025 or 800-635-5535.

Roanoke, Virginia

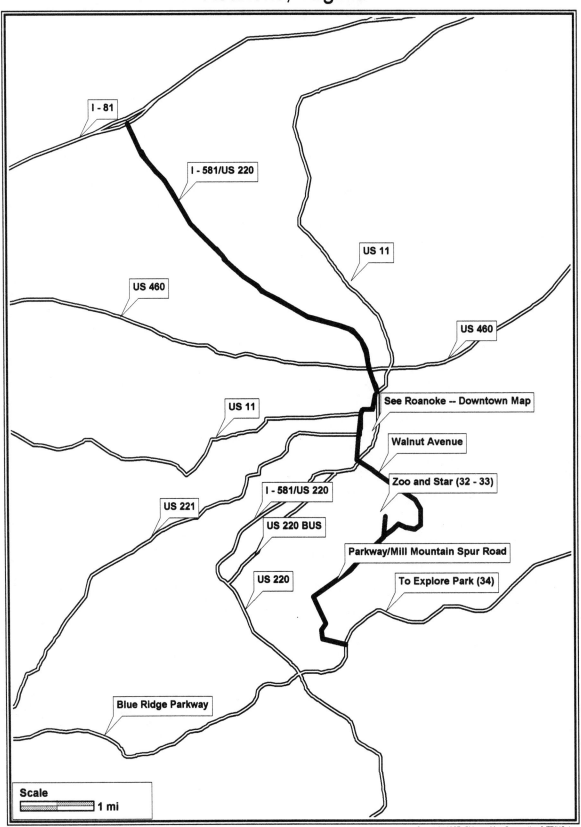

I - 81

I - 581/US 220

US 11

US 460

US 460

US 11

See Roanoke -- Downtown Map

Walnut Avenue

Zoo and Star (32 - 33)

I - 581/US 220

US 221

US 220 BUS

Parkway/Mill Mountain Spur Road

To Explore Park (34)

US 220

Blue Ridge Parkway

Scale
1 mi

Roanoke -- Downtown

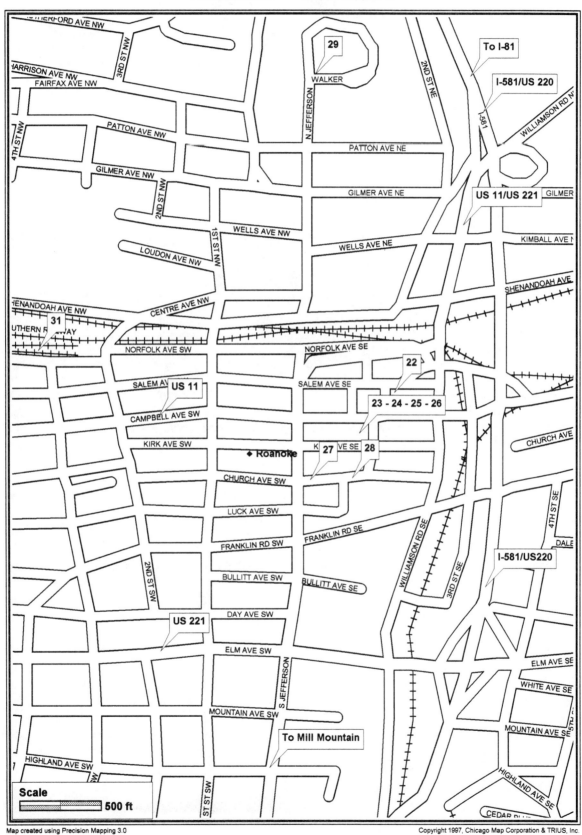

6-2 Roanoke's Farmers Market — Photo courtesy of the
Roanoke Valley Convention and Visitors Bureau

The following five attractions are a part of an art, science, history, culture, and theater complex called Center in the Square. All of them are located at One Market Square except The Arts Council of the Blue Ridge.

23.   The Art Museum of Western Virginia exhibits contemporary and traditional works in all mediums and features folk art from the Virginia mountains.   Art from Egypt, Japan, and Africa is also displayed. Workshops, tours, camps, lectures, and classes are offered for adults and children. Children are especially favored in a part of the museum called **ArtVenture: A Children's Center.** More than 2000 square feet of exhibitions and many special activities are of special interest to children.

24.   The Science Museum of Western Virginia and Hopkins Planetarium maintains five permanent exhibits   and frequently offers touring exhibits.   Many

opportunities for interactive experiences are provided, along with displays relating to light, anatomy, weather, animals, ocean creatures, sound, and computer science. The Planetarium conducts programs relating to all aspects of astronomy.

25.   The Roanoke Valley History Museum contains artifacts and other materials about the Roanoke area from prehistoric to modern times. Information about noteworthy people, railroads, and wars affecting the area, along with tools, documents, weapons, and a store from the 1890's are also included.

26.   Mill Mountain Theater presents musicals, dramas, classics, and children's plays and music. It is the only professional theater operating full-time in southwestern Virginia. The main stage and box office is in Circle in the Square with another facility, **Theater B - Center on Church,** at 20 East Church Avenue.

27. The Arts Council of the Blue Ridge, also at 20 East Church Avenue, provides display space for artists, juried exhibitions, art activities for high school students, art sales, and a regional newsletter reporting on subjects of interest to artists. An Artists Registry and Resource Library is maintained that serves hundreds of artists and dozens of art and culture organizations.

28. Fire Station Number One, at Church Avenue and Market Street, was built in 1906 and still serves the city as a firehouse. It was placed on the National Register of Historic places in 1972. This is a great place to visit with children. The firemen welcome visitors and will show you the old building and modern equipment. They will even slide down the original brass firepole if you ask them and they're not too busy.

29. The Catholic Historical Museum, at 624 North Jefferson Street, presents artifacts relating to the history of the Catholic Church in the Roanoke area. The museum is adjacent to **Saint Andrew's Church,** a local landmark of imposing size and stature, constructed in 1900. The museum aids in research by maintaining records and files from Catholic churches throughout the area. You should call for an appointment before visiting since the museum is frequently closed. 540-982-0152.

30. The Harrison Museum of African-American Culture is located at 523 Harrison Avenue. Displays show and explain examples of African-American history, art, and culture including works by local, regional, and national artists. The building was the first black public high school in southwestern Virginia.

31. The Virginia Museum of Transportation is located at 303 Norfolk Avenue in a restored railway freight station.

Railroads have played a very important part in the history of Roanoke and southwestern Virginia and this museum contains exhibits that preserve that heritage. Steam and diesel locomotives, railroad cars, railroad artifacts, antique automobiles, buggies, model trains, airplanes, and other transportation equipment make up the collection. This museum has the largest display of locomotives in the United States.

From downtown Roanoke, drive south on Jefferson Street (VA 116). Just before you get to I - 581 (the 1200 block on Jefferson), turn east on Walnut Avenue, then go under I - 581. Continue east on Walnut Avenue for about 3 miles to Parkway/Mill Mountain Spur Road and a sign directing you to the Mill Mountain Zoo. Turn right and go to:

32. Mill Mountain Zoo. This ten-acre zoo offers a fine collection of more than one hundred native and exotic animals. Paths wind throughout the various habitat areas. There are places for children to touch goats and other small mammals and a variety of educational programs in the summer. This zoo was recently accredited by the American Zoo and Aquarium Association. Picnic spots and rest rooms are also provided.

33. The Mill Mountain Star is a 100-foot tall metal star, the largest man-made star in the world. Located close to the zoo, it's so large you can't possibly miss it. It is visible for miles during the day, and brightly lit, can be seen from even farther away at night. An observation deck close to the star provides a spectacular view of Roanoke in the valley far below.

Go back to the Parkway/Mill Mountain Spur Road, turn right, and continue 3.7 miles southwest to the Blue Ridge Parkway, Milepost 120.5.

6-3 Virginia's Explore Park — Photo courtesy of the
Roanoke Valley Convention and Visitors Bureau

Drive 5.5 miles northeast on the Parkway to Milepost 115 to Virginia's Explore Park sign and 1.5 miles south to:

34. Virginia's Explore Park, at 3900 Rutrough Road, is an outdoor museum of local history and culture. Covering 1,300 acres, this park contains houses, barns, a farm, a schoolhouse, a blacksmith shop, and many other features in a setting recreating frontier, colonial, and more recent life.

Interpreters demonstrate and explain the lifestyles of these people who were ancestors to many of us. A typical Tutelo Indian Village is under construction. The park also provides picnic areas, rest rooms, a museum shop, hiking trails, and a **Regional Information Center.** 540-427-1800.

Return to the Parkway, Milepost 115.

CHAPTER 7 - ROUTE 7

Roanoke/Salem, VA
Smith Mountain Lake, VA
Ferrum, VA

ROUTE 7

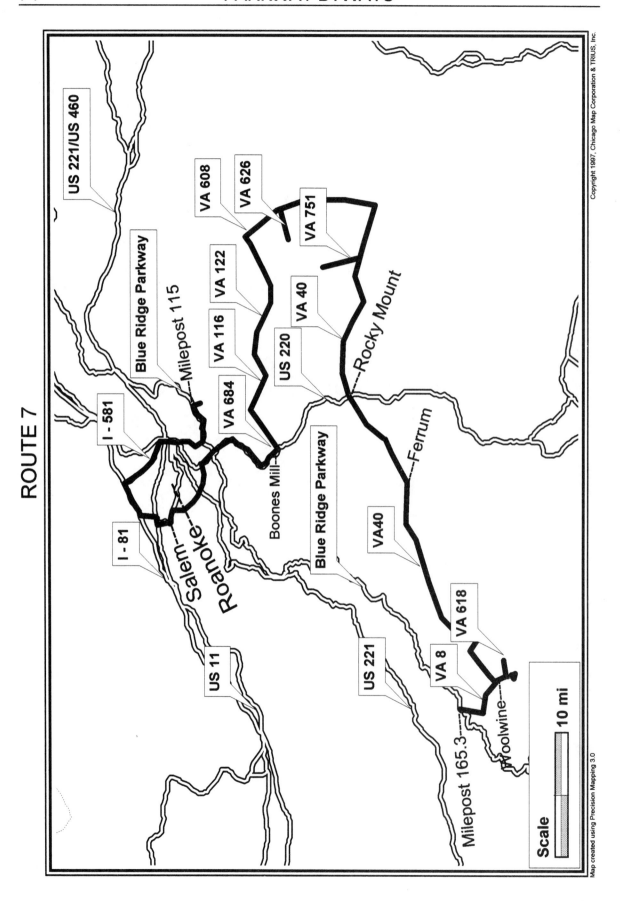

US 221/US 460

Blue Ridge Parkway

Milepost 115

VA 608

VA 626

VA 751

VA 122

VA 116

VA 40

US 220

VA 684

Rocky Mount

Ferrum

I - 581

I - 81

Salem

Roanoke

Boones Mill

Blue Ridge Parkway

VA40

VA 618

US 11

US 221

VA 8

Woolwine

Milepost 165.3

Scale

10 mi

The Roanoke/Salem - Smith Mountain Lake - Ferrum Route tours the Virginia counties of Roanoke, Bedford, Franklin, and Patrick. It is about 175 miles long. Although the byways traveled are quite different, the attractions listed for Roanoke and Salem can also be visited on Route 6. This trip begins at Milepost 115 on the Blue Ridge Parkway at the road to Virginia's Explore Park and continues in a clockwise direction to Milepost 165.3 at Tuggle Gap.

THE BYWAYS —

Route 7 starts with visits to Virginia's Explore Park, attractions on Mill Mountain, and in Roanoke and Salem. The roads and streets traveled are quite scenic because this community contains such a unique and interesting mix of old houses, quiet parks, and modern business buildings. You will enjoy driving around in the downtown area or in almost any residential neighborhood.

From Roanoke, Route 7 proceeds down the mountains and around Smith Mountain Lake, one of the most scenic areas of central Virginia. Frequent glimpses of the clear blue lake water complement views of the mountains and add another dimension to your trip.

This loop concludes with an unusually attractive section of Virginia Highways (VA 40 and VA 8) that take you back up into the mountains. The VA 8 portion is a Virginia Byway.

THE TOWNS —

Roanoke and Salem have an extremely diverse background involving railroads, commerce, manufacturing, and cultural activities. Home to 230,000 people, this is the largest metropolitan area in southwest Virginia. Festivals are very prominent here — Roanoke's Festival in the Park attracts 350,000 people annually and Salem's Fair draws about 200,000. Museums, art exhibits, musical and theatrical performances, and recreational facilities are fully integrated into everyday life. The Center in the Square/City Market complex in Roanoke is one of the most exciting downtown areas in the United States. Combine these cultural advantages with a great climate, excellent health care, and a low crime rate and you have an outstanding community to visit or place to live.

The charming Franklin County town of Rocky Mount is more than 200 years old but is quite progressive with many new businesses and industries. Ferrum is essentially Ferrum College with a beautiful campus and the Blue Ridge Institute which orchestrates many activities relating to Virginia folklore.

THE ATTRACTIONS —

Starting at Milepost 115 on the Blue Ridge Parkway at the sign to Virginia's Explore Park, drive 1.5 miles south to:

Roanoke, Virginia

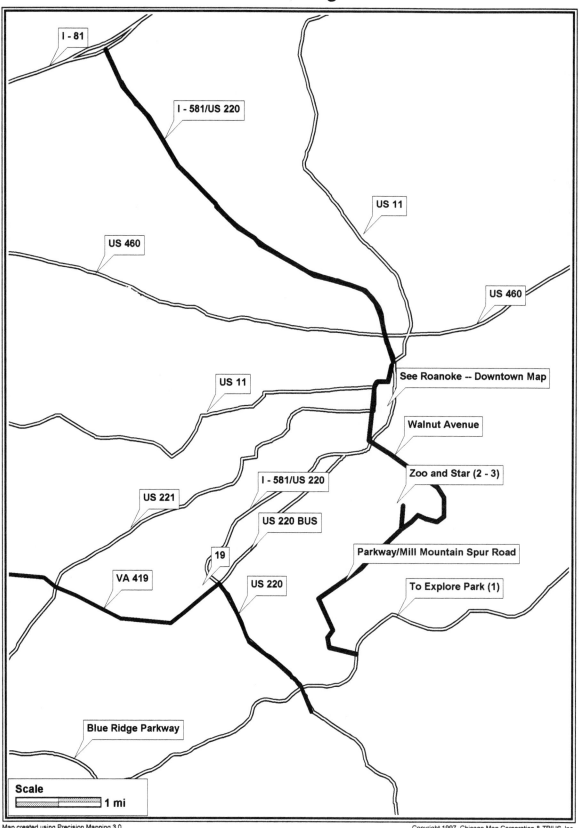

I - 81

I - 581/US 220

US 11

US 460

US 460

US 11

See Roanoke -- Downtown Map

Walnut Avenue

Zoo and Star (2 - 3)

I - 581/US 220

US 221

US 220 BUS

Parkway/Mill Mountain Spur Road

19

VA 419

US 220

To Explore Park (1)

Blue Ridge Parkway

Scale
1 mi

Roanoke -- Downtown

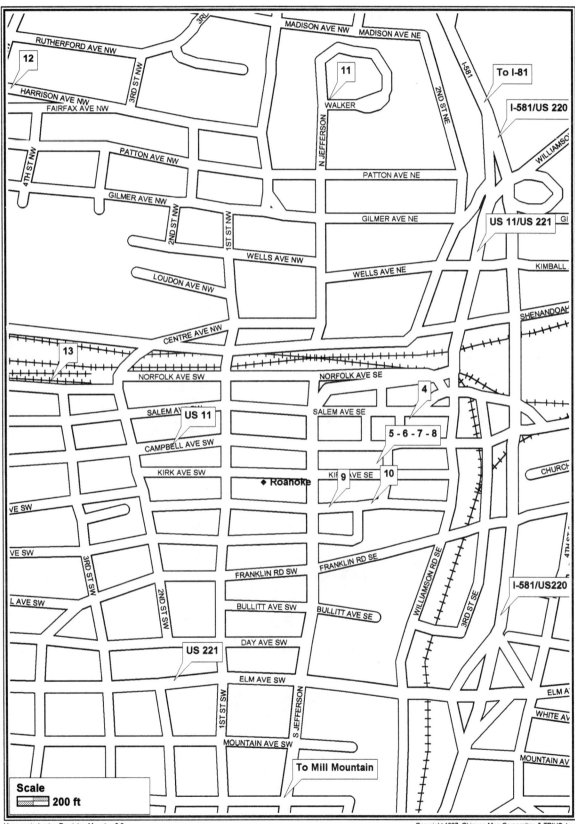

1. Virginia's Explore Park, an outdoor museum of local history and culture. Covering 1,300 acres, this park contains houses, barns, a farm, a schoolhouse, a blacksmith shop, and many other features in a setting recreating frontier, colonial, and more recent life. Interpreters demonstrate and explain the lifestyles of these people who were ancestors to many of us. A typical Tutelo Indian Village is under construction. The park also provides picnic areas, rest rooms, a museum shop, hiking trails, and a **Regional Information Center.** 540-427-1800.

Return to the Parkway, then drive 5.5 miles southwest to the Parkway/Mill Mountain Spur Road. Go 3.7 miles northeast to a sign directing you to:

2. Mill Mountain Zoo. This ten-acre zoo offers a fine collection of more than one hundred native and exotic animals. Paths wind throughout the various habitat areas. There are places for children to touch goats and other small mammals and a variety of educational programs in the summer. This zoo was recently accredited by the American Zoo and Aquarium Association. Picnic spots and rest rooms are also available.

3. The Mill Mountain Star is a 100-foot tall metal star, the largest man-made star in the world. Located close to the zoo, it's so large you can't possibly miss it. It is visible for miles during the day, and brightly lit, can be seen from even farther away at night. An observation deck close to the star provides a spectacular view of Roanoke in the valley far below.

Return to the Parkway/Mill Mountain Spur Road, then drive northwest down the mountain to:

7-1 Ruby the Tiger, a favorite at Mill Mountain Zoo —
Photo courtesy of the Roanoke Convention and Visitors Bureau

Roanoke, Virginia

The Roanoke Festival in the Park is a fantastic eleven-day event occurring in late May/early June. Involving more than three thousand volunteers, and attracting thousands of visitors, this is a must-visit activity. Concerts, art shows, fireworks, a carnival, foods of all kinds, children's activities, a river race, bike and road races, and a parade are among the many featured adventures.

Go under I-581, turn north on Jefferson Street (VA 116), then drive to:

4. The Roanoke Valley Visitor Information Center at 114 Market Street. Be sure to stop here before you explore the city. You won't want to miss the many festivals, shows, and performances, and they will know about them all. Ask for information about a walking tour of downtown Roanoke including the fascinating **Farmer's Market.** 540-342-6025 or 800-635-5535.

The following five attractions are a part of an art, science, history, culture, and theater complex called Center in the Square. All of them are located at One Market Square except **The Arts Council of the Blue Ridge.**

5. The Art Museum of Western Virginia exhibits contemporary and traditional works in all mediums and features folk art from the Virginia mountains. Art from Egypt, Japan, and Africa is also displayed. Workshops, tours, camps, lectures, and classes are offered for adults and children. Children are especially favored in a part of the museum called **ArtVenture: A Children's Center.** More than 2000 square feet of exhibitions and many special activities are of special interest to children.

6. The Science Museum of Western Virginia and Hopkins Planetarium maintains five permanent exhibits and frequently offers touring exhibits. Many opportunities for interactive experiences are featured, along with displays relating to light, anatomy, weather, animals, ocean creatures, sound, and computer science. The Planetarium conducts programs relating to all aspects of astronomy.

7. The Roanoke Valley History Museum contains artifacts and other materials about the Roanoke area from prehistoric to modern times. Information about noteworthy people, railroads, and wars affecting the area, along with tools, documents, weapons, and a store from the 1890's are also featured in the displays

8. Mill Mountain Theater presents musicals, dramas, classics, and children's plays and music. It is one of only two professional theaters operating full-time in southwestern Virginia. The main stage and box office is in Circle in the Square with another facility, **Theater B - Center on Church,** at 20 East Church Avenue.

9. The Arts Council of the Blue Ridge, also at 20 East Church Avenue, offers display space for artists, juried exhibitions, art activities for high school students, art sales, and a regional newsletter reporting on subjects of interest to artists. An Artists Registry and Resource Library is maintained that serves hundreds of artists and dozens of art and culture organizations.

10. Fire Station Number One, at Church Avenue and Market Street, was built in 1906 and still serves the city as a firehouse. It was placed on the National Register of Historic places in 1972. This is a great place to visit with children. The firemen welcome visitors and will show you the old building and modern equipment. They will even slide down the original brass firepole if you ask them and they're not too busy.

11. The Catholic Historical Museum, at 624 North Jefferson Street, presents artifacts relating to the history of the Catholic Church in the Roanoke area. The museum is adjacent to Saint Andrew's Church, a local landmark of imposing size and stature, constructed in 1900. The museum aids in research by maintaining records and files from Catholic churches throughout the area. You should call for an appointment before visiting since the museum is frequently closed. 540-982-0152.

12. The Harrison Museum of African-American Culture is located at 523 Harrison Avenue. Displays explain examples of African-American history, art, and culture including works by local, regional, and national artists. The building

was the first black public high school in southwestern Virginia.

13. The Virginia Museum of Transportation is located at 303 Norfolk Avenue in a restored railway freight station. Railroads have played a very important part in the history of Roanoke and southwestern Virginia and this museum contains exhibits that preserve that heritage. Steam and diesel locomotives, railroad cars, railroad artifacts, antique automobiles, buggies, model trains, airplanes, and other transportation equipment make up the collection. This museum has the largest display of locomotives in the United States.

From downtown Roanoke, drive 6.4 miles northwest on I - 581 to I - 81, then 4 miles southwest on I - 81 to VA 311. Go 1.5 miles south on VA 311 to:

7-2 An antique car at the Virginia Museum of Transportation —
Photo courtesy of the Roanoke Valley Convention and Visitors Bureau

Salem, Virginia

Salem's major festival is the annual Salem Fair. The dates are in early July and the place is the Salem Civic Center. A large antique car show is held annually during Old Salem Days in mid-September.

14. The Salem Visitor's Center, at 1001 Boulevard, is in the Salem Civic Center. Ask for the brochure describing the **Historic Salem Walking Tour.** If you're a baseball fan, the Class A affiliate of the Colorado Rockies, the Salem Avalanche, plays in a stadium close to the Civic Center. 540-375-3004 or 888-827-2536

15. Lake Spring Park is at the corner of West Main and Green Streets. This downtown park is a place to walk, fish, rest, and get a glimpse of local people and their activities.

16. The Salem Farmers Market, at Main and Broad Streets, will provide a nice change of pace for you. Visitors enjoy a profusion of natural, colorful sights and intriguing smells.

17. Roanoke College, 221 College Lane, operates art galleries that display traditional and contemporary works of both regional and nationally known artists. The campus of this downtown college is characterized by shady lawns and historic buildings, the oldest built in 1847.

18. The Salem Museum is located at 801 East Main Street in Longwood Park. Regional history, Civil War history, education, and early photography are featured in this museum in the Williams-Brown House, circa 1845. A fitness trail and a wide variety of playground equipment are available in the park.

From downtown Salem, drive 2.6 miles southeast on US 11 to VA 419 (Electric Road), then 6.2 miles southeast on VA 419 to:

19. To the Rescue Museum. Located on the upper level of Tanglewood Mall, this is a national museum devoted to emergency rescue equipment, techniques, artifacts, and interactive displays. Information about Julian Stanley Wise, who founded the emergency rescue movement in the United States, is featured.

From Tanglewood Mall, drive 1 block north to US 220, then go 10 miles southeast on US 220 to Boones, Mill and VA 684. Drive 6.7 miles northeast on VA 684 to VA 116. Drive 5.1 southeast on VA 116 to VA 122 at Burnt Chimney. Travel 5.5 miles northeast on VA 122 to:

20. The Booker T. Washington National Monument. This park is dedicated to the preservation of the memory and accomplishments of this great former slave who became world-famous as an author, educator, speaker, college president, and statesman. He was born here on April 5, 1856 and died in 1915. The visitor center provides park rangers to answer questions, exhibits, a bookstore, along with a reconstruction of the farm of Washington's "owner", James Burroughs. Demonstrations of farm life before the Civil War will add another dimension to your visit.

Drive 9 miles northeast to Moneta and VA 608. Go 6.4 miles southeast on VA 608 to VA 626, then travel 2 miles southwest on VA 626 to:

21. Smith Mountain Lake State Park. Facilities include primitive camping, a dumping station, cold water showers, pit toilets, boat launching (motor boats permitted), paddleboat rentals, fishing pier, hiking trails, swimming, and picnic tables, a snack bar, a visitors center, programs, and some facilities for the disabled.

Return to VA 608 and go 18 miles southeast on VA 608/VA 605 to VA 40. Drive 2.7 miles west on VA 40 to VA 751 and a sign indicating the route to the Smith Mountain Lake Dam site. Turn north and follow the signs along VA 751, VA 777, and VA 908 (about 8 miles) to:

22. **Smith Mountain Dam,** a part of a two-lake electricity generating system that also includes Leesville Lake and Dam. Water flows through the Smith Mountain Dam into Leesville Lake. When the demand for electricity is lower, some of this water is pumped back into Smith Mountain Lake to restart the process. Electricity is generated when water flows through either dam. A visitors center at the dam, operated by Appalachian Power Company, contains exhibits that explain how the dam was built and how electricity is generated. You can watch a large model of the project which demonstrates a typical operating cycle.

Return to VA 40, then drive 23 miles west to:

Rocky Mount, Virginia

The Rotary Independence Day Celebration and the Lords Acre Sale, on the third weekend in October, are festivals of interest.

23. **The Franklin County Chamber of Commerce** is located at 261 Franklin Street. Ask here if the furnace at the former **Washington Iron Works** is open to visitors. This furnace, dating from the Revolutionary War period, is on private property and may be off-limits at the time of your visit. Also ask for information about performances at the Blue Ridge Dinner Theatre and other activities at nearby Ferrum College. 540-483-9542.

7-3 Smith Mountain Lake — Photo courtesy of the
Bedford Area Chamber of Commerce

24. The Hale Ford Academy, at 102 Bernard Road, is a restored school building and museum of education which portrays school life in the late nineteenth century.

Drive 10 miles southeast on VA 40 to:

Ferrum, Virginia

The Ferrum College Folklife Festival, held the fourth Saturday in October, has more visitors than any other folk festival in Virginia. Arts, crafts, food, music, and dramatic performances are featured.

25. The Blue Ridge Institute and Farm Museum is the major site in Virginia for the preservation of Blue Ridge Mountain folklore. The museum consists of log buildings and fields representing a German-American farmstead. Interpreters in costume use tools, equipment, and methods common in the nineteenth-century to demonstrate life on the early farms. Crops and produce are grown, food is prepared, and household chores are performed according to the traditions of long ago. This Institute is an important cultural resource and should be on your travel agenda if at all possible

26. The Stanley Library Art Galleries, on the campus of Ferrum College, present art shows by students and professional artists.

27. The Blue Ridge Dinner Theatre presents several plays each summer using professional and student actors.

Travel 22 miles southwest on VA 40 to VA 8 at Woolwine. Go 1.5 miles south on VA 8 to VA 618. Drive 1 mile east on VA 618, then 0.1 miles south on VA 869 to:

28. The Bob White Covered Bridge. This structure was built in 1921 and served local residents for more than 50 years. It has been replaced by a modern bridge but is maintained for its historic value.

Return to VA 8, then drive 1 mile south to VA 615. Go 0.2 miles west on VA 615 to:

29. Jacks Creek Covered Bridge, which also has been replaced by a modern bridge, but is being preserved as a reminder of the "good old days." It was built in 1914.

Return to VA 8, then travel 9 miles northwest to the Blue Ridge Parkway, Milepost 165.3 at Tuggle Gap.

Radford, VA
Pearisburg, VA
New River Trail State Park, VA

ROUTE 8

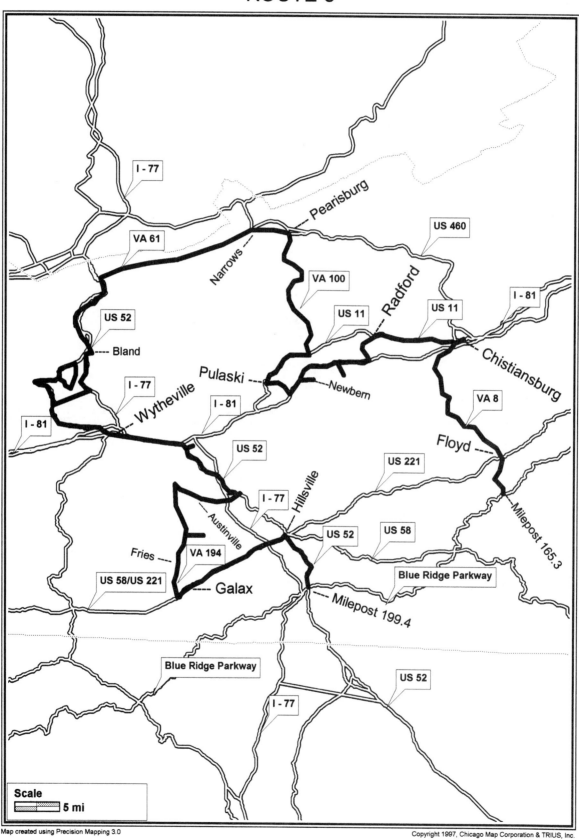

Scale
5 mi

The Radford - Pearisburg - New River Trail State Park Route tours the Virginia counties of Floyd, Montgomery, Pulaski, Giles, Bland, Wythe, and Carroll. It is about 275 miles long. Although the byways are quite different, the attractions listed for the Wytheville, Bland, and Big Walker Mountain area can also be visited on Route 10. This trip begins at Milepost 165.3 on the Blue Ridge Parkway and continues in a counterclockwise direction to Milepost 199.4 at Fancy Gap.

THE BYWAYS —

Almost all of Route 8 travels on byways of exceptional beauty and charm, including the three short sections of interstate highway. Double your pleasure — plan to drive both clockwise and counterclockwise on this route as soon as you can.

Route 8 starts with a scenic section of VA 8, a Virginia Byway from the Parkway through Floyd almost to Christiansburg. The terrain consists of beautiful hills and valleys with larger mountains in the background.

VA 100, from Dublin to Narrows, makes several transitions from mountains to valleys resulting in the usual scenic bonus characteristic of this part of Virginia. The area around the New River at Pearisburg and Narrows is exceptionally scenic. If you have time, drive on other nearby roads and highways, especially US 460, both east and west of Pearisburg.

The entire length of VA 61, from Narrows to Rocky Gap, winds through a narrow valley along bold and beautiful Wolf Creek. Stop occasionally to watch and listen to this exciting stream.

After you reach Bland, the next section of Route 8 runs through one of the most interesting and scenic areas in Virginia — the Big Walker Mountain area. There is a little backtracking but the views are so magnificent and the attractions are so numerous that you won't mind the extra miles. Most of the roads in this section are Virginia Byways and the part on US 52 is also a National Forest Scenic Byway.

The section of US 52/VA 94 south of Fort Chiswell is interesting and unique as it runs through the New River Valley. Frequent views of the river mixed with views of hills and mountains add to the variety.

THE TOWNS —

The text in this chapter lists more than a dozen picturesque Virginia villages and towns. All of them are as appealing as they are different. Spend as much time as you can walking along the sidewalks, talking to the people, and driving on the local streets.

Newbern, Narrows, Austinville, and Fries are small villages that have a special historical significance. All of them are very old. All are on or very close to the New River, which contributed to their early existence. These early communities exhibit a nineteenth-century lifestyle that is very interesting to contemporary travelers.

Floyd, Christiansburg, Pulaski, Pearisburg, Bland, and Hillsville are typical county seat towns with a few industries and other businesses in addition to the usual government offices. All of them contain many old houses and other buildings reflecting the early settlement of Virginia.

Radford, Wytheville, and Galax are larger towns with more industry and business activity. They also have more art centers, museums, educational institutions, parks, and other cultural amenities. Radford University and Bisset Park in Radford, the Chautauqua Festival in Wytheville, and the Old Fiddlers Convention in Galax are especially noteworthy.

THE ATTRACTIONS —

Starting at Milepost 165.3 on the Blue Ridge Parkway, drive 6 miles north on VA 8 to:

Floyd, Virginia

Visit Floyd in early October for the Arts and Crafts Festival. Quilts are a featured attraction but many other kinds of hand-crafted items are also available. The festival is held at Floyd High School, Baker Street and Woods Gap Road.

A unique mini-festival of music is held every weekend at **Cochran's General Store,** 206 South Locust Street. Friday nights bring mountain music and dancing. Gospel music fans celebrate on Saturday nights.

8-1 Floyd County Courthouse — Photo courtesy of the Floyd County Chamber of Commerce

1. Floyd Chamber of Commerce is at 107 East Main Street. Operating hours are from 7:00 AM to 12:00 noon on Tuesdays and Thursdays. Ask for a brochure describing a self-guided walking tour of downtown Floyd, or if the office is closed, get one at Cochran's General Store at 206 South Locust Street. 540-745-4407.

Travel 21 miles north on VA 8 to:

Christiansburg, Virginia

The Wilderness Trail Festival, held on the third Saturday in September, is a special occasion in Christiansburg. Arts and crafts are displayed; music, games, and great food are enjoyed by residents and visitors alike.

2. The Christiansburg-Montgomery County Chamber of Commerce is located at 205 West Main - Number 4. 540-382-4251.

3. Montgomery Museum and Lewis Miller Art Center is located at 300 South Pepper Street. This museum exhibits items relating to the history of Montgomery County and southwestern Virginia. Art works of Lewis Miller, a primitive folk artist, is featured. The building, built in the mid-nineteenth century, was the home of the Pepper family.

4. The Historic Christiansburg Depot Museum, on Depot Street, is located on the site where an earlier depot was burned by the Union Army in 1864.

5. The Palette Art Gallery, located east of downtown Christiansburg at 2840 Roanoke Street (US 460), is a non-profit organization that displays works of artists from Montgomery County and the surrounding area.

Drive 10 miles west on US 11 to:

Radford, Virginia

The Brush Mountain Arts and Crafts Fair is a new festival for Radford. It is held in early April at the Dedmon Center, an unusual air supported sports complex on the campus of Radford University. This is a major event for the town with many art and crafts exhibits, live entertainment, and activities for children.

6. The Radford Chamber of Commerce is located at 1126 Norwood Street (US 11). Ask for information about the new Radford Heritage Museum under development by the Radford Heritage Foundation in the historic home, Glenco. The scheduled opening is July 4, 1998. 540-639-2202.

7. The Bondurant Center for the Arts, at 1115 Norwood Street, owned and operated by Radford University, houses an authentic German restaurant, studio and lecture space, an art gallery, and a gift shop. Art from all over the world is displayed.

8. The Flossie Martin Gallery and the Burde Sculpture Courtyard are on the campus of Radford University, which is close to the Chamber of Commerce. Go east on Norwood Street to Adams Street (at the large Radford University sign) and turn south. The Gallery and Courtyard are on the right. Contemporary and traditional artists — national and regional — working in both two and three dimensions are featured. Ten new sculptures are exhibited in an annual competition in the Courtyard. One of these works is purchased and installed on the campus.

9. Bisset Park and Wildwood Park, located across Norwood Street from each other, are delightful places to, swim, play, exercise, or just relax and enjoy nature.

Both parks are just north of the junction on Norwood Street where US 11 turns right and crosses the New River and VA 232 goes southwest to I - 81. Bisset Park is a large park along the river with a swimming pool, jogging trails, tennis courts, and picnic shelters. Wildwood Park, on the southeast side of Norwood Street, is quieter and more nature oriented with places to walk and rest.

10. *The Long Way Home* is an outstanding historical drama presented in an outdoor amphitheater. The facility is located on VA 232 just north of Interstate 81. The drama is presented during the months of July and August on Thursday through Sunday at 8:00 PM. The story concerns Mary Draper Ingles, who was captured by Indians, escaped, and influenced the French and Indian War. This performance has been designated as "Virginia's Historical Drama of the Commonwealth."

Drive 0.3 miles south on VA 232 to I - 81, then go 4 miles west to Exit 101 and VA 660. Travel 3 miles south on VA 660 to:

11. **Claytor Lake State Park,** a large park with many facilities including four campgrounds with over 100 campsites, many of which have electric and water hookups. Showers, toilets, and a dumping station are provided. Twelve housekeeping cabins are also available. The park features swimming with a beach, bathhouse, and a lifeguard. A Marina provides a launching ramp, slip rental, fuel, food, motor and rowboat rentals, and supplies. Hiking trails, great fishing in Claytor Lake, a playground, picnic areas with grills, and horseback riding are additional features.

The park office and visitor center is in the historic **Howe House** built by Haven B. Howe in the late nineteenth-century. Exhibits relating to nature and early settlers are on display. Visit Howe House on Labor

Day weekend for the annual **Claytor Lake Arts and Crafts Festival** featuring pottery, stained glass, baskets, woodwork, painting, plus a wide variety of foods and entertainment.

Return to I - 81, then drive 3 miles west to Exit 98 and frontage road F-047. Go 1 mile southwest on F-047 to VA 611, then drive northeast on VA 611 to:

Newbern, Virginia

More than 25,000 people visit Newbern on the second weekend in October for the Newbern Fall Festival of Arts and Crafts. This festival specializes in delicious food, antiques, crafts, music, art, and pets.

12. **The Wilderness Road Regional Museum** is a group of buildings which include a large house and restored outbuildings. Artifacts from 1810 to 1865, such as furniture, documents, photos, and other materials relating to southwestern Virginia are displayed. This museum is owned and operated by the New River Historical Society. The area around the Museum, called Newbern Historic District, contains many other old buildings on the National Register of Historic Places.

Return to I - 81, then drive 4 miles southwest to Exit 94 and VA 99. Turn northwest on VA 99, then go 3.6 miles to downtown:

Pulaski, Virginia

The Depot Days Festival is a major event in Pulaski. It is held in late June and features arts and crafts, a car show, food vendors, bands, activities for children, and exhibits relating to trains, railroads, and other kinds of transportation.

13. The Chamber of Commerce is located at the restored **Pulaski Railway Station** on Washington Avenue. This station, built in 1886, was donated to the town by the Norfolk and Western Railroad in 1989 and restored in 1994. 540-980-1991.

14. The Raymond F. Ratcliffe Memorial Museum, also located at the Pulaski Railway Station, displays model railroads and artifacts relating to the history of Pulaski and Pulaski County.

15. The Fine Arts Center for the New River Valley, at 21 West Main Street and at **The Womens Club Annex** at 44 West Fourth Street, is a regional art center offering musical and dramatic performances and exhibitions by amateur and professional artists. Art classes, workshops, and outreach programs are conducted throughout the year.

16. The Pulaski County Courthouse, at 52 West Main Street, was constructed in 1896, burned in 1989, and rebuilt in 1992. A stone arch which now serves as the entrance to the building, was constructed for the entrance to the Pulaski County exhibit at the Jamestown Exposition in 1907. Displays feature the history of African Americans and exhibit other items of local historical interest. This is a handsome building that combines Queen Anne and Romanesque architecture. The courthouse was built of "Peak Creek" sandstone.

17. Jackson Park, located at Washington Avenue and Second Street, is an attractive downtown park with cannons from the Civil War and World War I plus a gazebo, used for musical concerts, and a pleasant fountain.

18. The New River Trail State Park is a major attraction in southwestern Virginia. It is a Rails-to-Trails conversion park running for 57 miles through the Virginia counties of Pulaski, Wythe, Carroll, and Grayson and the towns of Pulaski and Galax. Since the trail is a former railroad bed, the surface is quite wide and level and suitable for use by physically disabled persons. The park offers hiking, biking, horseback riding, and cross country skiing. Motorized vehicles are not allowed. There are more than a dozen places to picnic and fishing opportunities abound in the New River (39 miles), Chestnut Creek (12 miles) and Claytor Lake (1.5 miles).

The Virginia Department of Conservation and Recreation has prepared a great brochure describing this trail. Copies are available at Chambers of Commerce/ Welcome Centers in Wytheville, Fort Chiswell, Pulaski, Galax, Independence, and many other places in Virginia. You can also call 540-699-6778 for the brochure and other information about the park.

Parking and access points to the trail are included in the text of this book according to their location along the route traveled.

The Pulaski parking and access point is located about 2 miles northwest of I - 81 on VA 99. Turn at Xaloy Drive. Xaloy Drive is also about 2 miles east of downtown Pulaski on VA 99.

From downtown Pulaski, drive 7 miles northeast on US 11 to VA 100, then 21 miles north on VA 100 to:

Pearisburg, Virginia

Visit Pearisburg in mid-June for the Festival Around Town.

19. The Giles County Chamber of Commerce is at 101 South Main Street. Ask for their interesting brochure describing "Olde Towne Pearisburg — Established 1808." This is a downtown walking tour

8-2 Wytheville's Rock House Museum — Photo courtesy of the
Town of Wytheville

through the historic district that you won't want to miss. If you're ready for a strenuous hike — 1.5 miles one-way over steep and difficult terrain — ask for directions to **Angels Rest,** a place with spectacular views of the countryside. This is a segment of the Appalachian Trail on the mountain overlooking Pearisburg. 540-921-5000.

20. The Johnston House, at 208 North Main Street, is the oldest brick house in Giles County. It was built in 1829 and is on the National Register of Historic Places. A museum in the house, displaying period furniture and artifacts relating to Pearisburg and Giles County, has recently been enlarged into a major historical resource.

21. The Giles County Courthouse, on the Public Square, is listed in the Virginia Landmarks Register and the National Register of Historic Places.

Drive 5 miles west on VA 100 to:

Narrows, Virginia

The Narrows Fall Festival in early October features music, street dancing, activities for children, rides, and contests along with the sale of art, crafts, and food.

The town park in Narrows offers a restful place to take a break from your driving.

Drive 21 miles southwest on VA 61 to Rocky Gap and I - 77, then go 4 miles south on I - 77 to:

22. The Rocky Gap Welcome Center. This Interstate Welcome Center, maintained by the Virginia Tourism Corporation, provides restrooms, drinks, food, and a world of information about Virginia attractions, restaurants, motels, etc.

Continue 2 miles south on I - 77 to Exit 58 and US 52, then drive 7 miles south on US 52 to:

Bland, Virginia

The Bland County Festival of Leaves , held during the second weekend in October, features art and photography, a storyteller, puppets, hay rides, quilts, antique cars, food sales, music, and a doll show plus many other fun things to do.

From Bland go 0.8 miles west on US 52 to I - 77. Drive 4 miles south on I - 77 to:

23. The Big Walker Tunnel, running for more than a mile under Big Walker Mountain, is an exciting experience for both the young and the young in heart.

Continue south on I - 77 to Exit 47 and VA 717. Go 4 miles southwest on VA 717 to:

24. Stony Fork Campground, a USDA Forest Service facility. There are sunny and shady campsites with picnic tables, fireplaces, lantern posts, fresh water, restrooms, warm showers, flush toilets, and a dump station. You can fish in Stony Fork Creek or walk on an interesting nature trail.

Drive 0.5 miles west on VA 717, then 4 miles northwest on US 52 to:

25. Monster Rock Hiking Trail. Park in the Big Walker Lookout parking lot and take a short trail to a large rock outcropping where there is a great view of the valley below and the mountains beyond.

From the Big Walker Lookout parking lot, drive 4 miles southeast on FS 206 to:

26. The Big Bend Picnic Area, which is a delightful place for picnics, with tables, grills, and fireplaces. Panoramic views from the 4,000 crest of Big Walker Mountain make this a very special site.

Return to US 52, then travel 3.3 miles northeast to VA 617.

27. The VA 617 Loop Trip runs for seven beautiful miles along Walker Creek at the base of Big Walker Mountain. The winding creek, open fields, rolling terrain, and well-kept farms make this Virginia Byway a truly delightful place.

Turn southwest at the junction of VA 617 and US 52, then drive 6.8 miles back up Big Walker Mountain, then go 6.5 miles south on US 52 to:

28. Dark Horse Hollow Picnic Area, a USDA Forest Service facility, is situated along US 52 on the banks of Stony Fork Creek. Picnic tables, grills, and vault toilets are provided.

Continue 7 miles southeast on US 52 to:

Wytheville, Virginia

A major festival in Wytheville in mid-June is the Chautauqua Festival in the Park. This festival extends over several days and features visual and performing arts; a place for residents and visitors to share in the area's culture, entertainment, and history. The Elizabeth Brown Memorial Park at Fourth and Spring Streets is the site for this delightful series of events.

29. The Wytheville - Wythe - Bland Chamber of Commerce and the Wytheville Area Convention and Visitor's Bureau are located in adjacent offices at 150 East Monroe Street. Either agency will be happy to give you information about the area. Ask for details about a walking tour of the downtown area. 540-223-3365 and 540-223-3355.

30. The Rock House Museum, at 205 North Tazewell Street, was the home of Wytheville's first resident physician, Dr. John Haller. Completed in 1823, this old house served as a hospital during the Civil War, and now contains many of Dr. Haller's possessions and other items related to Wythe Country history.

31. The Thomas J. Boyd Museum is located next to the Rock House Museum on Tazewell Street. Artifacts displayed include Wytheville's first fire truck and a variety of old farming and industrial machines. Historical and military information is also featured..

From downtown Wytheville, drive 8.4 miles east on US 11/US 52/ I - 77/I - 81 to Exit 80. Turn south on US 52, then immediately east on Factory Merchant Drive. Go 1 mile to the Outlet Mall and :

32. Southwest Highlands Gateway Visitor Center. This fine facility, maintained by the USDA Forest Service and other organizations, contains one of the most extensive collections of travel brochures in southwestern Virginia. Educational exhibits and guidance from helpful workers will add extra enjoyment to your trip.

Return to US 52, then drive 8 miles southeast to:

33. The Shot Tower Historical State Park, a historic structure that was used in the manufacture of lead shot in pioneer days. The tower is almost 200 years old. Lead was hoisted to the top of the tower, melted, poured through sieves, and dropped 150 feet into a container of water. This process created the round lead pellets called shot. Thomas Jackson, born in 1762, built and operated the tower until his death in 1824.

Drive 2.3 miles northeast on VA 608, then VA 623 to:

34. The Historic Foster Falls Village, the headquarters for the **New River Trail State Park.** The facility at Foster Falls provides access to the New River, boat launching, canoe and bike rentals, hiking, bicycling, horseback riding, fishing, and picnicking. A number of old buildings, dating back to the nineteenth-century, including a railroad depot, hotel, mill, and an iron furnace are also available for your inspection.

Return to US 52, then drive 2 miles south to VA 69. Travel 4 miles west on VA 69, then VA 636 to:

Austinville, Virginia

Formerly known as Lead Mines, this historic little town was the center of early lead mining activity. Settlers here wrote the "Fincastle Resolutions" which were later incorporated into the Declaration of Independence. Moses Austin managed the lead mines after the Revolutionary War and was the father of Stephen Austin who became known as the "Father of Texas."

Drive 5 miles west on VA 619 to VA 94, then go 2 miles southeast on VA 94 to Ivanhoe and VA 639, where parking for the **New River Trail State Park** is provided. Drive 5 miles south on VA 94 to VA 602, then go 4 miles east on VA 602 to:

35. The Byllesby Dam and The New River Campground. The dam is an interesting hydroelectric structure in the New River. This dam produces electricity by the run-of-the-river method. The whole river flows through the power house. There is no lake. Excess water can be diverted around the dam at flood times. **The New River Campground,** north of the dam on VA 737 and a USDA Forest Service facility, provides primitive camping along the river, drinking water, fishing, hiking trails, picnicking, and toilets. There is a great view of rock bluffs across the river.

Parking and an access point to the **New River Trail State Park** is provided at the dam or you can use your campsite as a base for exploring the trail.

Return to VA 94, then go 6 miles south to:

Fries, Virginia

This is a quaint town with many old buildings, a pleasant town park, and another parking and access point to the **New River Trail State Park.** Mount Vernon Mills, the town's major source of employment, closed in 1989.

Drive 9 miles south on VA 94 to US 58, then go 4 miles northeast on US 58 to:

Galax, Virginia

Galax does festivals in a big way. First, there's the Twin County United Way Festival in the Park, held on Memorial Day weekend, and highlighting food, children's games, booths with information about United Way agencies, concessions, etc. Felts Park, on Main Street is the location for this festival.

Bluegrass musicians and fans from around the world gather in Galax for the festival that has brought Galax recognition as the "World Capital of Old Time Country Music." This exciting event, The Old Fiddlers Convention, coinciding with Fiddlefest, a downtown street festival, occurs on the second weekend in August. In addition to the great music, arts and crafts sales, food, and activities for children are featured.

36. The Galax-Carroll-Grayson Chamber of Commerce is at 405 North Main Street. 540-236-2184.

8-3 Fries Dam on the New River — Photo courtesy of the Grayson County Tourist Information Center and Linda Richardson

37. The Rooftop of Virginia Community Action Program maintains a large craft store at 206 North Main Street. Quilts, pottery, toys, baskets, antique furniture, and many kinds of handmade articles are just a few examples of the many fascinating items available for sale at this non-profit store.

38. The Jeff Matthews Memorial Museum is located at 606 West Stuart Drive. A wide variety of artifacts and memorabilia are on display including many stuffed animals, clothing from the turn of the century, pictures of Civil War veterans, a display of African items, a covered wagon, fossils from Alaska, etc.

Two more parking and access points lead to the **New River Trail State Park** in the Galax area. The first is downtown, where US 58 crosses Chestnut Creek, just east of Main Street. The second is northeast of downtown on Cliffview Road (VA 887/ VA 721), across from the Cliffview Mansion and the Cliffview Trading Post.

Drive 7.7 miles northeast on US 58 to VA 620, then 3 miles south on VA 620 to:

39. The Crooked Creek Wildlife Management Area. Operated by the Virginia Department of Game and Inland Fisheries, this facility provides 6 miles of trout fishing on Crooked Creek. Three miles of the stream are stocked with trout on five days in each week. A total of 1,600 acres of fields and woodland are available for hunting. Fishing permits and licenses, sandwiches, snacks, drinks, picnic tables, and restrooms are also available.

Return to US 58, then go 6 miles northeast to:

Hillsville, Virginia

Labor Day weekend in Hillsville brings the Annual Gun Show and Flea Market. This giant four day affair attracts thousands of sellers, shoppers, and gun collectors. It is sponsored by the Grover King Post 1115, VFW.

The Hillsville Arts and Crafts Show and Old Fashioned Day, featuring a farm display, health fair, arts, crafts, music, food, etc., make up the Old Mountain Home Week Celebration in mid-October.

40. The Carroll County Chamber of Commerce is located at 853 West Stuart Drive in the Hickory Hills Shopping Center. 540-728-5397.

41. The Carroll County Courthouse, on Main Street, is famous for a courtroom shoot-out that occurred on March 14, 1912. Five people were killed and two were wounded when a judge ruled against a member of the influential Allen family. The original charge was for disorderly conduct at a church meeting.

42. The Carroll County Historical Society Museum, located in a restored former post office building on Main Street, features information about the 1912 courthouse tragedy and other materials relating to Carroll County history. A model of a log cabin is also displayed.

Travel 5 miles south on US 52 to:

43. The J. Sidna Allen Home. This unusual large house is open to the public on most weekends. The Queen Anne style house is a Virginia Historic Landmark.

Drive 3 miles south on US 52 to Fancy Gap and the Blue Ridge Parkway at Milepost 199.4.

CHAPTER 9 - ROUTE 9

Martinsville, VA
Hanging Rock State Park, NC
Mount Airy, NC

ROUTE 9

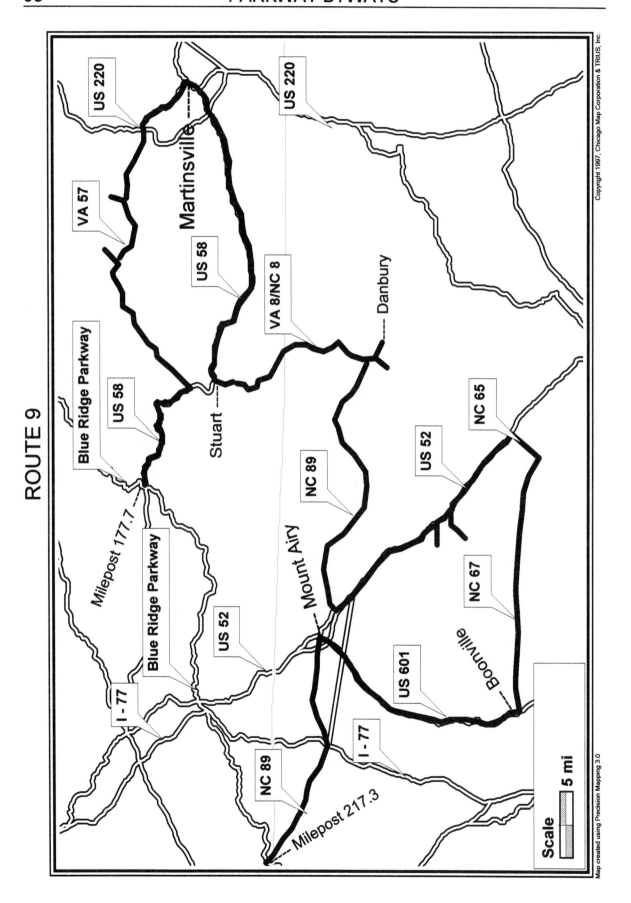

Copyright 1997, Chicago Map Corporation & TRIUS, Inc.

Map created using Precision Mapping 3.0

The Martinsville - Hanging Rock State Park - Mount Airy Route tours the Virginia counties of Patrick and Henry and the North Carolina counties of Stokes, Surry, and Yadkin. It is about 250 miles long. This trip begins at Milepost 177.7 on the Blue Ridge Parkway at the Meadows of Dan and continues in a clockwise direction to Milepost 217.3, close to Cumberland Knob.

THE BYWAYS —

Route 9 starts with a dramatic section of VA 8 as it winds down from the Parkway toward Stuart. This Virginia Byway features breathtaking views of Virginia's Piedmont, particularly at Lovers Leap and the Fred Clifton Park.

The loop starting on VA 8, continuing on VA 57 to Martinsville and returning on US 58 to VA 8 at Stuart, is a "foothills" area that is rugged but not mountainous. You will enjoy the rolling hills and well-kept farms.

A Virginia Byway, VA 8 south from Stuart, travels through scenic hill country and continues as NC 8 south to Danbury, North Carolina. The area around Danbury, Stokes County, is the only county in the United States that claims its own mountain range, the Sauratown Mountains. Majestic peaks and ridges provide panoramic views of the surrounding countryside, 1,700 feet below. Hanging Rock State Park is the perfect place to view these mountains up close.

9-1 Country Musicians — Photo courtesy of the
Floyd County Chamber of Commerce

A NC Scenic Byway, NC 89, takes you west toward Mount Airy through attractive farmland. Blue Ridge Mountain views dominate the horizon. As you travel southeast from Mount Airy, the enormous bulk of Pilot Mountain looms far above the farmland below. This is arguably the most spectacular sight on Route 9.

Returning to Mount Airy, you will finish this trip with a drive on NC 89 into the mountains and return to the Parkway.

THE TOWNS —

Martinsville, Virginia is a small city with diversified industry, several institutions devoted to arts and culture, and many fine old houses and other buildings.. The Virginia Museum of Natural History is especially noteworthy. Racing fans will surely want to visit the Martinsville Speedway for an abundance of fun and excitement.

Danbury, North Carolina, listed in the National Register of Historic places, is small, but offers several things to see and do. Dating back to 1849, Danbury was once well known as a mineral springs resort town.

Mount Airy, North Carolina, is everybody's hometown. Andy Griffith told us so much about his "Mayberry" that we can walk through Mount Airy expecting to meet an old friend at any moment. Proud to be called "The Friendly City," Mount Airy expresses, in fact, all those homespun virtues we saw portrayed in fantasy on the TV screen.

THE ATTRACTIONS —

From Milepost 177.7 on the Blue Ridge Parkway, drive 6.2 miles east on US 58 to:

1. **The Fred Clifton Park,** an exciting public park with several places to picnic and spectacular views of five counties. Lovers' Leap Wayside adjoins this lovely park.

Continue 6.5 miles southeast on US 58 to VA 8. Travel 4.3 miles northeast on VA 8 to VA 57, then 8 miles northeast on VA 57 to VA 346. Go 2 miles north on VA 346 to:

2. **Fairy Stone State Park.** This park, named after the small crystalline crosses found in the area, is one of Virginia's most attractive and well-equipped parks. A campground with water and electrical hookups, a dump station, showers, toilets, housekeeping cabins, picnicking, hiking trails, bicycle trails, swimming, bathhouse, rowboat and paddleboat rentals, fishing, and a snack bar, along with some facilities for disabled persons are provided. A 168-acre lake is a special feature of this park.

Return to VA 57, then drive 7 miles east to VA 904 (Philpott Dam Road). Go 1 mile north to:

3. **Philpott Lake Management Center.** Ask here for information about the multitude of recreational services provided at this US Army Corps of Engineers dam and lake. 10,000 acres of water and surrounding lands make up this great facility, believed by the Corps to be the most beautiful in Virginia. A few of the many services provided include campgrounds; boat launching, docking, and mooring; hiking trails, picnicking, swimming, and a museum.

Return to VA 57, then drive 12 miles southeast on VA 57 and US 220 to:

9-2 Martinsville's Indian Heritage Festival — Photo courtesy of the
Martinsville - Henry County Chamber of Commerce

Martinsville, Virginia

Visit Martinsville on the first Saturday in October for Octoberfest, a street festival held in the Uptown area.

NASCAR racing at Martinsville Speedway, on VA 976, brings a festival atmosphere to the community several times each year. Race fans will know when their favorite cars and trucks are in action. Auto shows provide classes for cars, trucks, and motorcycles.

3. The Martinsville - Henry County Chamber of Commerce is located at 115 Broad Street. Ask for their publication, *History - Old Homes - Other Historical Facts.* 540-632-6401.

4. The Virginia Museum of Natural History, at 1001 Douglas Avenue, is the main facility of this outstanding organization which also has branches at Blacksburg and Charlottesville. Natural history exhibits, galleries, field trips, lectures, Indian heritage studies, tours of research sites, and educational activities for schools are some of the services offered. Recent exhibits include "Rock Hall of Fame," "Our Age of Mammals," "Age of Reptiles," "Dan River People: Ancient Virginians and Their Environment," and "A Closer Look." Giant ground sloth tracks, dinosaur tracks, and ancient whale skeletons have been excavated and are on display.

5. The Piedmont Arts Association, an associate of the Virginia Museum of Fine Arts, is located at 215 Starling Avenue. This impressive cultural resource offers exhibits of fine arts, performing arts, workshops, displays, special events, and opportunities for educational experiences of all kinds.

6.   The Gray Lady, located on Church Street, is a striking historic home listed on the Virginia and National Registers of Historic Places. Although occupied by a real estate company, the building is open to the public during normal business hours.

7.   The Walker Fine Arts Center is located on the campus of Patrick Henry Community College, located north of uptown Martinsville. Take VA 108, VA 714, and VA 371 (College Street) to the college. The Fine Arts Center contains a 300-seat theater and features a variety of art exhibits.

Drive 20 miles west on US 58 to VA 626, then go 4 miles north on VA 626 to VA 787. Turn west to:

8.   The Reynolds Homestead is the restored birthplace of R. J. Reynolds, founder of the R. J. Reynolds Tobacco Company. This old house, now a Virginia and National Historic Landmark, contains many of the original furnishings. Blacksburg's Virginia Tech operates a Continuing Education Center at the site, offering festivals, art exhibitions, special events, and concerts.

Return to US 58, then travel 8 west miles to:

Stuart, Virginia

Here's a change-of-pace festival: Stuart's Summertime Beach Music Festival, held in mid-June at Wayside Park. This fun-filled event draws big-name bands and was ranked as one of the top beach music festivals by *USA Today.*

Visit Stuart in mid-August for the Virginia Peach Festival, at Rotary Field. Music and food are the main attractions.

9-3 Martinsville Speedway — Photo Courtesy of the Martinsville - Henry County Chamber of Commerce

9.   **The Patrick County Chamber of Commerce** is on South Main Street. 540-694-6012.

10.   **The Patrick County Historical Museum**, located at the Patrick County Library, exhibits documents and artifacts relating to mountain history and culture.

11.   **The Wood Brothers Racing Shop and Museum**, in the Patrick County Business Park on US 58, displays memorabilia depicting the history of one of racing's most successful organizations. Show cars and a souvenir shop are featured.

Drive 20 miles south on VA 8/NC 8 to:

Danbury, North Carolina

12.   **The Dan River ArtMarket** is an organization of artists from Stokes and Rockingham counties. Their gallery/shop, located in the restored Petree Building, offers baskets, pottery, glass, toys, jewelry, quilts, plus a number of other arts and crafts items. The ArtMarket is a project of the Stokes County Arts Council.

13. **Moratock Park** is a delightful park on Shepherd Mill Road, on the bank of the Dan River. This is the site of the **Moratock Iron Furnace**, built in 1843, and used to make bar iron during the Civil War.

Drive 1.7 miles northwest on NC 8 to NC 1001 (Hanging Rock Road). Turn west and follow signs to:

14.   **Hanging Rock State Park**, a large, natural area containing waterfalls, rugged cliffs, and quiet forests. Facilities offered in this 6,000-acre park include a campground (no hookups), showers, toilets, rental cabins, swimming, fishing, canoe and rowboat rental, a concession stand, 18 miles of

hiking trails, picnicking at more than 100 tables, an observation tower, bridle trails, nature programs, and lots of great scenery.

Return to NC 8, turn northwest and go 2 miles to NC 89. Follow NC 89 northwest for 27 miles to US 52 BUS then go 12.4 miles southeast to NC 2053 (Pilot Mountain Park Road).

15.   **Pilot Mountain State Park - Mountain Section.** This section of the park features distinctive Pilot Mountain, a National Natural Landmark, which towers more than 1,400 feet above the surrounding countryside. In addition to great views in all directions from strategic overlooks, the park offers restrooms, places to picnic, and trails to hike.   A 5.5-mile "Corridor Trail," starting at the base of the mountain, connects the Mountain and River sections of the park. Both hiking and horseback riding are permitted on the Corridor Trail.

Return to US 52, then drive 2 miles southeast to the Pinnacle Exit and NC 1147 (Perch Road).   Follow the brown historic site signs southwest to Horne Creek Living Historical Farm. Continue 0.4 miles to:

16.   **Pilot Mountain State Park - River Section.** This part of the park features trails for hiking and horseback riding and places to picnic.   The Corridor Trail from the Mountain Section of the park terminates here. A part of the River Section is across the Yadkin River which is normally shallow at this point and may be waded or you may reach the park from the town of East Bend, as described later in this chapter.

Retrace your route 0.4 miles to:

17.   **The Horne Creek Living Historical Farm,** a cultural and historical laboratory where specialists are reconstructing a family farm from the late nineteenth century.   This

site, administered by the North Carolina Department of Cultural Resources, is dedicated to the study, preservation, and interpretation of North Carolina's rural heritage. As you visit the farm, you may see archaeologists at work, farming operations, buildings under construction, cooking, butchering, and many other activities characteristic of early farm life. This is a wonderful place, filled with educational opportunities, which will fascinate everyone regardless of age.

Return to US 52, then drive 11 miles southeast to NC 65. Go 5 miles southwest on NC 65 to NC 67 then 10 miles west on NC 67 to East Bend. To visit the Yadkin County part of the Pilot Mountain State Park - River Section (south side of the Yadkin River), drive northwest on Main Street, then north on Fairground Road, Shady Grove Church Road, and Shoals Road to the park.

From East Bend, travel 11 miles west on NC 67 to US 601 at Boonville, then go 21 miles north on US 601 to:

Mount Airy, North Carolina

Among Mount Airy's many festivals, two are especially noteworthy. The Mayberry Days Festival is held on the last weekend in September and the Autumn Leaves Festival, featuring bluegrass and old time music, is on the second weekend in October.

18. The Mount Airy Visitors Center is at 615 North Main Street. Ask them for the brochure describing a tour of the historic town and about current performances at the Andy Griffith Playhouse. Check out their "world's largest collection of Andy Griffith memorabilia." 336-789-4636 or 800-576-0231.

19. The Mount Airy Museum of Regional History, at 301 North Main Street, is a new facility displaying artifacts and conducting educational programs relating to Surry County and the surrounding area.

20. The Andy Griffith Playhouse, at Rockford and Graves Streets, was used as a gymnasium and auditorium for the City of Mount Airy. The Surry Arts Council leased the building in 1975 and converted it into a theater and arts center.

Drive 21 miles northwest on NC 89 to NC 18, then 0.8 mile west to the Blue Ridge Parkway, Milepost 217.3.

Wytheville, VA
Hungry Mother State Park, VA
Jefferson, NC

ROUTE 10

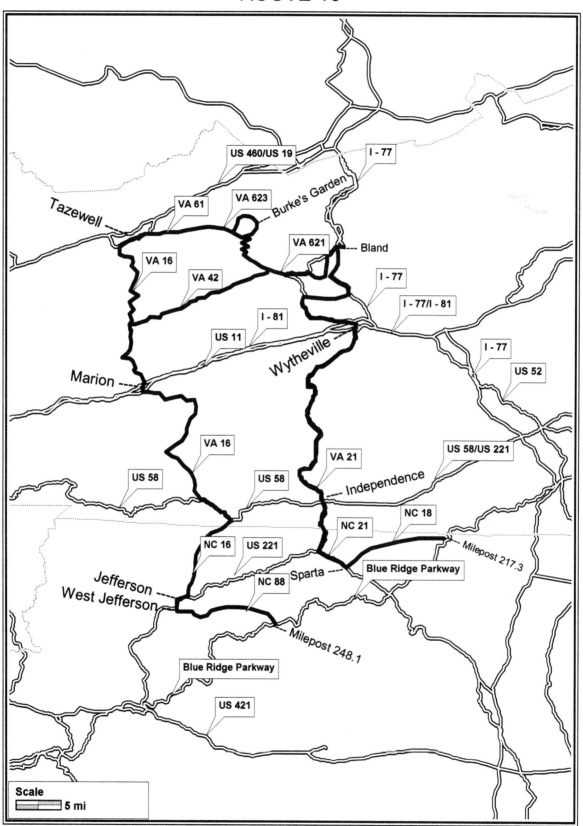

The Wytheville - Hungry Mother State Park - Jefferson Route tours the Virginia counties of Grayson, Wythe, Tazewell, and Smyth, and the North Carolina counties of Alleghany and Ashe. It is about 230 miles long. Although the byways are quite different, the attractions listed for Wytheville, Bland, and the Big Walker Mountain area can also be visited on Route 8 and the attractions listed for the Jefferson/West Jefferson area can also be visited on Routes 11 and 12. This trip begins at Milepost 217.3 on the Blue Ridge Parkway and continues in a counterclockwise direction to Milepost 248.1 south of Laurel Springs.

THE BYWAYS —

One of the most beautiful road trips described in this book, Route 10 has it all. Most of it is on highways designated as Scenic Byways by Virginia or North Carolina and the rest of the route is just as interesting. This route should definitely be driven in both clockwise and counterclockwise directions, especially the section of VA 100/US 21 from Wytheville south to Sparta, and the Burke's Garden area.

Route 10 starts with a fifteen-mile section of NC 18 from the Parkway to Sparta, North Carolina, that could well have been a North Carolina Scenic Byway. US 21/VA 100 from Sparta to Wytheville is more of the same with great views of mountains, valleys, and bold streams..

The next section of Route 10 travels through one of the most interesting and scenic areas in Virginia — the Big Walker Mountain area. There is a little backtracking but the views are so magnificent and the attractions are so numerous that you won't mind the extra miles. Most of the roads in this section

are Virginia Byways and the part on US 52 is also a National Forest Scenic Byway.

You will remember the trip from Big Walker Mountain, through the Burkes Garden area to Tazewell, Virginia, as a special treat. Even the ten mile gravel section provides spectacular views of the valleys below and Burke's Garden is truly one-of-a-kind.

The entire 90-mile section of VA 16/NC 16/NC 88 from just south of Tazewell, Virginia, to Laurel Springs, North Carolina, is nothing less than spectacular. You will travel from rugged mountains to peaceful valleys time after time and be presented with fantastic views in every direction. The northern 55 miles of this section is a Virginia Byway; the southern 14 miles is a North Carolina Scenic Byway.

THE TOWNS —

Wythe County, formed in 1790, is the site of Wytheville, which was incorporated as the county seat in 1839. This historic town now serves the business, medical, educational, and cultural needs of a large area. Home to

25,000 Virginians, Wytheville is a great place to live or visit. Their wide, tree-lined Main Street is as attractive and well-maintained as any in Virginia. Summer visitors by the thousands enjoy the annual Chautauqua Festival and the many other cultural and recreational activities.

Sparta, Independence, Bland, Tazewell, Marion, and Jefferson/West Jefferson are typical county seat towns with unique differences that make them special. Sparta holds several fine festivals every year. Independence shows off its Historic 1908 Courthouse. Bland is small and quite picturesque. Tazewell is home to the Crab Orchard Museum and Pioneer Park. Marion offers the Hungry Mother State Park and the Mount Rogers National Recreation Area, and Jefferson/West Jefferson proudly presents the famous frescoes in St. Mary's Episcopal Church. As you drive or walk through these towns, compare the courthouses, an educational pastime your whole family will surely enjoy.

THE ATTRACTIONS —

From the Parkway, drive 15 miles southwest on NC 18 to:

Sparta, North Carolina

The Annual Specialty Vehicle Show, held in late-July/early-August is one of the major custom vehicle shows in the state. Cars, trucks, sports cars, vintage cars, and other machines are displayed and compete in many categories for trophies and prizes.

In late June, Sparta holds the Annual Blue Ridge Mountain Crafts Fair. Arts and crafts are featured, but there is plenty of food, music and other interesting things to do.

Visit Sparta in mid-July for the Alleghany County Fiddlers' Convention.

Late September brings the Mountain Heritage Festival featuring arts and crafts, demonstrations of mountain life, food, music, and sidewalk sales by merchants.

1. **The Alleghany County Chamber of Commerce** is located at 348 South Main Street. 336-372-5473 or 800-372-5473.

Travel 10 miles north on US 21 to:

Independence, Virginia

An Independence Day Festival is an appropriate thing to do in a town named Independence and they do it up right. Arts and crafts sales, country/bluegrass music, a parade, games, a barbeque, and fireworks are all part of the celebration.

The second Saturday in October brings the Mountain Foliage Festival and the exciting Grand Privy Race. Other features are a band festival, a parade, food, and arts and crafts sales.

2. **The Grayson Tourist Information Center and Historic 1908 Courthouse** is the place to stop on your visit to Independence. This grand old building also houses the Vault Museum, containing artifacts from a mountain homestead, and The Treasury, a gallery/shop featuring Grayson County arts and crafts. The 200-seat Baldwin Auditorium is used for concerts and plays. 540-773-3711.

Drive 29 miles north on US 21 to:

10-1 Grand Privy Race in Independence, Virginia — Photo courtesy of
Grayson County Tourist Information Center

Wytheville, Virginia

A major festival in Wytheville, held in mid-June, is the Chautauqua Festival in the Park. This festival extends over several days and features visual and performing arts. It's a place for residents and visitors alike to share in the area's culture, entertainment, and history. The Elizabeth Brown Memorial Park, at Fourth and Spring Streets, is the site for this delightful series of events.

3. **The Wytheville - Wythe - Bland Chamber of Commerce and the Wytheville Area Convention and Visitor's Bureau** are located in adjacent offices at 150 East Monroe Street. Either agency will be happy to give you information about the area. Ask for details about a walking tour of the downtown area. 540-223-3365 and 540-223-3355.

4. **The Rock House Museum**, at 205 North Tazewell Street, was the home of Wytheville's first resident physician, Dr. John Haller. Completed in 1823, this old house served as a hospital during the Civil War, and now contains many of Dr. Haller's possessions and other items relating to Wythe County history.

5. **The Thomas J. Boyd Museum** is located next to the Rock House Museum on Tazewell Street. Artifacts displayed include Wytheville's first fire truck and a variety of old farming and industrial machines. Historical and military information is also featured.

Drive 7 miles northwest on US 52 to:

6. **The Dark Horse Hollow Picnic Area**, a USDA Forest Service facility, situated along US 52 on the banks of Stony Fork Creek. Picnic tables, grills, and vault toilets are provided.

Go 2.4 miles northwest on US 52, then drive 0.5 miles east on VA 717 to:

7. Stony Fork Campground, a USDA Forest Service facility. Sunny and shady campsites with picnic tables, fireplaces, lantern posts, fresh water, restrooms, warm showers, flush toilets, and a dump station are available. You can fish in Stony Fork Creek or walk on an interesting nature trail.

Travel 4 miles east on VA 717 to I - 77, then go north on I - 77 to:

8. The Big Walker Tunnel. Running for more than a mile under Big Walker Mountain, the tunnel is an exciting experience for both the young and the young in heart.

Continue 4 miles north on I - 77, then drive 0.8 miles east on US 52 to:

Bland, Virginia

The Bland County Festival of Leaves , held during the second weekend in October, features art and photography shows, a storyteller, puppets, hay rides, a quilt show, an antique car show, food sales, music, a doll show plus many other fun things to do.

Drive 2.2 miles west on US 52 to VA 617.

9. The VA 617 Loop Trip runs for seven beautiful miles along Walker Creek at the base of Big Walker Mountain. The winding creek, open fields, rolling terrain, and well-kept farms make this Virginia Byway a truly delightful place.

At the junction of VA 617 and US 52, go 3.3 miles southwest on US 52 to:

10. Monster Rock Hiking Trail. Park in the Big Walker Lookout parking lot and take a short trail to a large rock outcropping where there is a great view of the valley below and the mountains beyond.

From the Big Walker Lookout parking lot, drive 4 miles southeast on FS 206 to:

11. Big Bend Picnic Area, which is a delightful place for picnics with tables, grills, and fireplaces. Panoramic views from the 4,000 crest of Big Walker Mountain make this a very special site.

Return to US 52, then travel 3 miles west on VA 621 to VA 42. Continue 1.5 miles west on VA 42 to VA 623.

There is a decision for you to make at this point. VA 623 north is crooked, steep, and gravel surfaced for the next 10 miles. The destination, Burke's Garden, is a lovely one-of-a-kind place, but if you don't want to deal with this road, drive 17 miles southwest on VA 42 to VA 16 and pick up Route 10 there.

If you decide to make this trip, go 12 miles north on VA 623 to:

12. Burke's Garden, described as Virginia's largest Rural Historical District and National Landmark. Surveyor James Burke discovered this spectacular land-locked valley in 1748. Announcing that he had found the "Garden of Eden," he returned the following year to settle the 400 acres promised him. When his promise was not fulfilled, Burke left the area, and others settled the valley. Burke's Garden is an enormous bowl shaped depression at the 3,000 foot level in the mountains. It has lush rolling fields of the finest soil and immaculate farm houses for the 280 residents. VA 623, VA 625 (East End Road), and VA 666 (Back Road), all Virginia Byways, create a circular loop drive. I suggest you travel both ways along

10-2 Historic Crab Orchard Museum and Pioneer Park
Photo courtesy of Tazewell County Tourism

this loop — about 12 miles each way — to capture the full effect of this wonderful place.

The Burke's Garden Fall Festival, on the last Saturday of September, is a special occasion in this unique community.

Depending on where you start in the valley, drive about 6 miles northwest on VA 623, then 5 miles west on VA 61, then 2 miles southwest on US 19 to:

Tazewell, Virginia

The American Mountain Heritage Festival, held at the Historic Crab Orchard Museum on July 4, and the Main Street Moments Festival in late July are special celebrations in Tazewell.

13. Tazewell County Tourism, located at the Crab Orchard Museum, is a good source of information about activities in Tazewell County. 540-988-6755 or 800-588-9401.

14. The Historic Crab Orchard Museum and Pioneer Park is 3 miles west of Tazewell on US 19/US 460. This living history museum features thirteen furnished stone and log houses, outbuildings, farming operations and equipment, and artifacts from the area, along with a large collection of weapons from the Civil War and many antiques. This is a large and impressive cultural resource; a highlight of Route 10. Festivals and interpretive programs are scheduled throughout the year. A replica of Witten's Fort, originally built in 1774 and reconstructed in 1926, is located at the Museum's entrance.

From downtown Tazewell, drive 3 miles southwest on US 460/US 19 BUS, then 26 miles south on VA 16 to:

15. Hungry Mother State Park.

The Hungry Mother Arts and Crafts Festival in mid-July is a major event for local residents and visitors to the area.

Hungry Mother State Park is known for its beautiful 108-acre lake and the diversity of features and activities, which include a campground with electrical/water hookups, showers, toilets, a dumping station, housekeeping cabins, picnicking, hiking trails, swimming and a bathhouse, boat launching, boat rentals, fishing, a snack bar, a restaurant, rental horses, a visitor center, interpretive exhibits and programs, and some facilities for people with disabilities.

Drive 5 miles south on VA 16, then US 11 to:

Marion, Virginia

The Downtown Marion Independence Day Chili Championship is a street festival of special interest. Enjoy the Fourth of July with a band concert, the chili contest, and a gigantic fireworks display.

16.   The Chamber of Commerce of Smyth County is at 124 Main Street. 540-783-3161.

17.   The Smyth County Historical Museum, located on Stadium Road east of downtown Marion and south of US 11, displays artifacts of Smyth County in a renovated 1838 school building.

From downtown Marion, go 7.3 miles east on VA 16 to:

10-3 Marion artist Ned Johnson works on a new creation at the 1997 Hungry Mother Arts and Crafts Festival — Photo courtesy of Suzanne Sukle, EZDOSIT!

10-4 View of the New River — Photo courtesy of the
Ashe Chamber of Commerce

18. Mount Rogers National Recreation Area. The headquarters for this great recreational and educational resource is located just off VA 16. Forest rangers will tell you about campgrounds, picnic areas, fishing spots, scenic drives, and other features of the 115,000-acre USDA Jefferson National Forest recreation area. Several interesting exhibits, a bookstore, and restrooms are featured.

Drive 5 miles south on VA 16 to:

19. The Raccoon Branch Campground in the Mount Rogers Recreation Area. The campground provides campsites without electrical/water hookups, flush toilets, a dumping station, stream fishing for trout, hiking trails, and horse trails. Information about other facilities in the area is available at the Mount Rogers Recreation Area headquarters.

Drive 33 miles south on VA 16 to US 221, then 3 miles southwest on US 221 BUS to:

Jefferson, North Carolina

20. The Historic Ashe County Courthouse is on Main Street. Built in 1904, it is a distinctive example of courthouse architecture from a century ago. Soon to be replaced by a new county government building, this fine old structure will probably get its "second wind" as a museum.

Continue 2 miles southwest on US 221 BUS to:

West Jefferson, North Carolina

Christmas in July, a festival celebrating one of Ashe County's most interesting products, Christmas trees, is held annually in early July. In 11 years, almost a million people have gathered to visit arts and crafts booths, eat a wide variety of delicious foods, look at displays of Christmas decorating products, and listen to some great music.

21. The Ashe Chamber of Commerce, at 6 North Jefferson Avenue in West Jefferson, is the place to get information about the area. The friendly staff will do everything possible to help you have a pleasant visit in Ashe County. 336-246-9550.

22. The Ashe County Arts Council, located in an impressive stone building at the east end of Main Street in West Jefferson, offers changing exhibits of arts and crafts along with musical performances, educational programs, and other assistance to artists and art patrons. Check out the enormous mural, recently completed by local artist, Jack Young, on the side of an adjacent building. The Arts Council actively and creatively promotes all kinds of artistic experience and is a major contributor to the cultural life of the community.

From downtown West Jefferson, drive 2 miles south on US 221 BUS (just past McDonald's) to Beaver Creek School Road, then go 0.6 miles west to:

23. Saint Mary's Episcopal Church, at 400 Beaver Creek School Road. This is one of two churches in Ashe County that are world-famous for religious frescoes created by artist Ben Long. Frescoes are works of art that combine plaster and pigments to make a textured painting. The other church

containing frescoes, described in Chapter 11, is located in Glendale Springs at Milepost 258.6 on the Blue Ridge Parkway.

Return to US 221 BUS, go 1 block southeast to US 221 BYPASS, then drive 1.4 miles north to NC 1152 (Mount Jefferson State Park Road). Go 3 miles east on NC 1152 to:

24. Mount Jefferson State Park. Located more than 1,600 feet above the surrounding countryside at an elevation of 4,900 feet, this park is one of the highest in North Carolina. In addition to great views from overlooks and the mountain's summit, the park offers hiking trails, picnic tables with grills, interpretive programs, and rest rooms.

Return to US 220 BYPASS, then drive 3.4 miles northeast to NC 16/NC 88. Go 3.5 miles southeast to the New River, then 1.4 miles east on NC 88 to NC 1590 (Wagoner Access Road). Travel 1 mile north to:

25. New River State Park. This unusual park is designed for people who take canoe trips on the New River. Access to the river is provided, plus parking space for vehicles, picnic facilities, drinking water, and rest rooms. Fishing is a major activity as the river is stocked with muskellunge and its tributaries are stocked with brown and brook trout. Primitive camping is available here and at other points along the river.

Return to NC 88, then go 9 miles east to NC 18, then drive 2 miles southeast to the Blue Ridge Parkway, Milepost 248.1.

Elkin, NC
W. Kerr Scott Lake, NC
Blowing Rock, NC

ROUTE 11

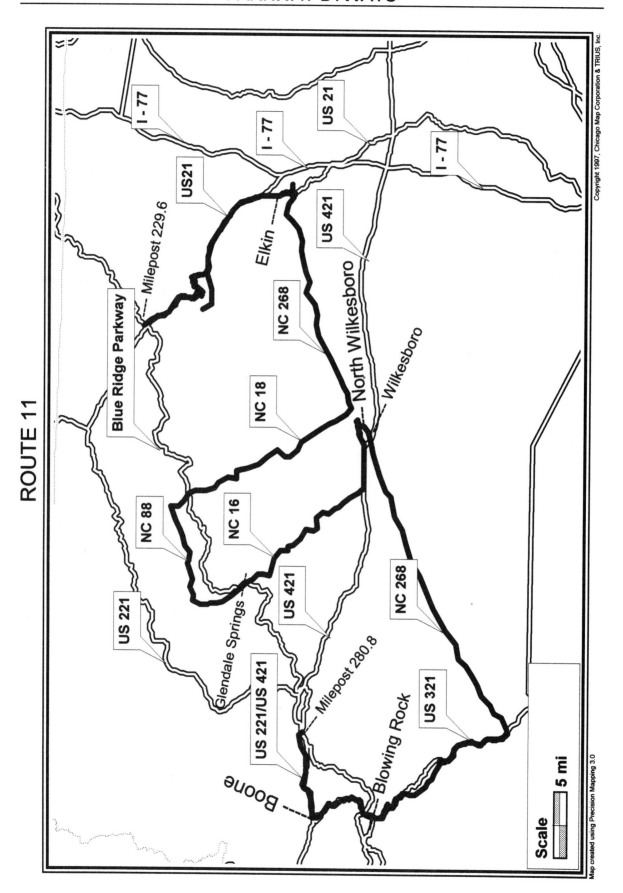

I - 77

I - 77

US 21

I - 77

US21

US 421

Milepost 229.6

Elkin

NC 268

Blue Ridge Parkway

North Wilkesboro

Wilkesboro

NC 18

NC 88

NC 16

US 221

Glendale Springs

US 421

NC 268

US 221/US 421

Milepost 280.8

US 321

Boone

Blowing Rock

Scale
5 mi

Copyright 1997, Chicago Map Corporation & TRIUS, Inc.

Map created using Precision Mapping 3.0

The Elkin - W. Kerr Scott Lake - Blowing Rock Route tours the North Carolina counties of Surry, Wilkes, Ashe, Caldwell, and Watauga. It is about 180 miles long. Although the byways are quite different, the attractions listed for the Glendale Springs area can also be visited on Routes 10 and 12 and Blowing Rock/Boone attractions can also be visited on Route 14. This trip starts at Milepost 229.6 and continues in a clockwise direction to Milepost 280.8.

THE BYWAYS —

Route 11 provides **two** trips down the southeastern slopes of the Blue Ridge Mountains to the North Carolina Piedmont with returns to the Parkway. As a result, you will see many fantastic views as you see the valleys from the mountains, then the mountains from the valleys. These mountain/valley "transition" byways often result in more scenic opportunities than roads that stay in either the mountains or the valleys.

NC 268, which you will travel for 60 miles through the Yadkin Valley, from Elkin to US 321 south of Blowing Rock, is an exception to this pattern, however. Great views of the mountains are plentiful, the Yadkin Valley is quite attractive in its own right, and you will get many glimpses of the scenic Yadkin River and W. Kerr Scott Lake..

THE TOWNS —

The towns of Route 11 are unusually varied. Included are factory/farming communities like Elkin/Jonesville and Wilkesboro/North Wilkesboro. Residents of these towns are primarily working people, employed in manufacturing plants, on farms, in trade and service businesses, and in local government.

The sophisticated resort town of Blowing Rock attracts a large number of summer visitors, many of whom have homes in the area. Although farming and industrial enterprise is virtually non-existent, retail trade is very active throughout the year. Tourism is a major focus during the spring, summer, fall, and the winter skiing season. Commercial attractions such as The Blowing Rock, Tweetsie Railroad, and Grandfather Mountain attract thousands of visitors to Blowing Rock and Boone.

Boone is a typical college town centered around the activities at Appalachian State University. Responding to Boone's reputation as the "coolest spot in the south," summer vacationers come by the thousands. When the snow starts falling, skiers are very much in evidence as they hurry to the area's many ski resorts.

All of the towns along Route 11 offer a wide variety of distinctive architecture in houses and other buildings. Many other features are described below.

THE ATTRACTIONS —

From the Parkway, drive 10.4 miles south on US 21 to NC 1002, then 4.4 miles west to the John P. Frank Parkway. Turn north, then go 2 miles to:

1. **Stone Mountain State Park.** This exciting park contains a gigantic dome-shaped mountain. Wind and water wore away softer surrounding rock to expose the enormous granite mass that gives the park its name. Stone Mountain offers tent/trailer/RV camping (without hookups), hot showers, toilets, a dump station, backcountry camping, horse trailer parking, a bridle trail, hiking trails, three waterfalls, picnicking, and more than 17 miles of trout fishing streams. This great park covers more than 13,000 acres and is one of North Carolina's finest.

Return to US 21, then drive 12 miles south to:

Elkin, North Carolina

Late October brings a unique event to Elkin, the Yadkin Valley Pumpkin Festival. From the Great Pumpkin Weigh-in, there's something happening every minute, including contests, food, music, a 5K-road race, live entertainment, a juried art show, a parade, and much more.

2. **The Greater Elkin - Jonesville - Arlington - Chamber of Commerce and Welcome Center** is at 116 East Market Street in Elkin. Ask for their brochure titled *Historic Downtown Elkin Walking Tour.* 336-526-1111.

3. **The Foothills Art Council,** located in the historic former home of Dr. Hugh Clay Salmons at 129 Church Street, promotes and displays the work of area artists. A lighted garden on the property is a special feature. Check out the exhibit, "Elkin in the '90s: A Century Ago," a documentary about the town's early history.

11-1 Stone Mountain — Photo courtesy of the Wilkes Chamber of Commerce

4. The Richard Gwyn Museum, in the 1850 home of Elkin's founder, Richard Gwyn, is on Church Street next to the Foothills Arts Council. This building is the oldest one in Surry County to have been used as a church or school. It was rescued from destruction in 1953 by the Jonathan Hunt Chapter of the Daughters of the American Revolution.

5. The Elkin Municipal Park, located on NC 268, is a terrific place to take a break. Here are a few of its many attractions: tennis courts, an outdoor swimming pool, a hiking trail, a children's playground, a band shell, and a covered picnic pavilion.

Drive 19 miles southwest on NC 268 to NC 18, then go 21 miles north on NC 18 to Laurel Springs and NC 88. Go 9 miles west on NC 88 to NC 1590 (Wagoner Access Road), then 1 mile north on NC 1590 to:

6. New River State Park. This unusual park is designed for people who take canoe trips on the New River. Access to the river is provided, plus parking space for vehicles, picnic facilities, drinking water, and rest rooms. Fishing is a major activity as the river is stocked with muskellunge and its tributaries are stocked with brown and brook trout. Primitive camping is available here and at other points along the river.

Return to NC 88, then travel 1.4 miles southwest to NC 16 at the New River, then drive 4.2 miles south on NC 16 to:

Glendale Springs, North Carolina

7. Holy Trinity Episcopal Church is one of two churches in Ashe County that are world-famous for religious frescoes created by artist Ben Long. Frescoes are works of art that combine plaster and pigments to make a textured painting. The other church containing frescoes, described in Chapters 10 and 12 in this book, is at 400 Beaver Creek School Road in West Jefferson.

8. The Northwest Trading Post, at Milepost 258.6 on the Blue Ridge Parkway, is a unique place to buy products produced by artisans in a surrounding eleven-county area. Mountain arts and crafts, baskets, toys, quilts, jewelry, antiques, jellies, hams, and baked goods are just a few of the items featured in this great non-profit establishment. All profits are donated to local charities.

Drive 16 miles south on NC 16 to NC 1304, then 3 miles west to NC 1346. Go 2 miles north to NC 1348, then travel 1.3 miles north to:

9. Rendezvous Mountain Educational State Forest. This fine facility provides a series of trails featuring "talking trees" that give information on forestry and ecology. There are several places to picnic along the way.

Return to NC 16, then drive 3 miles south to US 421, then go 5 miles east on US 421/US 421 BUS to:

North Wilkesboro, North Carolina

The Brushy Mountain Apple Festival is held on the first weekend in October. This exciting event, attracting over 160,000 people each year, features old-timey arts and crafts such as basket making and quilting, plus cider and molasses making. There is a constant sound of country music and lots of appetizing food and drink.

10. The Wilkes Chamber of Commerce is located at 717 Main Street. Ask for the brochure about the Old Wilkes Walking Tour, which describes historic buildings in Wilkesboro. 336-838-8662.

11-2 Wilkes County Courthouse — Photo courtesy of Wilkes Chamber of Commerce

11. The Wilkes Art Gallery is 0.8 miles north of the Chamber of Commerce at Elizabeth Street, Hinshaw Street, and Finley Avenue. (Ask at the Chamber office for more information and detailed directions.) Works of local and nationally recognized artists are displayed.

Drive 2 miles southwest on NC 268 to:

Wilkesboro, North Carolina

The big event in Wilkesboro is the MerleFest, a four-day music festival honoring Merle Watson, deceased son of the famous musician, Doc Watson. Held on the last weekend in April at the Wilkes Community College Gardens, the festival attracts bluegrass and acoustic music fans from around the world. Almost 100 artists and groups appear, making this one of the largest festivals of its kind anywhere.

12. The Wilkes County Courthouse, built in 1902, is a grand example of courthouse architecture in the early 1900s.

13. The Old Wilkes Jail Museum, located behind the Wilkes County Courthouse, once housed Thomas C. Dula, subject of the famous folk song, *Tom Dooley.* This building is one of the few remaining examples of nineteenth-century jails in the state.

14. The Robert Cleveland House, a log cabin built in the 1770s in western Wilkes County, was restored and moved to its present location behind the Old Wilkes Jail.

From downtown Wilkesboro, drive 1 mile southwest on NC 268 to Collegiate Drive, then go 0.6 miles southwest to:

15.   The Wilkes Community College Gardens. This is the perfect place for a walk in a beautiful natural setting. A hiking trail through the gardens, along the

Moravian Creek, and around a duck pond is a special feature. Along with the hiking trail and many flowers and plants, the Eddy Merle Watson Memorial Garden for the Senses provides a place to enjoy the pleasures of touch and fragrance. Braille labels identify the plants.

16. The John A. Walker Community Center, on a hill above the College, presents a full schedule of professional musical and other performances. Get more information at the Welcome Center in the College Gardens or at the Wilkes Chamber of Commerce.

Return to NC 268. Go 3 miles west to NC 1178 (Reservoir Road), then drive 0.6 miles north to:

17. The Dam Site Park — The W. Kerr Scott Dam and Reservoir. The Project Manager's office is located here along with a welcome center, picnic tables with grills, a boat launching ramp, and an interpretive nature trail. Covering 1,470 acres, this large lake has many kinds of recreational activities available at several locations. Included are hiking trails, campgrounds (with and without hookups); boat launching, docking, mooring, rentals, and repairs; sporting equipment, bait, a restaurant, developed picnic areas, showers, shelters, toilets, dumping stations, swimming, hunting, fishing piers, and canoe launching. Ask for information on facilities and services at the Project Manager's office. You can also get information about the lake at Bandit Roost Park (see below).

Return to NC 268, then drive 2 miles west to:

18. Bandit Roost Park, one of the major campgrounds on the reservoir, where you may choose to camp and/or get information about other recreation sites.

From Bandit Roost Park, drive 23 miles southwest on NC 268 to US 321, then go 4.6 miles northwest on US 321 to NC 1370 (Kirby Mountain Road). Travel 0.5 miles northwest on NC 1370 to NC 1371 (Waterfall Road), then drive 1.6 miles north on NC 1371 (the gravel section is short and in good condition) to:

19. Silvervale Falls, a spectacular 100 foot waterfall that is located very close to NC 1371. You can see it from your car but will enjoy it more if you leave your car and listen to as well as watch the cascading water.

Go 1.7 miles north on NC 1371 to US 321, then drive 7 miles northwest on US 321/US 321 BUS to:

Blowing Rock, North Carolina

Festivals in Blowing Rock come in groups. First, there's Art in the Park, a world class juried arts and crafts show, that happens on Saturdays toward the middle of every month from May to October. Over one hundred of the finest artisans display their best works. The second group of festivals is the Concert in the Park series which occurs on Sundays toward the end of each of the summer months.

20. The Blowing Rock Chamber of Commerce is located next to Blowing Rock Memorial Park on Main Street. 828-295-7851 or 800-295-7851.

21. The Blowing Rock Memorial Park is located in the heart of town on Main Street. Tennis courts, facilities for basketball and volleyball, a playground, and restrooms are available along with comfortable benches where you can rest and observe the local scene.

22. Annie Cannon Memorial Park, Broyhill Park, and The Blowing Rock Swimming Pool are west of Main Street. In addition to swimming, you can enjoy walking trails, a gazebo, a covered picnic pavilion, and a delightful lake.

23. The Glen Burney Trail can be accessed from a parking lot at the Annie Cannon Memorial Park. This ancient trail runs along New York Creek to the Cascades at 0.8 miles, Glen Burney Falls at 1.2 miles, and Glen Marie Falls at 1.5 miles. The two waterfalls are about 50 feet high. The trail is steep with many slippery rocks and quite an adventure. You can get a trail guide brochure at the Blowing Rock Chamber of Commerce.

24. The Blowing Rock Stage Company, on Sunset Drive just east of Main Street, presents a variety of professional drama, comedy, and music performances during the summer months. Ask for show names, dates, and times at the Chamber of Commerce.

Drive 6.6 miles north on US 321/US 221 to:

25. The North Carolina High Country Host Visitor Center, at 1700 Blowing Rock Road (US 221/US 321). This center serves a six-county area with travel information and helpful advice and is a major resource for anyone traveling in northwest North Carolina. 828-264-1299 or 800-438-7500.

Travel 2 miles northwest on US 321 BUS to downtown:

Boone, North Carolina

Horn in the West is a summer-long outdoor historical drama performed in the Daniel Boone Amphitheater located on Horn in the West Drive southeast of downtown Boone. It has been performed in Boone since 1953.

11-3 Linn Cove Viaduct — Photo courtesy of the Boone Convention and Visitors Bureau and Judi Scharns

This play, commemorating the efforts of Daniel Boone and others to achieve independence from English domination, is presented nightly (except Monday) from mid-June through mid-August. The Cherokee Fire Dance is a special event in the show.

An Appalachian Summer Festival is a collection of cultural events including theater, dance, and music performances by the North Carolina Symphony and others. An outdoor sculpture competition and classes in art, music, photography, and dance are other features. Most events occur on the campus of Appalachian State University.

26. The Boone Area Chamber of Commerce, at 208 Howard Street, is an important source for information about Boone and the surrounding area. 828-262-3516 or 828-264-2225 or 800-852-9506.

27. The Jones House, at 604 West King Street, is the downtown community, art, and cultural center for Boone. Celebration of arts and humanities takes place in a large house listed on the National Register of Historic Places.

Note: The next two attractions are located on the main campus of ASU which is in the midst of a major construction program. Parking and traffic congestion can be quite a problem. Call the University at 828-262-2000 for current information on where to park and perhaps to arrange a guided tour.

28. The Appalachian Collection, housed in ASU's **Belk Library,** is a treasure of more than 15,000 books, musical recordings, photographs, newspaper articles, artifacts, and other historical information about the mountains and mountain people. This unique repository not only has many unusual items, but also distinctive ways of presenting them. You won't want to miss it!

29. The Catherine Smith Gallery, in Farthing Auditorium on the ASU campus, offers art and sculpture exhibits. While on campus, look for the many fine outdoor sculptures acquired by ASU over the years.

30. The Appalachian Cultural Museum, located in ASU's University Hall on University Hall Drive, also exhibits a variety of environmental and historical items that preserve the cultural heritage of the region. The Appalachian Collection and this outstanding museum are major assets for the people of Appalachia.

31. The Hickory Ridge Homestead is adjacent to the *Horn in the West* theater on Horn in the West Drive. Open on weekends from May to October and daily (except Monday) during Horn season, this is a living history museum portraying mountain life in the 1700s. A farmer's market is also held on Saturdays from May to October.

32. The Daniel Boone Native Gardens, also on the grounds of *Horn in the West*, exhibit plants native to the Blue Ridge Mountains. A visit to this beautiful and restful place is an educational as well as entertaining experience.

33. The Watauga Recreation Complex and Greenway Trail, at State Farm Road between Dale Street and Hunting Hills Lane, provides an indoor pool, lighted tennis courts; facilities for basketball, volleyball, and horseshoes; and a playground for children. Now under construction with more than two miles in use, the Greenway Trail offers walking, biking, jogging, and cross country skiing.

Drive 7.5 miles east on US 221/US 421 to the Blue Ridge Parkway, Milepost 280.8.

CHAPTER 12 - ROUTE 12

Whitetop Mountain, VA
Abingdon, VA
Mountain City, TN

ROUTE 12

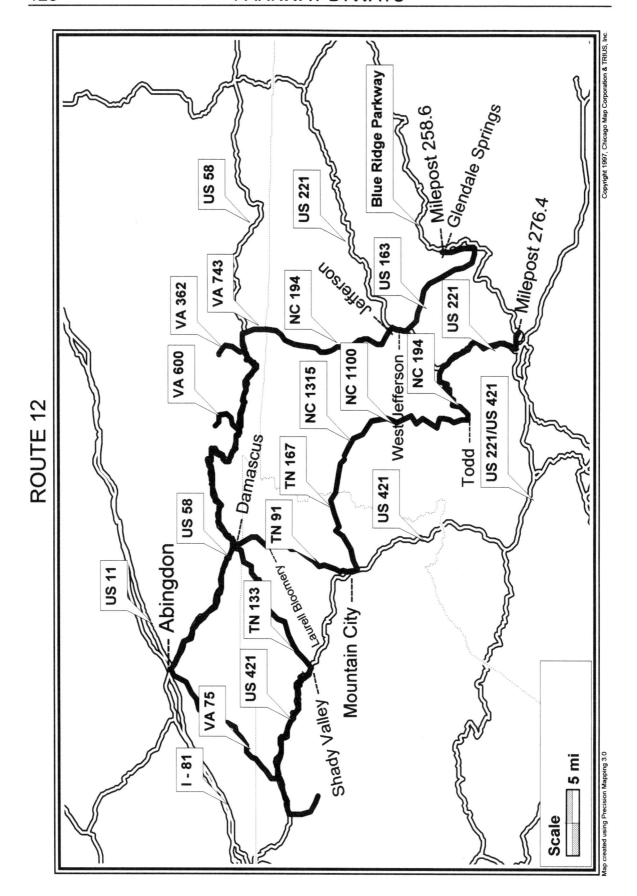

Blue Ridge Parkway

Milepost 258.6

Glendale Springs

Milepost 276.4

US 58

US 221

US 163

US 221

Jefferson

NC 194

VA 743

VA 362

NC 194

West Jefferson

VA 600

NC 1100

NC 1315

US 221/US 421

Todd

Damascus

TN 167

US 421

US 58

TN 91

Laurell Bloomery

US 11

TN 133

Abingdon

US 421

Mountain City

Shady Valley

VA 75

I - 81

Scale

5 mi

Copyright 1997, Chicago Map Corporation & TRIUS, Inc.

Map created using Precision Mapping 3.0

The Whitetop Mountain - Abingdon - Mountain City Route tours the Virginia counties of Grayson and Washington, the Tennessee county of Johnson, and the North Carolina county of Ashe. It is about 205 miles long. Although the byways are quite different, the attractions listed for Jefferson/West Jefferson can also be visited on Route 10, the attractions listed for Glendale Springs can be visited on Route 11, and the attractions listed for Mountain City can also be visited on Route 14. This trip starts at Milepost 258.6 on the Blue Ridge Parkway and continues in a counterclockwise direction to Milepost 276.4 at Deep Gap.

THE BYWAYS —

Route 12 has as much if not more great scenery per mile than any byway in this book. It starts with a pleasant mountain trip across Ashe County, North Carolina, from Glendale Springs through Jefferson/West Jefferson to the Virginia line. Mountains, valleys, picturesque villages, farms, and bold streams are abundant in this varied landscape.

US 58, a Virginia Byway, changes your journey from interesting to spectacular as it travels from Rugby, Virginia, to Damascus. The 22-mile section of US 58 plus two fantastic side trips to Grayson Highlands State Park and White Top Mountain is one of the most dramatic drives covered in this book. Enormous mountains, panoramic views, beautiful valleys, and frequent views of exciting Whitetop Laurel Creek will make your day.

The next part of the trip, from Damascus through Abingdon to Holston Valley, Tennessee, lowers the dramatic intensity just a little — you wouldn't want to get "scenery overload."

The final one hundred miles of Route 12 picks up the excitement again on US 421 to Shady Valley, a Tennessee Scenic Parkway, then along TN 133 and magnificent Beaverdam Creek to Damascus. VA 91/TN 91 south of Damascus, called the Daniel Boone Heritage Trail, picks up another wild stream called Laurel Creek. From Mountain City to Creston, North Carolina, you will encounter another beautiful Laurel Creek, then drive through more great mountains on your way back to the Parkway. The section on NC 194 from Todd to Baldwin is a North Carolina Scenic Byway.

THE TOWNS —

Jefferson, and West Jefferson, North Carolina, are interesting "twin" towns featuring prosperous business districts, historic buildings, and very friendly people. You will enjoy your visit to these fine communities.

Chartered in 1778, Abingdon is the oldest American town west of the Blue Ridge Mountains. It is one of southwestern Virginia's most important centers for arts, culture, historic architecture, great festivals, and retail trade. Abingdon is a Virginia Historic Landmark.

THE ATTRACTIONS —

Glendale Springs, North Carolina

1. The Northwest Trading Post, at Milepost 258.6 on the Blue Ridge Parkway, is a unique place to buy products produced by artisans in a surrounding eleven-county area. Mountain arts and crafts, baskets, toys, quilts, jewelry, antiques, jellies, hams, and baked good goods are just a few of the items featured in this great non-profit establishment. All profits are donated to local charities.

2. Holy Trinity Episcopal Church is one of two churches in Ashe County that are world-famous for religious frescoes created by artist Ben Long. Frescoes are works of art that combine plaster and pigments to make a textured painting. The other church containing frescoes is at 400 Beaver Creek School Road in West Jefferson.

A more scenic alternative is to drive 10 miles north on NC 16 along the New River to Jefferson/West Jefferson. This highway is scheduled for widening, however, and if construction has started, you may want to take the route described below.

Drive 2.5 miles south on NC 16 to US 163, then go 11 miles northwest on US 163 to:

West Jefferson, North Carolina

Christmas in July, a festival celebrating one of Ashe County's most interesting products, Christmas trees, is held annually in early July. In 11 years, almost a million people have gathered to visit arts and crafts booths, eat a wide variety of delicious foods, look at displays of Christmas decorating products, and listen to some great music.

12-1 Scene at the Christmas in July Festival — Photo courtesy of Bert Dollar

3. The Ashe Chamber of Commerce, at 6 North Jefferson Avenue in West Jefferson, is the place to get information about the area. The friendly staff will do everything possible to help you have a pleasant visit in Ashe County. 336-246-9550.

4. The Ashe County Arts Council, located in an impressive stone building at the east end of Main Street in West Jefferson, offers changing exhibits of arts and crafts along with musical performances, educational programs, and other assistance to artists and art patrons. Check out the enormous mural, recently completed by local artist, Jack Young, on the side of an adjacent building. The Arts Council actively and creatively promotes all kinds of artistic experience and is a major contributor to the cultural life of the community.

From downtown West Jefferson, drive 2 miles south on US 221 BUS to Beaver Creek School Road (just past McDonald's), then go 0.6 miles west to:

5. Saint Mary's Episcopal Church, at 400 Beaver Creek School Road, is one of two churches in Ashe County that are world-famous for religious frescoes created by artist Ben Long. Frescoes are works of art that combine plaster and pigments to make a textured painting. The other church containing frescoes is in Glendale Springs.

Return to US 221 BUS, then go 1 block southeast to US 221 BYPASS. Drive 1.4 miles north to NC 1152 (Mount Jefferson State Park Road), then travel 3 miles east on NC 1152 to:

6. Mount Jefferson State Park. Located more than 1,600 feet above the surrounding countryside at an elevation of 4,900 feet, this park is one of the highest in North Carolina. In addition to great views from

overlooks and the mountain's summit, the park offers hiking trails, picnic tables with grills, interpretive programs, and rest rooms.

Return to US 220 BYPASS, then drive 3.4 miles northeast to NC 16/NC 88. Go 3.5 miles southeast to the New River, then drive 1.4 miles east on NC 88 to NC 1590 (Wagoner Access Road). Travel 1 mile north to:

7. New River State Park. This unusual park is designed for people who take canoe trips on the New River. Access to the river is provided plus parking space for vehicles, picnic facilities, drinking water, and rest rooms. Fishing is a major activity as the river is stocked with muskellunge and its tributaries are stocked with brown and brook trout. Primitive camping is available here and at other points along the river.

Return to NC 88, then go 6.3 miles west to:

Jefferson, North Carolina

8. The Historic Ashe County Courthouse is on Main Street. Built in 1904, it is a distinctive example of courthouse architecture from a century ago. Soon to be replaced by a new county government building, this fine old structure will probably get its "second wind" as a museum.

Drive 1.6 miles west on NC 88 to NC 194, then go 3.7 miles north on NC 88/NC 194 to Warrensville. Bear right on NC 194 and continue 13.4 miles northeast to the Virginia state line and VA 743. Go 3.7 miles north on VA 743 to US 58, then drive 3.3 miles west on US 58 to VA 362. Travel 4.8 miles northeast, then northwest to:

12-2 View from Grayson Highlands State Park — Photo courtesy of the
Galax-Carroll-Grayson Chamber of Commerce

9. Grayson Highlands State Park. This park provides many breathtaking views of the mountains in addition to a variety of services for visitors. Camping with electrical/water hookups, a dumping station, showers, toilets, picnicking, bridle trails, bicycle trails, and groceries are provided. A visitor center with interpretive programs, and some facilities for disabled persons are also available.

Return to US 58, then drive 8 miles west to VA 600. Go 2 miles northwest on VA 600, then bear left on an unnumbered road and go 3 miles up the mountain to:

10. White Top Mountain, more than a mile high at 5,520 feet, is one of Virginia's highest. Fantastic views in every direction abound. There are no developed facilities, only a great place to see the world.

Return to US 58, then drive 18 miles west to:

Damascus, Virginia

11. The Virginia Creeper National Recreation Trail runs through Damascus which is located near the midpoint. Covering 34 miles between Abingdon, Virginia, and the Virginia-North Carolina line, this trail uses the abandoned right-of-way of the Virginia-Carolina Railroad. It was originally a Native American footpath and later served our nation's pioneers on their journeys through the mountains. The name, Virginia Creeper, came from early locomotives "creeping" slowly up the steep grades. Open to hikers, bicycle riders, and horseback riders, the trail runs through spectacular mountain scenery and is a major recreational resource. Visit the red caboose in Damascus for more information.

Drive 10.4 miles northwest on US 58 to I - 81, then go 2.6 miles southwest on I - 81 to Exit 17 and US 58 A (Cummings Street). Turn north to:

Abingdon, Virginia

Attracting 200,000 visitors annually, and held during the first two weeks of August, the Virginia Highlands Festival is a major event in Abingdon. Featured attractions are a large regional antique market and a juried arts and crafts show of national significance. In addition, music, performing arts, photography, creative writing, lectures, workshops, demonstrations, tours, and many more activities are scheduled during this exciting celebration.

If you're in the Abingdon area in mid-September, attend the Washington County Fair and Burley Festival.

12. The Abingdon Convention and Visitors Bureau is located at 335 Cummings Street (Exit 17 on I - 81). Ask for the brochure, *A Walking Tour of Main Street.* 540-676-2282 or 800-435-3440.

13. The William King Regional Arts Center, at 415 Academy Drive, offers traveling museum exhibitions from around the country, along with concerts, lectures, workshops, and classes. A special emphasis is placed on educational activity and interaction between artists and the people of southwest Virginia and northeastern Tennessee. A museum store, The Looking Glass, offers books, artistic products, gifts, jewelry, and original artworks. The building is a Virginia Historic Landmark.

14. The Barter Theatre — The State Theatre of Virginia is located at 127 Main Street. This historic, even famous, theater offers a wide variety of drama, comedy, and music performances throughout the year. The reputation of this fine organization for consistently outstanding presentations is worldwide.

15. The Washington County Courthouse and Historical Society of Washington County, at Main and Court Streets, was built in 1869. A special feature is the World War I memorial stained glass window designed by the Tiffany Studio. This impressive building contains many records used in historical and genealogical research.

16. The Arts Depot, located at 314 Depot Square, houses a collection of nonprofit art and cultural organizations. Art works of local and regional artists are displayed and offered for sale. Several artists maintain studios in the building which was built in 1870 by the Virginia and Tennessee Railroad.

17. The Cave House, built in 1857, is home to a cooperative of more than one hundred local craft workers. The house is in front of caves that, according to local legend, held wolves that attacked Daniel Boone's dogs in 1760.

18. The Fields-Penn 1860 House Museum, at 208 West Main Street, circa 1858, is typical of Abingdon's early houses. It now serves as a Visitor's Center and museum for the town.

19. The Virginia Creeper National Recreation Trail. The Abingdon trail head is just off Green Spring Road south of Main Street. Covering 34 miles between Abingdon and the Virginia-North Carolina border, this trail uses the abandoned right-of-way of the Virginia-Carolina Railroad. It was originally a Native American footpath and later served our nation's pioneers on their journeys through the mountains. The name, Virginia Creeper, came from early locomotives "creeping" slowly up the steep grades. Open to hikers, bicycle riders, and horseback riders, the trail runs through spectacular mountain scenery and is a major recreational resource.

12-3 Arts Depot — Photo courtesy of the Abingdon Convention and Visitors Bureau

From the Abingdon Convention and Visitors Bureau on Cummings Street, drive 10 miles southwest on VA 75 to the Tennessee State Line and TN 44. Continue 0.6 miles southwest on TN 44 to:

20. Observation Knob Park, provided for your enjoyment by Sullivan County, Tennessee. This park offers camping, picnicking, a playground for children, and access to South Holston Lake.

Drive 1.6 miles southwest on TN 44 to US 421 at Holston Valley, then go 3.4 miles southwest on US 421 to TN 2373 (Emmett Road) and a sign indicating the route to South Holston Dam. Drive about 3 miles southeast, following signs, to:

21. South Holston Lake and Dam, a Tennessee Valley Authority project that impounds the South Holston River for power generation, flood control, and recreation. It was completed in 1950 and is a part of a series of dams and lakes.

Picnicking, a visitors reception building, facilities for canoes and rafts, restrooms, and provision for fishing are offered at the dam site.

Return to US 421, then go 8.8 miles east to Denton Valley Road. Drive 1.6 miles north to Jacobs Creek Road and:

22. The Jacobs Creek Recreation Area, a USDA Forest Service facility. This lakeside park offers camping, boating, fishing, a hiking trail, picnicking, swimming, warm showers, toilets, and drinking water

Return to US 421, then drive 6.3 miles southeast to:

Shady Valley, Tennessee

This picturesque community in a beautiful valley celebrates with the Shady Valley Cranberry Festival in early October.

From Shady Valley, travel 10 miles northeast on TN 133 to:

23. Backbone Rock Recreation Area. This area, managed by USDA Forest Service, is the site of an unusual tunnel through a rock outcropping called Backbone Rock. A campground, fishing, picnicking, hiking trails, toilets, and drinking water are available. Be sure to visit Backbone Falls on Trail 198. The scenery along Beaverdam Creek and the rugged rocks is spectacular.

Continue 2 miles northeast on TN 133 to the Virginia state line and VA 716, then go 2 miles northeast on VA 716 to US 58 in Damascus. Drive 1.4 miles southeast on US 58, then go 2 miles southeast on VA 91 to the Tennessee state line and TN 91. Travel 4.4 miles south on TN 91 to:

Laurel Bloomery

This tiny, quaint village hosts an Old Time Fiddlers Convention in late August.

Drive 7.5 miles south on TN 91 to:

Mountain City, Tennessee

The Mountain Heritage Days and Rodeo in mid-August is an excellent time to visit Mountain City.

24. The Johnson County Welcome Center and Museum, at 716 South Shady Street (US 421), is located in an impressive 10,000 square foot building. A campground with hook-ups and a picnic area are provided. 423-727-5800.

25. The Ralph Stout Park is just north of the downtown area on US 421. A walking trail, playground, restrooms, picnic area, and vending machines are featured in this fine park.

Drive 2.5 miles south on US 421 to TN 167, then go 7.2 miles east on TN 167 to the North Carolina state line and NC 1315 (Big Laurel Road). Go 7.6 miles southeast to NC 88, then drive 1.5 miles southwest to NC 1100 at Creston. Look at the beautiful old church on your left as you cross the bridge, then go 11 miles south on NC 1100 to:

Todd, North Carolina

The New River Festival, held in mid-October, offers handmade arts and crafts, canoe trips, delicious food, and an extensive variety of mountain music.

26. The Elkland School Art Center, located just north of Todd on NC 1100 (Three Top Road), is an nonprofit school dedicated to experiential growth through the arts. A wide variety of study opportunities are provided for local and regional artists in a spacious 12,000 foot former elementary school. Visitors, more than welcome at this unique facility, will enjoy watching the exciting process of artistic endeavor.

Travel 7 miles northeast on NC 194 to US 221, then go 9 miles south on US 221 to US 421 at Deep Gap. Drive 0.8 miles east to the Blue Ridge Parkway, Milepost 276.4.

CHAPTER 14 - ROUTE 14

The New River, NC
Banner Elk, NC
Boone, NC

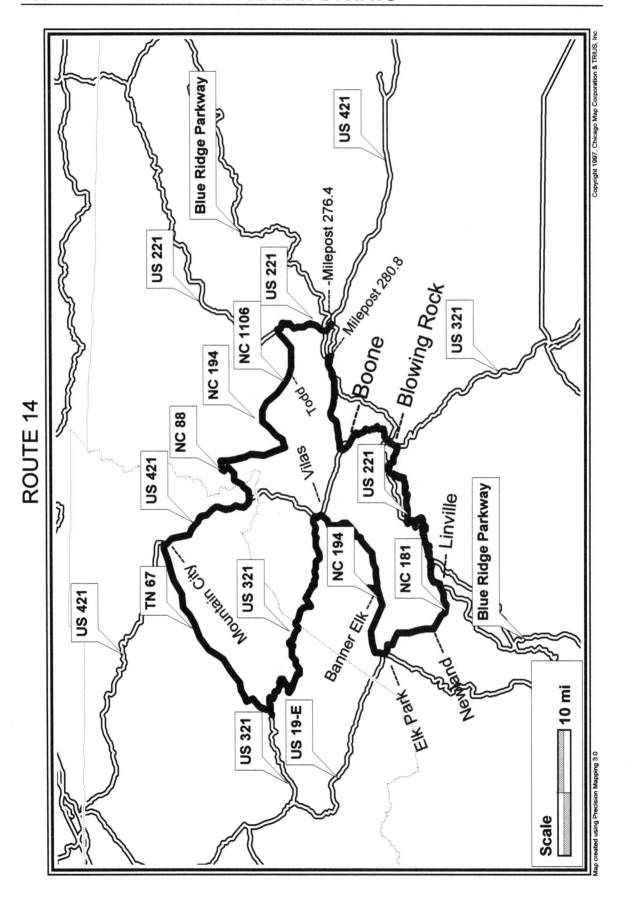

The New River - Banner Elk - Boone Route tours the North Carolina counties of Ashe and Watauga and the Tennessee county of Johnson, It is about 180 miles long. Although the byways are quite different, the attractions listed for Mountain City and Todd can also be visited on Route 12, the attractions listed for Blowing Rock/Boone can be visited on Route 11, and the attraction listed for Elk Park can be visited on Route 16. This trip starts at Milepost 276.4 on the Blue Ridge Parkway near Deep Gap and continues in a counterclockwise direction to Milepost 280.8.

THE BYWAYS —

The first byway featured on Route 14 runs from Fleetwood, North Carolina, to Todd, North Carolina, along the New River. This section of Railroad Grade Road (NC 1106 and NC 1100) is a study in tranquility as the river flows sedately through a valley between gentle mountains.

NC Highways 194, 1335, 1340, 1341, 1118, 88 and TN 67, the route from Todd to Trade, Tennessee, is quite a contrast to the road along the river. Higher mountains and deeper valleys create a much more dramatic effect, including many views that are as impressive as any mentioned in this book. The NC 194 segment of this section is a NC Scenic Byway and the other roads are equally spectacular.

US 321 from TN 67 to North Carolina state line is a Tennessee Scenic Parkway which provides many scenic views of Watauga Lake and the Watauga River.

NC 194, a NC Scenic Byway, from US 321 at Vilas to Elk Park is a wonderland of mountains and valleys and includes a side trip toward the summit of Beech Mountain. The mountain/valley views from NC 184, on the way to and from this fine resort community, are breathtaking.

Last, but certainly not least, is the section of US 221 from Linville, North Carolina, to Blowing Rock, North Carolina — also a NC Scenic Byway. This highway both provides fantastic views of Grandfather Mountain and of the North Carolina Piedmont, which extends to the southeast as far as the eye can see.

THE TOWNS —

The towns along Route 14 are quite different in size and character. Todd is a historic logging town that used to be much larger, but is now centered around the stove in the fine old country store. Mountain City and Newland are typical county seat towns. Valle Crucis is a special attraction. This picturesque community, including the surrounding rural area, is a great place to shop, dine, and experience the unique ambience. Banner Elk is well known for skiing and Lees McRae College. Beech Mountain, at 5,505 feet, is the highest town in the eastern United States. Linville, almost unchanged for more than one hundred years, is an exclusive resort community.

The sophisticated resort town of Blowing Rock attracts a large number of summer visitors, many of whom have homes in the area. Although farming and industrial enterprise is virtually non-existent, retail trade is very active throughout the year. Tourism is a major focus during the spring, summer, fall, and the winter skiing season. Commercial attractions such as The Blowing Rock, Tweetsie Railroad, and Grandfather Mountain attract thousands of visitors to Blowing Rock and Boone.

Boone is a typical college town centered around the activities at Appalachian State University. Responding to Boone's reputation as the "coolest spot in the south," summer vacationers come by the thousands.

When the snow starts falling, skiers are very much in evidence, as they hurry to the area's many ski resorts.

THE ATTRACTIONS —

From the Parkway, drive 0.8 miles west on US 421 to US 221, then go 6.2 miles north on US 221 to NC 1106 (Railroad Grade Road — just past a large red brick school building). Travel 8 miles southwest on NC 1106 to NC 1100, then 4 miles northwest on NC 1100 to:

Todd, North Carolina

The New River Festival, held in mid-October, offers handmade arts and crafts, canoe trips, delicious food, and an extensive variety of mountain music.

14-1 Scene from a general store in Todd, North Carolina —
Photo courtesy of Bert Dollar

1. The Elkland School Art Center, located just north of Todd on NC 1100 (Three Top Road), is a nonprofit school dedicated to experiential growth through the arts. A wide variety of study opportunities are provided for local and regional artists in a spacious 12,000-foot former elementary school. Visitors, more than welcome at this unique facility, will enjoy watching the exciting process of artistic endeavor.

Drive 7 miles southwest on NC 194 to NC 1335 (Meat Camp Road). Go 12 miles north on NC 1335, NC 1340, NC 1341, and NC 1118 to NC 88. (This is one continuous paved road despite the many route numbers.)

When you reach NC 88, take note of the beautiful Sutherland Methodist Church, a worthy subject for any photographers in your party.

Drive 3.7 miles southwest on NC 88 to the Tennessee state line and TN 67. Continue 1.7 miles southwest on TN 67 to US 421 at Trade, Tennessee, then go 10.5 miles north of US 421 to:

Mountain City, Tennessee

The Mountain Heritage Days and Rodeo in mid-August is an excellent time to visit Mountain City.

2. The Johnson County Welcome Center and Museum, at 716 South Shady Street (US 421), is located in an impressive 10,000-square-foot building. A campground with hook-ups and a picnic area are provided. 423-727-5800.

3. The Ralph Stout Park is just north of the downtown area on US 421. A walking

trail, playground, restrooms, picnic area, and vending machines are featured in this large, well-equipped park.

From Mountain City, drive 18 miles southwest on TN 67 to US 321, then 3.6 miles west on TN 67/US 321 to:

4. The Watauga Point Recreation Area, a USDA Forest Service day use area. Facilities for swimming, hiking, fishing, and hunting are provided along with rest rooms and drinking water. Camping is not permitted.

Travel 27 miles east on US 321 to NC 194, then 4.4 miles southwest on NC 194 to:

Valle Crucis, North Carolina

Drive 6.6 miles southwest on NC 194 to NC 184 and:

Banner Elk, North Carolina

Late October in Banner Elk brings Octoberfest, which culminates in the Wooly Worm Festival, currently celebrating twenty years of weather prognosticating. (Coloration of the winner of Wooly Worm "races" allegedly predict the severity of winter.) Crafts, food, games, and music are also featured.

5. The Avery/Banner Elk Chamber of Commerce is located in High Country Square. 828-898-5605 or 800-972-2183.

6. Lees McRae College, located on a beautiful campus in Banner Elk, offers a variety of cultural performances throughout the year which are open to the public. Inquire at the college for more information.

14-2 A scene from Banner Elk's Woolly Worm Festival —
Photo courtesy of the Avery/Banner Elk Chamber of Commerce

Go 4.4 miles north on NC 184 to:

Beech Mountain, North Carolina

7. The Beech Mountain Area Chamber of Commerce is located at 403A Beech Mountain Parkway. 828-387-9283 or 800-468-5506.

Return to NC 194, then drive 6.5 miles west on NC 194 to US 19. Go 0.8 miles west on US 19 to:

Elk Park, North Carolina

Travel 0.3 miles west on US 19 to NC 1303, then go 0.4 miles north on NC 1303 to NC 1305, then drive 4.4 miles north on NC 1305 to:

8. The Elk River Falls, a USDA Forest Service attraction. This is an exceptionally beautiful waterfall where the entire Elk River plunges over a 85-foot cliff. The areas at both the top and bottom of the falls are easily reached on a well marked trail. Places to picnic and hike are provided. This waterfall is somewhat remote, but well worth your time for a visit.

Return to Elk Park, then go 0.8 mile east on US 19 to NC 194. (Do not turn east toward Banner Elk.) Continue 0.2 miles southeast on NC 19/NC 194, then go 4.7 miles southeast on NC 194 to:

9. Waterfalls Park. Located on the east side of NC 194 just before you reach Newland, this interesting small park provides picnic tables and a hiking trail.

Drive 1 mile south on NC 194 to:

Newland, North Carolina

Visit Newland in late July for the Art on the Square festival. Enjoy arts and crafts plus good food and exciting music.

10. The Old Avery County Jail and Museum, located next to the courthouse, features artifacts from the earliest days of the county. It is one of the oldest jails still standing in North Carolina.

Drive 4.3 miles east on NC 181 to:

Linville, North Carolina

Visit Linville in late June for Singing on the Mountain, a one-day event celebrating traditional and contemporary gospel music. Attended by thousands, this famous festival will celebrate its seventy-fifth anniversary in 1999

The Grandfather Mountain Highland Games and Gathering of Scottish Clans, held annually in mid-July, is a world-class event attended by thousands of Scottish (and friends of Scottish) people. Picnics, footraces, Scottish folk music, dancing, a parade, and a wide variety of athletic competitions are among many exciting activities featured at this outstanding festival.

Travel 17 miles northeast on US 221 to:

Blowing Rock, North Carolina

Festivals in Blowing Rock come in groups. First, there's Art in the Park, a world class juried arts and crafts show that happens on Saturdays toward the middle of every month from May to October. Over one hundred of the finest artisans display their best works.

The second group of festivals is the Concert in the Park series which occurs on Sundays toward the end of each of the summer months.

11. The Blowing Rock Chamber of Commerce is located next to Blowing Rock Memorial Park on Main Street. 828-295-7851 or 800-295-7851.

12. The Blowing Rock Memorial Park is located in the heart of town on Main Street. Tennis courts, facilities for basketball and volleyball, a playground, and restrooms are available along with comfortable benches where you can rest and observe the local scene.

13. Annie Cannon Memorial Park, Broyhill Park, and The Blowing Rock Swimming Pool are west of Main Street. In addition to swimming, you can enjoy walking trails, a gazebo, a covered picnic pavilion, and a delightful lake.

14. The Glen Burney Trail can be accessed from a parking lot at the Annie Cannon Memorial Park. This ancient trail runs along New York Creek to the Cascades at 0.8 miles, Glen Burney Falls at 1.2 miles, and Glen Marie Falls at 1.5 miles. The two waterfalls are about 50 feet high. The trail is steep with many slippery rocks and quite an adventure. You can get a trail guide brochure at the Blowing Rock Chamber of Commerce.

15. The Blowing Rock Stage Company, on Sunset Drive just east of Main Street, presents a variety of professional drama, comedy, and music performances during the summer months. Ask for show names, dates, and times at the Chamber of Commerce.

Drive 6.6 miles north on US 321/US 221 to:

16. The North Carolina High Country Host Visitor Center at 1700 Blowing Rock Road (US 221/US 321). This center serves a six-county area with travel information and helpful advice and is a major resource for anyone traveling in northwest North Carolina. 828-264-1299 or 800-438-7500.

Travel 2 miles northwest on US 321 BUS to downtown:

Boone, North Carolina

Horn in the West is a summer-long historical drama performed in the Daniel Boone Amphitheater located on Horn in the West Drive southeast of downtown Boone. It has been performed in Boone since 1953. This play, commemorating the efforts of Daniel Boone and others to achieve independence from English domination, is presented nightly (except Monday) from mid-June through mid-August. The Cherokee Fire Dance is a special event in the show.

An Appalachian Summer Festival is a collection of cultural events including theater, dance, and music performances by the North Carolina Symphony and others. An outdoor sculpture competition and classes in art, music, photography, and dance are other features. Most events occur on the campus of Appalachian State University, sponsor of the festival.

17. The Boone Area Chamber of Commerce, at 208 Howard Street, is an important source for information about Boone and the surrounding area. 828-262-3516 or 828-264-2225 or 800-852-9506.

18. The Jones House, at 604 West King Street, is the downtown community, art, and cultural center for Boone. Celebration of arts and humanities takes place in a large house listed on the National Register of Historic Places.

14-3 Boone Creek - Rushing Water — Photo courtesy of the
Boone Convention and Visitors Bureau and Judi Scharns

Note: The next two attractions are located on the main campus of ASU which is in the midst of a major construction program. Parking and traffic congestion can be quite a problem. Call the University at 828-262-2000 for current information on where to park and perhaps to arrange a guided tour.

19. The Appalachian Collection, housed in ASU's **Belk Library,** is a treasure of more than 15,000 books, musical recordings, photographs, newspaper articles, artifacts, and other historical information about the mountains and mountain people. This unique repository not only has many unusual items, but also distinctive ways of presenting them. You won't want to miss it!

20. The Catherine Smith Gallery, in Farthing Auditorium on the ASU campus, offers art and sculpture exhibits. While on campus, look for the many fine outdoor sculptures acquired by ASU over the years.

21. The Appalachian Cultural Museum, located in ASU's University Hall on University Hall Drive, also exhibits a variety of environmental and historical items that preserve the cultural heritage of the region. The Appalachian Collection and this outstanding museum are major assets for the people of Appalachia.

22. The Hickory Ridge Homestead is adjacent to the *Horn in the West* theater on Horn in the West Drive. Open on weekends from May to October and daily (except Monday) during Horn season, this is a living history museum portraying mountain life in the eighteenth century. A farmer's market is also held weekly on Saturdays from May to October.

23. The Daniel Boone Native Gardens, also on the grounds of Horn in the West, exhibit plants native to the Blue Ridge Mountains. A visit to this beautiful and restful place is an educational as well as entertaining experience.

24. The Watauga Recreation Complex and Greenway Trail, at State Farm Road between Dale Street and Hunting Hills Lane, provides an indoor pool and lighted tennis courts; facilities for basketball, volleyball, and horseshoes; and a playground for children. Now under construction with more than two miles in use, the Greenway Trail provides a place for walking, biking, jogging, cross country skiing, and enjoying this beautiful natural environment.

Drive 7.5 miles east on US 221/US 421 to the Blue Ridge Parkway, Milepost 280.8 near the Parkway Elementary School..

Morganton, NC
Lake Lure, NC
Little Switzerland, NC

ROUTE 15

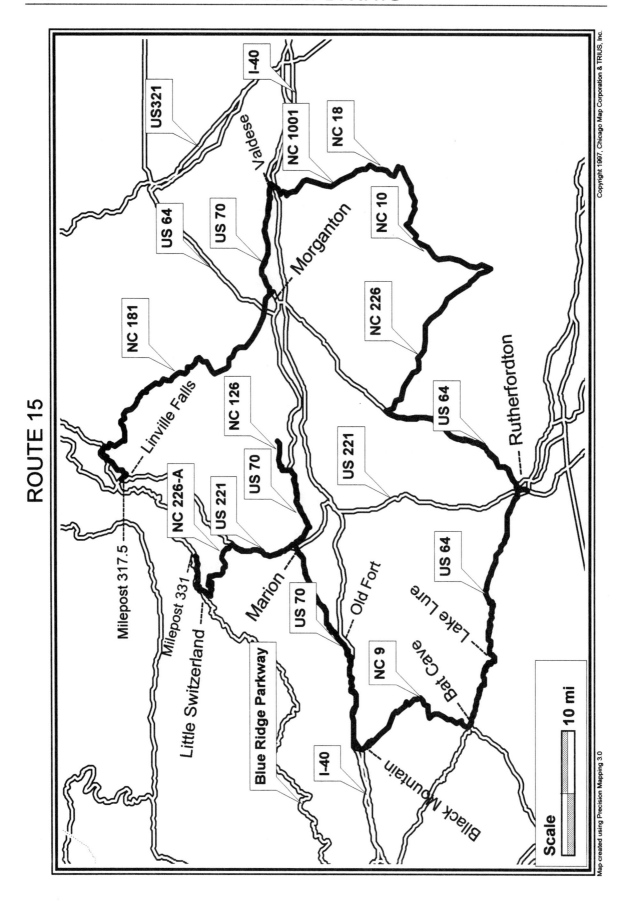

Scale

10 mi

The **Morganton - Lake Lure - Little Switzerland Route** tours the North Carolina counties of Burke, Cleveland, Rutherford, McDowell, and Buncombe. It is about 220 miles long. Although the byways are quite different, the attractions listed for Little Switzerland and Linville Falls can also be visited on Route 16. This trip starts at Milepost 317.5, on the Blue Ridge Parkway near Linville Falls, and continues in a clockwise direction to Milepost 331 at the Museum of North Carolina Minerals.

THE BYWAYS —

Route 15 starts on NC 181, which from the Parkway to Morganton, provides great views of the mountains and countryside below. Unusual 4,000-foot tall Hawksbill Mountain is a striking landmark on your right as you descend.

NC 226, from Polkville toward Marion, travels through the First Broad River Valley. Designated as a NC Scenic Byway, this stretch of highway presents a contrast between the valley and the surrounding mountains. As you drive southwest on US 64, note beautiful Cane Creek on your left.

US 64 and NC 9 travel through an incredibly varied scenic area on the way west from Lake Lure to Chimney Rock, then to Bat Cave, and finally north up the mountains to Black Mountain. Everything is here: picturesque Lake Lure, the exciting Broad River, quaint villages, spectacular rock formations, and majestic mountains. Understandably, the entire section is a NC Scenic Byway.

THE TOWNS —

The towns on Route 15 might be divided into three groups.

Morganton, Rutherfordton, and Marion are prosperous, middle-sized communities — similar in many ways but unique in others, mainly architectural diversity. All three are county-seat towns that offer scenic streets lined with historic homes and other fine old buildings. They are all engaged in many activities relating to arts, crafts and culture. Industry, business, and trade are common to the three towns.

Linville Falls, Lake Lure, Bat Cave, Black Mountain, Old Fort, and Little Switzerland are smaller towns, focusing on summer residents, tourism, and business..

Valdese is a small town steeped in the history and culture of the Waldensians, who came to the United States from the Croatian Alps of Italy in the late 1800s.

THE ATTRACTIONS —

From the Parkway, drive 0.6 miles southeast on US 221 to:

Linville Falls, North Carolina

Travel 0.7 miles southeast on NC 183 to:

1. The Linville Gorge Visitor Center. A stop at this USDA Forest Service information office is very important for anyone wanting to visit Linville Gorge, a

15-1 Old Burke County Courthouse — Photo courtesy of Burke Travel and Tourism Commission and John Payne, Photographer

spectacular wilderness area along the Linville River. The river, falling 2,000 feet in twelve miles, runs through the deepest gorge in the United States east of the Grand Canyon. Ask about hiking permits and the condition of the four-mile road (NC 1238) south to **Wiseman's View,** one of the best places to see this famous natural wonder. Restrooms, maps, brochures, and other information about the wilderness area are also available.

Return to NC 183, then go 3.5 miles northeast on NC 183 to NC 181. Drive 24 miles southeast on NC 181 to Saint Mary's Church Road (NC 1414), then north to:

2. The Quaker Meadows Plantation, a historical restoration project of the Historic Burke Foundation. Scheduled for opening in the fall of 1998, this historic site dates back to the Revolutionary War era.

Return to NC 181, then drive 2 miles southeast to:

Morganton, North Carolina

Morganton festivals include Riverfest, celebrated on the third Saturday in May on the banks of the Catawba River. Exhibits, bands, storytellers, a canoe race, and a variety of excellent foods are provided.

Early June brings Festival on the Square, which celebrates the start of summer with arts, crafts, food, and great music.

Morganton is also home to the largest street festival in Western North Carolina, the Historic Morganton Festival, held in mid-September. A juried arts and crafts show, a food fair, activities for children, basketball, roving entertainers, and all kinds of music, performed on four stages are featured. More than 40,000 people attend this exciting event every year.

3. A Visitor Information Center, The Historic Burke Foundation, and **The Heritage Museum** are all located in the **Old Burke County Courthouse** on Courthouse Square. The fine old courthouse, part of Morganton's Downtown National Register District, was constructed in 1837 and once was the summer seat of the North Carolina Supreme Court. Ask at the Information Center for a brochure describing many other Morganton buildings listed on the National Register of Historic Places. 828-433-6793.

4. The Jailhouse Gallery, also located on Courthouse Square, offers art and craft exhibits and sales for the Burke County Arts Council. Several rooms feature permanent and traveling exhibits, workshops, and contests.

5. The Senator Sam J. Ervin, Jr. Library and Museum is located south of the downtown area at 1001 Burkemont Avenue on the campus of Western Piedmont Community College. The college provides space for a replica of Senator Ervin's home library, which includes 7,500 books and other memorabilia relating to his family life and distinguished political career. Ervin is best remembered as the chairman of the Senate Watergate Committee.

6. The Catawba River Greenway Park is 2.5 miles west of the Visitor Information Center on Air Park Drive, just north of Carbon City Road (US 70). This enjoyable park offers picnicking, hiking trails, canoeing, and fishing.

Go 8 miles east on US 70 to:

Valdese, North Carolina

Visit Valdese in late July to mid-August for a performance of the drama, *From This Day Forward,* performed by the Old Colony Players. This play presents the story of the Waldensians, who settled in the Valdese area in 1893. The Waldensians came to the United States from the Croatian Alps of Italy after being persecuted for their religious beliefs. The Waldensian Festival, featuring arts, crafts, food, and music, is held each year at the end of the theater season..

7. The Old Rock Schoolhouse, at 402 Main Street, houses the Rock School Arts Gallery which offers art exhibits, concerts, and other entertainment.

8. The Waldensian Museum, located at 109 East Main Street, contains artifacts relating to the life of the Waldensians in Italy and after they emigrated to the United States.

9. The Waldensian Trail of Faith, on North Church Street, depicts the history of the Waldensians in a compound of buildings and monuments.

10. McGalliard Falls Park, also located on North Church Street, features a 45-foot waterfall, places to picnic, hiking trails, tennis courts, a playground for children, and a replica of an old gristmill.

From Valdese, drive 2.2 miles east on US 70 to NC 1001, then go 7 miles south on NC 1001 to NC 18. Travel 8.7 miles south on NC 18 to NC 10, then continue 16 miles southwest on NC 10 to NC 226. Drive 17 miles northwest on NC 226 to US 64, then go 16 miles southwest on US 64 to US 221. Drive 1 mile south on US 221 to:

15-2 Winter at McGalliard Falls in Valdese - Photo courtesy of
Burke County Travel and Tourism Commission and
Bob Hinceman, photographer

Rutherfordton, North Carolina

11. The Rutherford County Tourism Development Authority is located at 162 North Main Street. 828-286-1110 or 800-849-5998.

From Rutherfordton, go 1 mile north on US 221 to US 64, then 19 miles west on US 64 to:

Lake Lure, North Carolina

12. A Public Beach on Lake Lure and several **Picnic Areas** along the Broad River in the Chimney Rock area and behind the Town Hall in Lake Lure are provided for visitors.

Travel 6 miles west on US 64 to:

Bat Cave, North Carolina

Go 16.3 miles north on NC 9 to:

Black Mountain, North Carolina

The annual Sourwood Festival, held in mid-August, features arts and crafts, food, and entertainment. This is a street festival in the downtown Historic District.

13. The Black Mountain/Swannanoa Chamber of Commerce Visitor Center is located at 201 East State Street (US 70). 828-669-2300 or 800-669-2301.

14. The Black Mountain/Swannanoa Art Center and Swannanoa Valley Museum, in adjacent buildings at State Street and Dougherty Street, offer adventures in art and history.

15. The Old Depot, at Sutton Avenue and Black Mountain Avenue, is a nonprofit art gallery in a restored depot. Exhibiting a variety of arts and crafts, this gallery represents more than 75 artisans. Constructed about 1893, the depot building is on the National Register of Historic Places.

Drive 9 miles east on US 70/I - 40 to:

Old Fort, North Carolina

Pioneer Day, held on the third Saturday in April, celebrates Old Fort's colorful history. Arts, crafts, food, and entertainment are featured.

Visit Old Fort on the third Saturday in October for Oktoberfest. A street dance with live music, food, crafts, and entertainment are some of the fun things happening at this entertaining event.

Mountain music fills the town every Friday night as hundreds of people get together to play, sing, and dance. Saturday night is just as exciting, as fans enjoy modern country music. The location of all these festivities is a hall next to the Fire Department on Main Street.

16. The Railroad Museum and Old Fort Chamber of Commerce, at Main Street and Catawba Avenue, are located in a Southern Railway depot from the 1890's. History of the railroad is depicted through exhibits of tools, signal lights, signs, and furniture. Note the distinctive **Arrowhead Monument,** a landmark to generations of visitors to Old Fort, many of whom came by rail. 828-668-4244 or 800-237-6111.

17. The Mountain Gateway Museum, on Mauney Avenue, displays early tools, photographs, documents, housewares, musical instruments, songbooks, furniture, pottery, and other items relating to pioneer life. Two log cabins and an outdoor amphitheater, which presents educational and living history programs, are also located on the museum grounds. This fine museum, located on the banks of historic Mill Creek, also provides a picnic area.

Travel 9 miles northeast on US 70 past the intersection with NC 80 to:

18 The Carson House Museum. Colonel John Carson, an Irish immigrant who grew rich by trading in real estate and farming, starting building this house, using walnut logs, about 1790. His estate covered 8,000 acres which were devoted to the production of corn and cattle. Now a private nonprofit museum, the old house displays artifacts, furniture, clothing, tools, home furnishings, and other memorabilia relating to McDowell County history. The Carson House is listed on the National Register of Historic Places.

Go 1.5 miles northeast to US 221 BYPASS, then 2 miles south to:

19. The McDowell Chamber of Commerce and Visitors Center. Located at 629 Tate Street in an impressive new building, the McDowell Chamber of Commerce will provide you with information about Marion and McDowell County. 828-652-4240.

Drive east on Tate Street to downtown:

Marion, North Carolina

Marion's Mountain Glory Festival, held in mid-October, features arts, crafts, food, and entertainment in celebration of the coming of autumn to the mountains.

15-3 Lake James State Park — Photo courtesy of the
McDowell County Tourism Development Authority

20. The McDowell County Tourism Development Authority, located at 10 East Court Street, Suite 212, is another source for information about the area. 828-652-1103 or 888-233-6111.

21. The McDowell Arts and Crafts Center, at 24 South Main, presents theatrical performances, maintains an art gallery for local artists, hosts the Appalachian Potters Market, and sponsors touring performers in the public schools.

From downtown Marion, travel 5 miles northeast on US 70 to NC 126, then turn north on NC 126 and follow signs (about 3 miles) to:

22. Lake James State Park. This fine state park offers backpack camping with tent sites, fireplace/grills, picnic tables, and drinking water. Other facilities include a boat ramp, fishing, hiking trails, a picnic area, swimming, a washhouse, and restrooms.

Return to Marion, then go 6 miles north on US 221 to:

23. The Woodlawn Picnic Area, a North Carolina Department of Transportation facility. A special feature of this roadside park is a one-mile fitness trail with guided exercise stations.

Continue 3 miles north on US 221 to NC 226. Drive 1.3 miles northwest on NC 226 to NC 226A, then go 10 miles northwest on NC 226A to:

Little Switzerland, North Carolina

Travel 3 miles east on NC 226A to:

24.   The North Carolina Minerals Museum and **The Mitchell Area Chamber of Commerce.** Stop here to see extensive exhibits of gem stones, minerals, and the industrial operations of mining and mineral processing. Friendly staff members of the Mitchell Area Chamber of Commerce, located in the same building, will answer your questions about the Spruce Pine area which is described in the next chapter on Route 16. 828-765-9483 or 800-227-3912.

Return to the Blue Ridge Parkway.

Roan Mountain TN/NC
Erwin, TN
Spruce Pine, NC

ROUTE 16

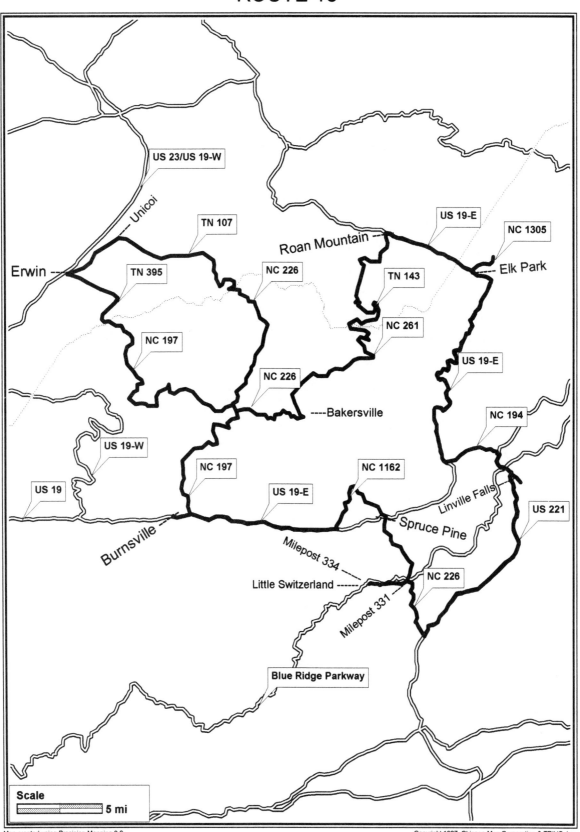

US 23/US 19-W

Unicoi

TN 107

US 19-E

NC 1305

Roan Mountain

Erwin

TN 395

NC 226

TN 143

Elk Park

NC 197

NC 261

US 19-E

NC 226

NC 194

Bakersville

US 19-W

NC 197

NC 1162

US 19

US 19-E

Linville Falls

US 221

Burnsville

Milepost 334

Spruce Pine

Little Switzerland

NC 226

Milepost 331

Blue Ridge Parkway

Scale
5 mi

Map created using Precision Mapping 3.0

Copyright 1997, Chicago Map Corporation & TRIUS, Inc.

The Roan Mountain - Erwin - Spruce Pine Route tours the North Carolina counties of McDowell, Avery, Yancey, and Mitchell and the Tennessee county of Unicoi. It is about 200 miles long. Although the byways are quite different, the attraction listed for Elk Park can also be visited on Route 14, the attractions listed for Linville Falls and Little Switzerland can also be visited on Route 15, and the attractions listed for Burnsville and Erwin can also be visited on Route 18. This trip starts at Milepost 331 on the Blue Ridge Parkway near The North Carolina Minerals Museum and continues in a counterclockwise direction to Milepost 334 at Little Switzerland.

THE BYWAYS —

Route 16 starts with a trip down the mountains on NC 226, then back up again on US 221 to Linville Falls. Great views of the mountains and valleys are visible around every turn. Note the unusual railroad configurations east of NC 226. These are The Loops, a famous design of railroad engineers to get trains up and down the steep mountains. The Loops can also be seen from the Blue Ridge Parkway, Milepost 328.6, where a sign describes them in greater detail.

US 19, north of the Parkway toward Elk Park, is graced by the exciting presence of the North Toe River rushing alongside.

A Tennessee Scenic Parkway, TN 143, first runs along the Doe River, then ascends 6,000-foot Roan Mountain. Breathtaking vistas occur frequently on the way up to Carver Gap, then a new series of great views takes over on the way down to Bakersville on NC 261.

From Bakersville, NC 226 to Iron Mountain Gap, then TN 107 transports you back over the mountains to Tennessee, where this delightful process is repeated — up on TN 395, then down on NC 197 to Burnsville. The large river along NC 197 is the mighty Nolichucky. Fabulous sights are constantly in view as you make these transitions from valleys to mountains and vice versa. Bold mountain streams are frequent close-by companions as you drive along, adding a musical note whenever you stop for a break.

THE TOWNS —

The towns of Route 16 are quite a diverse collection.

Erwin and Burnsville are larger towns built around industry, trade, and the operation of county governments. Both have distinctive homes and other buildings.

Elk Park, Roan Mountain, Bakersville, and Unicoi are smaller towns, primarily engaged in retail trade. Bakersville is the county seat of Mitchell County.

Spruce Pine is focused on mining, manufacturing, tourism, and retail trade; Linville Falls and Little Switzerland cater to summer residents and visitors from the Blue Ridge Parkway.

The rural area of Route 16 contains many towns with unusual names — some along the route, some close by on the backroads. Here are a just few of the quaint and distinctive names: Plumtree, Frank, Buladean, Cranberry, Backwoods, Toecane, Loafers Glory, Pigeon Roost, Day Book, Bandana, Ledger, and Wing. The young-at-heart in your party will enjoy a game of finding these names, and others, on roadside signs.

THE ATTRACTIONS —

From the Parkway, drive 0.2 miles northwest to:

1. The North Carolina Minerals Museum and **The Mitchell County Chamber of Commerce.** Stop here to see extensive exhibits of gem stones, minerals, and the industrial operations of mining and mineral processing. Friendly staff members of the Mitchell Area Chamber of Commerce, located in the same building, will answer your questions about the area. 828-765-9483 or 800-227-3912.

Travel 5.4 miles south on NC 226 to US 221, then 14 miles northeast on US 221 to:

Linville Falls, North Carolina

Travel 0.7 miles southeast on NC 183 to:

2. The Linville Gorge Visitor Center. A stop at this USDA Forest Service information office is very important for anyone wanting to visit Linville Gorge, a spectacular wilderness area along the Linville River. The river, falling 2,000 feet in twelve miles, runs through the deepest gorge in the United States east of the Grand Canyon. Ask about hiking permits and the condition of the four-mile road (NC 1238) south to **Wiseman's View,** one of the best places to see this famous natural wonder. Restrooms, maps, brochures, and other information about the wilderness area are also available.

Return to the Parkway on NC 183 and US 221, then drive 1.3 miles northwest on US 221 to NC 194. Travel 4 miles west on NC 194 to US 19E, then go 17 miles north on US 19E to:

Elk Park, North Carolina

Travel 0.3 miles west on US 19 to NC 1303, then go 0.4 miles north on NC 1303 to NC 1305, then drive 4.4 miles north on NC 1305 to:

3. The Elk River Falls, a USDA Forest Service attraction. This is an exceptionally beautiful waterfall, where the entire Elk River plunges over a 65-foot cliff. The areas at both the top and bottom of the falls are easily reached on a well marked trail. Places to picnic and hike are provided. This waterfall is somewhat remote, but well worth your time for a visit. It is one of the mot impressive waterfalls listed in this book.

16-1 Roan Mountain Rhododendron Gardens — Photo courtesy of
the Mitchell County Chamber of Commerce

Return to US 19E, then go 1.6 miles northwest on US 19E to the Tennessee state line. Continue 4.7 miles northwest on US 19E to TN 143 and:

Roan Mountain, Tennessee

Drive 2 miles south on TN 143 to:

4.   The Roan Mountain State Resort Park. One of Tennessee's largest and most diversified state parks, Roan Mountain offers cabins, two campgrounds with water and electrical hookups, a restaurant, picnic facilities with tables and grills, seven hiking trails, a large swimming pool, tennis courts, cross country skiing, playgrounds, horseshoes, badminton, volleyball, ping-pong, drinking water, and restrooms. Educational programs of all kinds are presented frequently during the summer months.

Travel 9.4 miles south on TN 143 to the North Carolina state line, NC 261, then 3 miles west on NC 1348 to:

5.   The Roan Mountain Rhododendron Gardens. Catawba rhododendron grows in great natural profusion on this 6,000-foot mountain. Blooming in mid-June, thousands of these plants provide a remarkable experience of botanical beauty.   These gardens, covering more than 600 acres, are the largest of their kind in the world.   The USDA Forest Service maintains this famous site and staffs an information booth. Hiking trails, picnic areas, scenic views, drinking water, and restrooms are available.

Drive 13 miles southeast on NC 261 to:

Bakersville, North Carolina

Celebrating the colorful flowers that blanket the area, the Rhododendron Festival is attended by thousands every year. Held in mid-June since 1947, visitors enjoy great food, crafts, beauty pageants, street dances, and other kinds of entertainment.

6. The Mitchell County Courthouse, built in 1907, is a fine example of early Neo-Classical Revival architecture. It is listed on the National Register of Historic Places.

Drive 16 miles northwest on NC 226 to the Tennessee state line and TN 107, then go 7 miles northwest on TN 107 to:

7. The Limestone Cove Campground, a USDA Forest Service facility that provides tent pads, lantern posts, grills, and vault toilets. A picnic area on Indian Creek is across the highway from the campground.

16-2 Red Fork Falls in Unicoi County, Tennessee — Photo courtesy of the Erwin/Unicoi County Chamber of Commerce

Travel 3 miles northwest on TN 107 to:

Unicoi, Tennessee

Visit Unicoi on the third weekend in May for the Strawberry Festival. In addition to foods featuring strawberries, you will enjoy arts and crafts exhibits, music, and other entertainment.

Travel 2.7 miles southwest on TN 107 to:

8. The Erwin National Fish Hatchery. This hatchery, operated by the USDI Fish and Wildlife Service, produces 14 million rainbow trout eggs annually that are sent to other hatcheries, to research laboratories, and to other countries. A picnic pavilion is provided for visitors.

9. The Unicoi County Heritage Museum was once the house provided for superintendents of the National Fish Hatchery. Built in 1903 and renovated in the 1980's, this grand old house now contains exhibits of antique furniture, clothing from the early 1900's, locally manufactured pottery, arts and crafts, railroad memorabilia, a replica of Erwin's Main Street shops, an old school house, an amphitheater, a nature trail, and much more.

Continue 0.6 miles southwest on TN 107 to:

10. The Unaka Ranger District Office, at 1205 North Main (TN 107). Pick up information here on Cherokee National Forest campgrounds, recreational sites, and other services.

Drive 2 miles southwest on TN 107 to:

Erwin, Tennessee

The Apple Festival, held in early October, features arts and crafts displayed by more than 300 vendors. Attendance usually exceeds 60,000 people who come for gospel singing, a show and sale for collectors of Blue Ridge Pottery, square dancing, apple orchard tours, apple cooking contests, and many other kinds of delicious food.

11. The Unicoi County Chamber of Commerce is located at 100 South Main Avenue. 423-743-0942.

From downtown Erwin drive 0.6 miles northeast on TN 107 to TN 385, then go 3 miles southeast to:

12. The Rock Creek Recreation Area, a USDA Forest Service campground and day use area. Among the featured services are campsites, some with electrical hookups; hiking trails, picnic tables, a swimming pool, a bike trail, and an amphitheater.

Go 4 miles south on TN 395 to the North Carolina state line and NC 197. Continue 27 miles southeast on NC 197 to:

Burnsville, North Carolina

Burnsville residents and visitors enjoy several festivals each year. Among these are the Spring Arts Festival in late May; the Yancey County Clogging/Arts and Crafts Show in mid-June; and the Mount Mitchell Crafts Fair in early August. All are held on the Burnsville town square — all feature arts, crafts, food, entertainment, and other fun-things.

13. The Yancey County Chamber of Commerce is located at 106 West Main Street. 828-682-7413 or 800-948-1632.

14. The Rush Wray Museum of Yancey County History, a North Carolina Regional Historic Site, is behind the Chamber of Commerce. Artifacts and other Yancey County historical information are on display.

16-3 A festival on the Burnsville town square — Photo courtesy of
the Yancey County Chamber of Commerce

15. The Parkway Playhouse, northeast of downtown Burnsville on Green Mountain Drive, presents musical and theatrical performances by the **Burnsville Little Theater** and other groups.

16. The Toecane Ranger District Office, USDA Forest Service, is located on US 19E BYPASS, about 0.25 miles east of Main Street. Get information here about facilities available in the Pisgah National Forest.

Go 11 miles east on US 19E to NC 1160 (at the Penland School sign), then drive 3 miles north on NC 1160 and NC 1162 (Penland Road) to NC 1164 (Penland School Road). Go northwest on NC 1164 to:

17. The Penland School of Crafts. Internationally renowned, the Penland School offers classes in wood, clay, glass, metal work, photography, and other arts and crafts. Instructors and students come from all over the world to teach and study here; many former students have built studios and live in the area. The Penland Visitor Center exhibits crafts and provides information about the school and local artisans.

Return to NC 1162, then drive 1 mile north on NC 1162/NC 1242 to NC 226. Travel 4 miles southeast of NC 226 to:

Spruce Pine, North Carolina

The North Carolina Mineral and Gem Festival is held on the first full weekend in August. Both retail and wholesale shows attract the attention of thousands of visitors who are interested in jewelry, pearls, silver, gold, diamonds, mineral specimens, and lapidary supplies.

Mid-September brings a Revolutionary War reenactment called the Overmountain Victory Celebration. Military camps feature costumed volunteers reliving the experiences of our pioneer ancestors in authentic settings. Demonstrations of the lifestyle of the period are presented. The name Overmountain refers to the 1780 march of American soldiers from Abingdon, Virginia, "over the mountains" to encounter British soldiers at Kings Mountain, South Carolina.

Visit Spruce Pine in mid-October for the Fall Celebration of the Arts. Glass, clay, fiber, metal, wood, and paper objects are displayed by contemporary and traditional artists in a juried competition. Prizes are given for outstanding works.

18. The Riverwalk Park, across the North Toe River from Downtown Spruce Pine, features places to picnic, a walking trail, restrooms, and playground equipment.

19. The Mitchell County Chamber of Commerce, also listed as the first attraction on this route, is located 5 miles south of Spruce Pine on NC 226. 828-765-9483 or 800-227-3912.

Drive 5 miles south on NC 226 to NC 226A, then go 3 miles west on NC 226A to:

Little Switzerland, North Carolina

Drive north to the Blue Ridge Parkway, Milepost 334.

Asheville, NC
Looking Glass Falls, NC
Highlands, NC

ROUTE 17

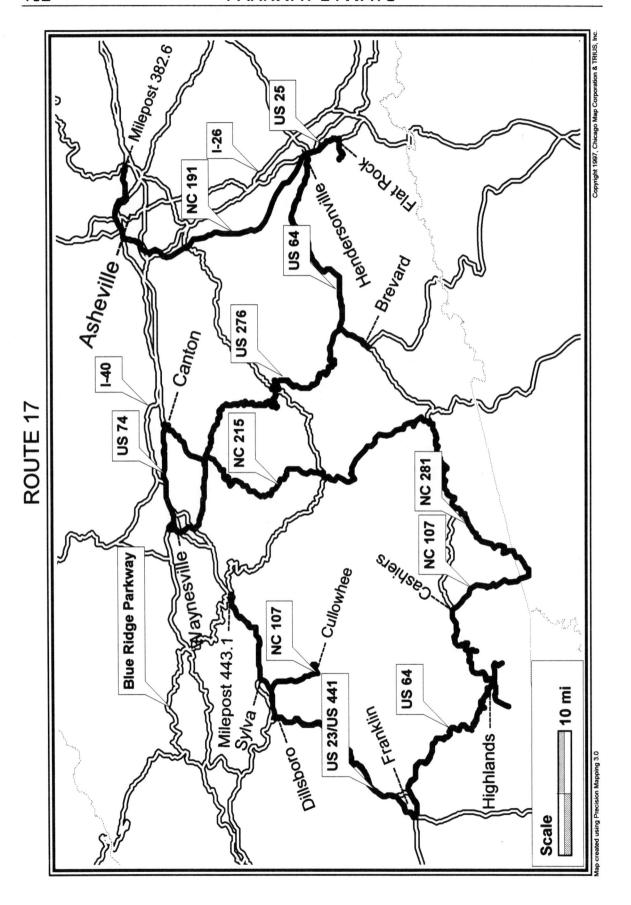

Milepost 382.6

US 25

I-26

NC 191

Flat Rock

US 64

Asheville

Hendersonville

Brevard

Canton

US 276

I-40

US 74

NC 215

NC 281

NC 107

Cashiers

Blue Ridge Parkway

Waynesville

Milepost 443.1

Sylva

NC 107

Cullowhee

Dillsboro

US 23/US 441

US 64

Franklin

Highlands

Scale

10 mi

The Asheville - Looking Glass Falls - Highlands Route tours the North Carolina counties of Buncombe, Henderson, Transylvania, Jackson, and Haywood. It is about 270 miles long. Although the byways are quite different, the attractions listed for Asheville can also be visited on Route 18 and the attractions listed for Franklin, Dillsboro, Sylva, and Cullowhee can also be visited on Route 19. This trip starts at Milepost 382.6 on the Blue Ridge Parkway near the Folk Art Center and continues in a clockwise direction to Milepost 443.1 at Balsam Gap.

THE BYWAYS —

Route 17 includes all of two NC Scenic Byways, the Forest Heritage and the Whitewater Way, plus a long section of the Waterfall Byway. It just doesn't get any more interesting and entertaining than this.

First, US 276 passes by two special water attractions, Looking Glass Falls and Sliding Rock, then crosses the mountain ridge at the Parkway. The trip continues with a descent to Waynesville and Canton followed by another mountain crossing on NC 215 to the French Broad River and Rosman. Spectacular views are common as you drive from valleys to mountains, then repeat the process.

A scenic drive on NC 281, the NC Whitewater Way Byway, takes you to North Carolina's highest and perhaps most dramatic waterfall, Whitewater Falls. From the handy parking lot, it's only a five-minute walk to the falls.

You think it couldn't get any better, then it does with a NC Waterfall Byway trip through the gorgeous Cullasaja Gorge. Everything is here: towering waterfalls, a wild river crashing around giant boulders, and fantastic mountains — all visible from or near a comfortable highway. You really don's want to miss it!

THE TOWNS —

Incredibly diverse and distinctive, Asheville is the largest city on Route 17. The variety of things to see and do is truly amazing. Historic and unusual architecture is everywhere. Artistic, cultural, religious, and educational exhibits and activities abound, and shopping opportunities are never ending. Almost any kind of recreational experience is readily available. Although commercial and not listed as attractions in this book, Biltmore Estate and the Grove Park Inn are architectural and historical landmarks. Asheville is simply a fantastic place to visit or live.

Hendersonville, Flat Rock, Brevard, Cashiers, and Highlands are sophisticated towns, catering to retirees, visitors, devotees of music and culture, and discriminating shoppers. All five towns have a pleasing ambience that you will enjoy immensely.

Asheville, North Carolina

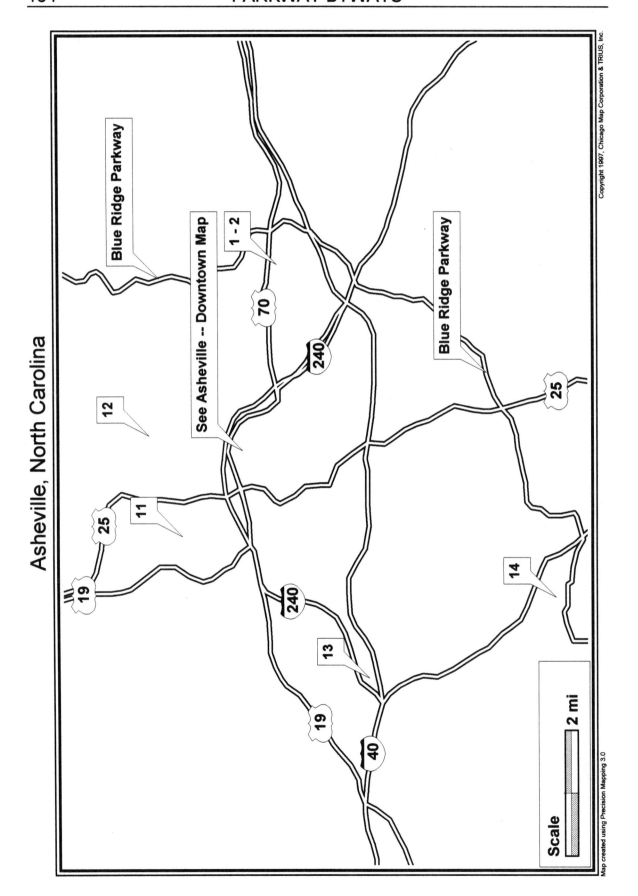

Blue Ridge Parkway

See Asheville -- Downtown Map

Blue Ridge Parkway

Scale

2 mi

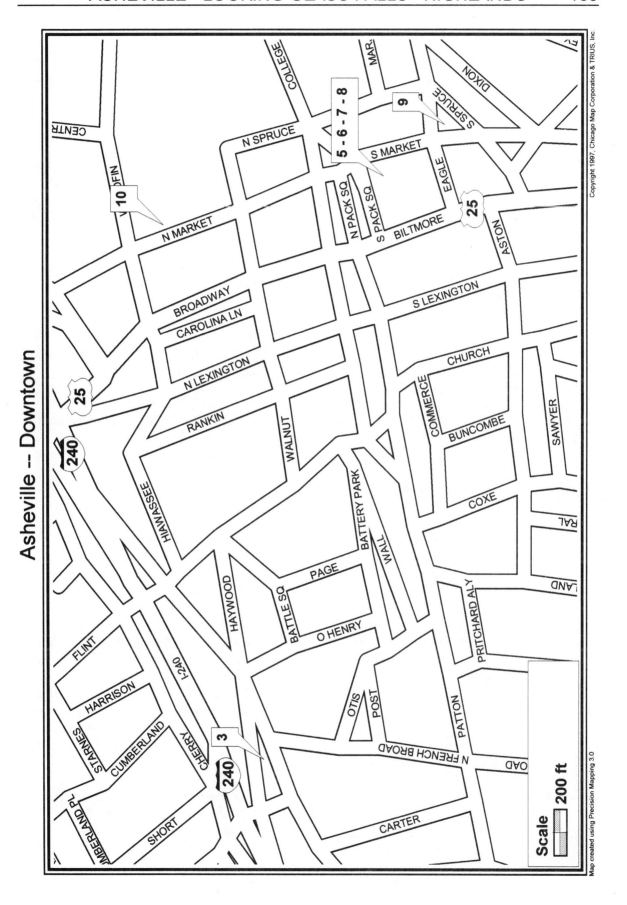

Asheville -- Downtown

Scale
200 ft

Dillsboro, Sylva, Waynesville, and Canton happily entertain their many visitors, and engage in retail trade, business, county government, and industry.

Cullowhee is essentially Western Carolina University plus supporting businesses and services.

THE ATTRACTIONS —

Asheville, North Carolina

Asheville holds about 150 festivals annually, appealing to every conceivable taste and interest. Call or write the Asheville Convention and Visitors Bureau for their brochure, *Mountain Festivals and Events* to get a detailed list. The address and phone numbers are listed below. Here are five of the most popular:

Shindig-on-the-Green "happens" every Saturday night during the summer. Celebrated by thousands over its long history, this tribute to all kinds of mountain music and dancing takes place at Asheville's City/County Plaza just east of Pack Square.

The Mountain Dance and Folk Festival is held in early July at the City/County Plaza and Diana Wortham Theater.

Bele Chere, an exciting downtown street festival, is celebrated in late July. This is one of Asheville's largest festival events.

Craft Fairs, sponsored by the Southern Highlands Craft Guild, are held at the Asheville Civic Center in mid-July and mid-October.

From the Parkway, drive 0.8 miles west on US 70 to NC 81 (Swannanoa River Road), then go 0.5 miles southwest on NC 81 to Azalea Road. Turn east, then drive to Gashes Creek Road and:

1. The Western North Carolina Nature Center, located at 75 Gashes Creek Road. This fine facility features a living museum of native Southern Appalachian wild animals, farm animals, and plants. A nature trail provides an opportunity to see this rich heritage in a natural environment.

2. The Buncombe County Recreation Park, located near the Nature Center on the banks of the Swannanoa River, offers amusement park rides, swimming, and places to picnic. Of special interest to families with children, there is something here for everyone.

Return to US 70, then travel 2 miles west to I-240. Drive 2.5 miles northwest on I-240 to the Montford Avenue (4-C) exit, then south on Montford Avenue and east on Haywood Street to:

3. The Asheville Convention and Visitors Bureau - Asheville Area Chamber of Commerce. This treasury of travel information is located at 151 Haywood Street, P. O. Box 1010, Asheville, NC 28802. 828-258-6109 or 800-257-1300.

4. The Asheville Urban Trail winds through Asheville's distinctive and historic downtown district. The buildings, constructed primarily in the period from 1880 to 1930, present a bold statement on architectural diversity. Explanatory plaques are located along the trail; more information is available at the Asheville Convention and Visitors Bureau.

The Pack Place Education, Arts, and Science Center includes the five following attractions:

17-1 Asheville Skyline — Photo courtesy of the
Asheville Convention and Visitors Bureau

5. The Asheville Art Museum, at 2 South Pack Square, features exhibits of twentieth-century art by national and local American artists and crafts relating to the Southern Appalachians. Educational programs for children and adults are also provided.

6. The Coburn Gem and Mineral Museum, at 2 South Pack Square, presents permanent and traveling exhibits of gems and minerals from North Carolina and the world. Hands-on involvement with minerals is available at some of the exhibits.

7. The Diana Wortham Theater, at 2 South Pack Square, presents a variety of musical, theatrical, and educational performances in a 500-seat auditorium. Plays, poetry, jazz, symphony music, ballet, modern dance, lectures, and many other kinds of performing arts are featured regularly.

8. The Health Adventure, at 2 South Pack Square, is a museum devoted to physical health and applied science. Hands-on learning opportunities are available for children of all ages. Examples of exhibit names are Body Works, Miracle of Life, and Brain Storm.

9. The YMI Cultural Center, located at the corner of Market and Eagle Streets (southeast across the street from the attractions listed above), features permanent and traveling exhibits relating to the history and culture of African-Americans.

10. The Thomas Wolfe Memorial State Historic Site, located at 52 Market Street, is the former home of the famous author. Originally known as "Old Kentucky Home," Wolfe called the rambling old boarding house, "Dixieland," and used it as the setting for his classic novel, *Look Homeward, Angel.* This attraction is a North Carolina Historic Site and is maintained by the Division of Archives and History, Department of Cultural Resources.

11. The Botanical Gardens, located at 151 W. T. Weaver Boulevard, are a part of the University of North Carolina - Asheville. Ten acres of gardens feature native plants in natural settings, walking trails, a visitors center, and a gift shop. This delightful place offers a beautiful and restful environment — the perfect site for a break on a busy day.

12. North Carolina Homespun Museum, at 111 Grovewood Road, presents the history of Biltmore Industries. The art of handweaving is portrayed with artifacts and demonstrations. An antique automobile museum, displaying old cars and a fire engine, is located at the same address.

If you have a few extra minutes, visit the **Grove Park Inn**, located near the Homespun Museum. Although a commercial establishment and not included as an attraction in this book, the Grove Park Inn is a spectacular example of hotel architecture. Built in 1913 out of enormous boulders, this unusual building is an Asheville landmark. The lobby is especially impressive.

From downtown Asheville, drive 0.7 miles west on Patton Avenue to I-240, then go 3.3 miles southwest on I-240 to NC 191 (Brevard Road). Drive 0.7 miles south on NC 191 to:

13. The Western North Carolina Farmers Market, at 570 Brevard Road, owned and operated by the State of North Carolina. This 36-acre facility provides farmers, growers, and artisans with a place to market their produce, flowers, jams and jellies, plants, and handmade crafts. A restaurant and a garden center are also available.

Travel 5 miles south on NC 191 to the Blue Ridge Parkway, then drive west on the Parkway to Fredrick Law Olmsted Way, and the entrance to:

14. The North Carolina Arboretum. A facility of the University of North Carolina, this multi-faceted complex features gardens, nature trails, horticultural exhibits, greenhouses, and the National Native Azalea Repository. The site covers more than 400 acres in the Bent Creek Research and Demonstration Forest — USDA Pisgah National Forest.

Return to the Parkway and NC 191. Drive 12 miles south on NC 191 to:

15. The Historic Johnson Farm. This unusual educational center, owned by the Henderson County Public Schools, features a large brick house circa 1870s, a museum, various outbuildings, nature trails, forests, fields, and streams. The farm is listed on the National Register of Historic Places.

Travel 3.5 miles southeast on NC 191 to US 25, then go 0.7 miles southeast to:

Hendersonville, North Carolina

Thousands of residents, visitors, and artists get together in early August for the Sidewalk Art Show. Held annually for forty years, this interesting event takes place on Hendersonville's Main Street.

The really big show happens on Labor Day weekend when the Apple Festival, celebrating Hendersonville's position as the

17-2 Jump Off Rock — Photo courtesy of Henderson County Travel and Tourism

largest apple producer in North Carolina, fills Main Street with fun-seeking people. Art, crafts, food, entertainment, and sporting events are featured.

16. The Visitors Center - Henderson County Travel and Tourism is located at 201 South Main Street. 828-693-9708 or 800-828-4244.

17.   Historic Hendersonville's Main Street, with its serpentine design, planter boxes, music, trees, and neat places to shop and eat, is one of the most attractive downtown districts covered in this book.

18.   The Historic Hendersonville Depot and Model Railroad, located at Seventh Avenue and Maple Street, is a special place for train buffs. The old depot, now painted in its original colors, houses an elaborate HO scale model railroad portraying the actual railroad layout in the Hendersonville area. The Carolina Special stopped running in 1968, but this model, a project of the

Apple Valley Model Railroad Club, maintains the heritage. A Southern Railway caboose is also on display.

19.   The Henderson County Curb Market, at the corner of Church Street and Second Avenue, sells items that are home grown, made, or crafted by residents of Henderson County. Shop here for fresh fruit and vegetables, baked goods, dairy products, jams and jellies, toys, quilts, and other kinds of local produce and products.

20. Wolfe's Angel is a statue frequently referred to in Thomas Wolfe's book, *Look Homeward, Angel*. It now resides in the Oakdale Cemetery on US 64 just west of downtown Hendersonville.

Drive about 4.5 miles west on Fifth Avenue, continuing as Laurel Park Highway to:

21. Jump Off Rock, a great place to view the mountains, valleys, and towns in the Hendersonville area. According to a local

17-3 Flat Rock Playhouse — Photo courtesy of
Henderson County Travel and Tourism

legend, an Indian maiden jumped to her death from this place after hearing that her Indian chief had been killed.

Return to Hendersonville, then drive 1 mile south on US 25 to US 176. Go 1 mile southeast on US 176 to Upward Road, then travel northeast on Upward Road, Beverly Avenue, and Substation Street to Gilbert Street, the Hendersonville Airport, and:

22.   The Western North Carolina Air Museum. More than a dozen restored and antique airplanes are displayed at this museum, the first of its kind in North Carolina. Air shows are held annually in the spring and fall. The museum is open on Wednesday, Saturday, and Sunday afternoons.

Return to US 25, then drive 2 miles south on US 25 to:

23.   The St. John in the Wilderness Episcopal Church. Built in 1833, the church served many prominent southern families over the years, and is now a part of the Episcopal Diocese of Western North Carolina. The church is listed on the National Register of Historic Places.

Continue 1 mile south on US 25 to:

Flat Rock, North Carolina

The Sandburg Folk Festival, held in late May at the Carl Sandburg Home, features crafts, food, and entertainment.

24.   The Flat Rock Playhouse, State Theater of North Carolina, is located at 2661 Greenville Highway (US 25). This highly regarded seasonal theater (May - October), presents a variety of dramas, musicals, comedies, and other theatrical delights for thousands of visitors every year. More that three hundred productions have been staged over fifty years. Call 828-693-0731 for schedules and reservations.

25. The Carl Sandburg Home National Historic Site, at 1928 Little River Road, was home to the famous poet, historian, and speaker for the last 22 years of his life. Called "Connemara," the 240-acre estate was the perfect place for Sandburg's writing and for his family to live. The main house, containing his library of 10,000 books, papers, and family artifacts, is furnished much like it was originally. Numerous outbuildings portray farm life in the 1800's.

From Flat Rock, drive 3.7 miles north on US 25 to US 64 in Hendersonville, then go 20 miles west/then southwest on US 64 to **Brevard, North Carolina.** This is a more direct route but misses the **Holmes Educational State Forest.**

Or, as an alternative, travel about 4 miles west on Little River Road (NC 1123) to Kanuga Road (NS 1127), then go about 5.6 miles southwest on NS 1127 to:

26. The Holmes Educational State Forest. Many trails throughout this delightful forest feature displays that explain the science of modern forestry. Picnic tables, a picnic shelter (with grills), and walk-in camping sites are also available.

Drive about 6 miles west/then north on Crab Creek Road (NC 1127/NC 1528) to US 64 at Penrose, then go 7.3 miles southwest on US 64 to:

Brevard, North Carolina

The Festival of the Arts has entertained Brevard residents and visitors for more than 25 years. Held annually in early July, this week-long event features fireworks, musical programs, arts, crafts, food, museum exhibitions, a flower show, and a forest tour.

27. The Brevard - Transylvania County Tourism Development Authority is located at 35 West Main Street. Arts and crafts by local artisans are exhibited here. 828-883-3700 or 800-648-4523.

28. The Brevard Music Center, at 1001 Probart Street, presents nationally renowned musicians during a summer season running from late June through the second weekend in August. Concerts are held daily that feature orchestras, bands, choral groups, opera, and chamber music.

29. The Silvermont Mansion, on East Main Street, is the 33-room former home of John and Elizabeth Silversteen. The family was involved in tanning, lumber, and other enterprises. Now on the National Register of Historic Places, the house serves the Brevard community as a meeting place, a senior center, and a recreation center with a playground, tennis and shuffleboard courts, a basketball court, and a picnic area. Opportunities for dancing and listening to music are frequently offered.

30. The Jim Bob Tinsley Museum and Research Center, located at 20 West Jordan Street, is devoted to the collecting and preservation of artifacts and memorabilia relating to the American cowboy, outdoor, and mountain life. Songs, art works, posters, sculptures, Indian relics, and many other objects on display are from the lifetime collection of Jim Bob and Dottie Tinsley and others. Born in Brevard in 1921, Tinsley later became famous as a performer of cowboy songs and as a cowboy music historian.

Drive 3.5 miles northeast on US 64 to US 276, then go about 1.5 miles northwest on US 276 to:

31. The Pisgah Ranger District Office. Stop at this USDA Forest Service facility for more information about the many recreational and educational opportunities in the Pisgah and Nantahala National Forests.

Go about 0.5 miles southeast on US 276 to

32. The Davidson River Campground and Sycamore Flats Recreation Area. The campground offers camping, trailer spaces, showers, a trailer dump station, restrooms, an amphitheater for educational programs, fishing, and hiking. The recreation area features picnic tables, restrooms, and fishing.

Drive about 4.5 miles northwest on US 276 to:

33. The Looking Glass Falls. This exciting waterfall can be viewed from your car but will be more enjoyable if you walk closer and listen as well as look at the magnificent sight

Go about 1 mile northwest on US 276 to:

34. The Moore Cove Falls Trail. This interesting waterfall requires a bit of walking (0.7 miles each way), but is well worth the effort.

Travel about 0.5 miles northwest on US 276 to:

35. The Sliding Rock Recreation Area. Here is a place where you can get really close to nature on a 60-foot rock waterslide into a pool below. This popular attraction features a bathhouse, restrooms, and lifeguards during the summer.

Drive about 3.5 miles northwest on US 276 to:

36. The Cradle of Forestry in America National Historic Site, the home of the first forestry school in the United States. **The Forest Discovery Center,** located at the site, offers exhibits on forestry and a historical film. Many of the exhibits feature opportunities for hands-on involvement. Additional services include a restaurant, a gift shop, guided trail walks, people working on crafts, and special programs on forestry, outdoor life, wildlife, and a birthday party for Smokey Bear (on August 9). The Cradle of Forestry is one of the most interesting and important attractions listed in this book.

Go about 24 miles northwest on US 276 to:

Waynesville, North Carolina

The Blue Ridge Arts and Crafters Freedom Festival of Crafts is held in early July at the Haywood County Fairgrounds at Lake Junaluska. Their fall show, Autumn Leaves Craft Festival, takes place in mid-October, also at the Haywood County Fairgrounds.

Folkmoot USA, NC International Folk Festival, a major 10-day event featuring music, food, and folk dancing, comes to Waynesville in mid-July.

The Church Street Arts and Crafts Show takes over Waynesville's downtown Main Street for a day in mid-October.

37. The Chamber of Commerce is located at 73 Walnut Street. 828-456-3021.

38. The Haywood County Tourism Development Authority is at 1233 North Main, Suite 1-40. 828-452-0152 or 800-334-9036.

39. Downtown Waynesville is a special attraction with its brick sidewalks, interesting places to shop, and fun places to eat. Enjoy a leisurely walk through this delightful town.

40. The Museum of North Carolina Handicrafts — Historic Shelton House, at 307 Shelton Street, was built between 1875 and 1880 for Stephen J. Shelton, a respected early citizen of Waynesville. The museum features exhibits of heritage crafts including hand carved dulcimers, pottery, quilts, handcrafted jewelry, Indian artifacts, and furniture of the late 1800's.

Drive 3 miles north on US 276 to US 19, then turn east to:

41. The Lake Junaluska — Lake Junaluska Heritage Museum and The World Methodism Museum. These museums feature displays that present the history of the Methodist Church.

Travel 3.8 miles east on US 19/US 23 to NC 1800 (Jones Cove Road), then go south to:

42. The Campus Arboretum of Haywood Community College. This charming place features an oak forest with trees more than one hundred years old and gardens containing roses, rhododendron, and other plants. A mill house and a pond also contribute to the pleasant environment.

Return to US 19/US 23, then drive 5.2 miles east to:

Canton, North Carolina

Kick up your heels every Friday night from May to August at Pickin' In The Park, a celebration of bluegrass music. These entertaining events take place at the Canton Recreation Park.

Visit Canton in early September for the Labor Day Festival. Special features are a parade and the annual Paper Boat Race on the Pigeon River.

43. The Canton Papertown Association, at 32 Main Street, is the place to get local information. 828-648-7925.

44. The Canton Area Historical Museum, on Park Street, specializes in the history of eastern Haywood County. Artifacts on display include Indian relics, tools, and pottery.

Drive 7 miles southwest on NC 215 to Bethel, North Carolina, then jog east and continue 8 miles southwest on NC 215 to:

45. Sunburst Campground, a USDA Forest Service campground, offers spaces for tents and trailers, picnic tables, and restrooms.

Go 9.6 miles south on NC 215 to:

46. The Bubbling Spring Branch Cascades, the most imposing and easiest to view of several waterfalls and cascades in the immediate area.

Travel 18.4 miles south on NC 215 to US 64, then go 9.5 miles west on US 64 past Lake Toxaway to NC 181. Drive 1.8 miles southwest on NC 281 to:

47. Drift Falls, Turtleback Falls, and Rainbow Falls. These waterfalls on the Horsepasture River are accessible along the same trail starting at NC 181. Be very careful around these falls. A number of people have fallen to their death in recent years.

Continue 6.8 miles southwest on NC 281 to:

48. Whitewater Falls. This is the highest and most spectacular waterfall listed in this book. Easily accessible on a short trail from a spacious parking lot, this scenic natural wonder will be a highlight of your trip.

Continue 1 mile south to the South Carolina State Line and SC 130, then continue 1 mile southwest to SC 413 Drive 2.2 miles southwest on SC 413 to SC 107, then travel 9.2 miles north on SC 107/NC 107 to:

Cashiers, North Carolina

The Chili Cook-off, held annually in mid-September, is the major Cashiers festival.

49. The Cashiers Area Chamber of Commerce is on NC 107 North at US 64. 828-743-5191.

Drive 4.7 miles southwest on US 64 to NC 1600 (Whiteside Mountain Road), then go south on NC 1600 to:

50. Whiteside Mountain. Almost 5,000 feet high and 2.000 feet above the surrounding valley, this great mountain provides panoramic views to the south, east, and west A two-mile loop trail along the mountain ridge opens up these exciting vistas

Return to US 64, then drive 5.6 miles southwest to:

Highlands, North Carolina

The Highlands Chamber Music Festival, running from mid-July through the first weekend in August, has been entertaining Highlands residents and visitors for more than a dozen years.

The Rotary Club Bar-B-Que, held on July 4, features great food, music, family games, skydivers, and fireworks.

Highlands Own Craft Show, displaying local arts and crafts, happens every year in mid-October at the Highlands Civic Center.

51. The Highlands Chamber of Commerce is located at 396 Oak Street. 828-526-2112.

52. The Highlands Visitors Center, USDA Forest Service, is on West Main Street. Get information here about facilities in the Nantahala National Forest. 828-526-3462.

53. The Highlands Nature Center and Biological Station, located on Horse Cove Road east of downtown Highlands, offers educational programs about animals and plants, botanical gardens, and nature walks.

54. The Bascom-Louise Gallery, also on Horse Cove Road, in the Hudson Library, provides exhibit space for local and regional artists, programs, performances, and workshops.

Drive 2.5 miles east on Horse Cove Road to Rich Gap Road (NC 1710), then turn right and go for about 150 feet to a parking area for:

55. The Fodderstack Poplar, the second largest yellow tulip poplar tree in North Carolina.

Return to Highlands.

56. The Highlands Parks and Recreation Civic Center is south of Foreman Street on US 64 (Cashiers Road). This extensive facility offers a swimming pool, picnic tables, tennis courts, a Nautilus room, and many other services.

17-4 A place to sit, rock, and look at the Smoky Mountains —
Photo courtesy of the Swain County Tourist Development Authority

57. The Highlands Playhouse is located on Oak Street near the Chamber of Commerce. Live musical and theatrical performances are presented from early June through late August.

From downtown Highlands drive west on US 64 (Main Street) to NC 106, then go 1.7 miles southwest to a USDA Forest Service sign for the Glen Falls Scenic Area and NC 1618 (Glen Falls Road). Go 1 mile south on NC 1618 to:

58. Glen Falls, accessible after a 1-mile hike over rather steep terrain. There are actually three waterfalls here; the highest two are the most impressive.

Return to Highlands, then drive 2.7 miles northwest on US 64 to:

59. Bridal Veil Falls. This famous waterfall has been enjoyed by millions of visitors over many years.

Travel 1 mile northwest on US 64 to:

60. Dry Falls. Accessible on a short paved trail, this beautiful waterfall on the Cullasaja River is a natural inspiration.

Go 0.7 miles northwest on US 64 to:

61. The Van Hook Glade Campground. This USDA Forest Service campground offers camping sites, picnic table, grills, and toilets.

62. The Cliffside Lake Recreation Area, near Van Hook Glade (a short hike or 1.5 miles by car), features a number of hiking trails, picnic tables, swimming, showers, and fishing.

Return to US 64, then drive 4.7 miles northwest to:

63. The Lower Cullasaja Falls. This spectacular waterfall can be viewed from

US 64 but be very careful where you park and in crossing the highway.

Continue 10 miles northwest on US 64 to:

Franklin, North Carolina

Visit downtown Franklin on any Saturday night from June through October for Pickin' on the Square.

Franklin is renowned for minerals and gems. The Macon County Gemboree in late July and the Annual Leaf Lookers Gemboree in early October celebrate this interesting activity.

Franklin's Foot Stompin' Festival, held in mid-October, features clogging competitions and exhibitions.

64. The Franklin Area Chamber of Commerce is located at 425 Porter Street. 828-524-3161 or 800-336-7829

65. The Smoky Mountain Host, at 4437 Georgia Road (US 23/US 441), provides information about several counties in western North Carolina and about the Great Smoky Mountains. 828-369-9606 or 800-432-4678

66. The Franklin Gem and Mineral Museum, located at 25 Phillips Street in the former county jail, exhibits unusual gems, mineral specimens, and a rock collection, plus educational displays, books on gems and minerals, and a wide variety of other materials.

67. The Macon County Historical Society Museum, at 36 West Main Street, displays historical memorabilia including documents, artifacts, and photographs.

68. The Scottish Tartans Museum and Heritage Center, located at 95 East Main Street, offers exhibits, a library, and other materials relating to tartan dress, the kilt, and weaving.

69. The Macon County Arts Association, at 6 East Main Street, features a variety of art works in their gallery, along with works to encourage interest in the arts in Macon County.

Drive 17.5 miles northeast on US 23/US 441 to:

Dillsboro, North Carolina

Visit Dillsboro in mid-June for the Heritage Day Festival. Arts and crafts are the featured attraction, but you will also enjoy great food, fiddling and banjo pickin'.

70. The Jackson County Visitor Information Center, located at the corner of Front and Depot Streets, is the place to pick up a brochure describing **Downtown Dillsboro.** This area is a fascinating place to walk, look at the unique buildings, shop, and eat.

Travel 2 miles east on US 23 BUS/NC 107 to:

Sylva, North Carolina

Greening Up the Mountains, an Earth Day celebration, is held in Sylva in late April.

71. The Jackson County Chamber of Commerce and the Jackson County Tourism Development Authority are located at 116 Central Street. Ask for a map of beautiful **Downtown Sylva,** another great place to walk and look at old buildings, especially the **Historic Jackson County Courthouse.** Call the Chamber or Tourism

Development Authority at 828-586-2155 or 800-962-1911.

Drive 1 mile east on US 23 BUS/NC 107, then go 5 miles south on NC 107 to:

Cullowhee, North Carolina

Mountain Heritage Day, rated among the top 200 art events in the United States, is held on the fourth Saturday in September at Western Carolina University. Among many exciting activities, dancing, singing, playing music, story telling, demonstrating crafts, and eating American/Indian foods, are featured. Annual attendance is more than 35,000.

72. The Mountain Heritage Center, at Western Carolina University, offers displays of historical information and artifacts relating to the area's culture and society. A permanent exhibit describes settlement of the area by Scotch/Irish people in the eighteenth century. Other exhibits portray handcrafts, farming, and family life. This fine center is a major resource for anyone interested in the history and culture of North Carolina mountain people.

Return to US 23 BUS at Sylva, then drive 10.5 miles northeast on US 23 BUS/US 23/US 74 to:

73. The Balsam Welcome Center, located on US 23/US 74 at the Blue Ridge Parkway. 828-452-7307

Return to the Parkway, Milepost 443.1 at Balsam Gap.

Jonesborough, TN
French Broad River, TN/NC
Asheville, NC

ROUTE 18

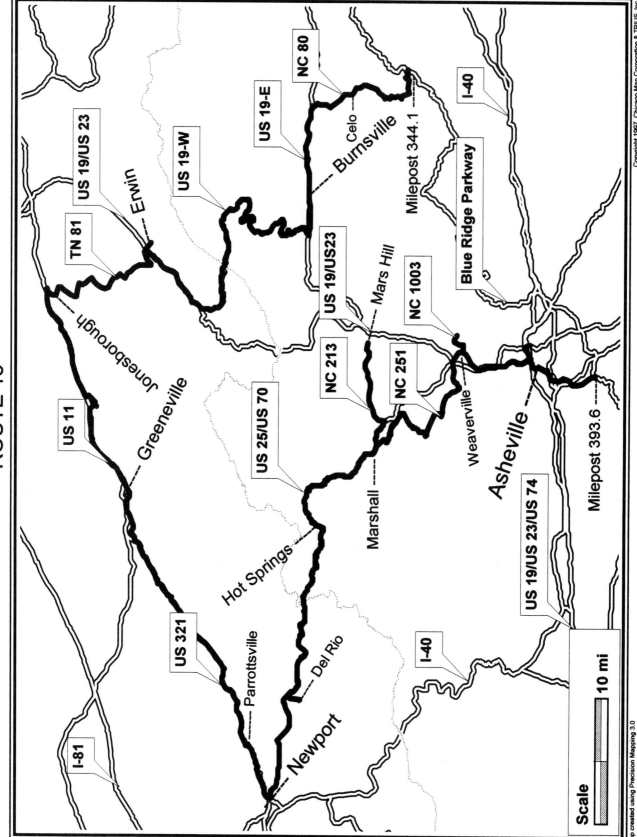

The Jonesborough - French Broad River - Asheville Route tours the North Carolina counties of Yancey, Madison, and Buncombe and the Tennessee counties of Unicoi, Washington, Greene, and Cocke. It is about 240 miles long. Although the byways are quite different, the attractions listed for Burnsville and Erwin can also be visited on Route 16 and the attractions listed for Asheville can also be visited on Route 17. This trip starts at Milepost 344.1 on the Blue Ridge Parkway at Buck Creek Gap and continues in a counterclockwise direction to Milepost 393.6 at NC 191 near the North Carolina Arboretum.

THE BYWAYS —

Route 18 starts with a trip down scenic NC 80 from the Parkway to Micaville. Note the rushing waters of the South Toe River.

West of Burnsville, US 19-W starts its winding mountain ascent along the delightful Cane River, following its every twist and turn. Since there is a large change in elevation, the river is often filled with whitewater rapids.

TN 81 from Erwin to Jonesborough, US 11/US 321 from Jonesborough to Greeneville, and US 321/US 411 from Greeneville to Newport is an unbroken series of Tennessee Scenic Parkways. The reason they were so designated is obvious to the traveler. Manicured valley fields, well-kept farmhouses, and picturesque towns are artistically arranged in front of the massive Appalachian Mountains rising to the south. The continuing panorama is a constant delight.

North Carolina Scenic Byways, US 25/US 70 in the Hot Springs area and NC 251 from Marshall toward Asheville, conclude Route 18. US 25/US runs through some interesting mountains and NC 251 follows the historic French Broad River.

THE TOWNS —

The city and towns of Route 18 are quite a varied mix.

Burnsville, Erwin, Newport, and Marshall are typical county seat towns devoted to county government, retail trade, business, and a little manufacturing and industry. Weaverville concentrates on retail trade and housing Asheville workers.

Jonesborough and Parrottsville are uniquely historical as two of the first three towns in Tennessee. Del Rio and Hot Springs are picturesque villages.

Greeneville/Tusculum is larger with a focus on the heritage of President Andrew Johnson, Tusculum College, plus more business, trade, and industry. Mars Hill is the quintessential college town, the home of Mars Hill College.

Incredibly diverse and distinctive, Asheville is the largest city on Route 18. The variety of things to see and do is truly amazing. Historic and unusual architecture is everywhere. Artistic, cultural, religious, and educational exhibits and activities abound, and shopping opportunities are never ending. Almost any kind of recreational experience is readily available. Although commercial and not listed as attractions in this book, Biltmore Estate and the Grove Park Inn are architectural and historical landmarks. Asheville is simply a fantastic place to visit or live.

THE ATTRACTIONS —

From the Parkway, drive 5.4 miles west, then north on NC 80 to:

1.   The Carolina Hemlocks Recreation Area. Tent and trailer camping, restrooms, picnic tables, drinking water, tubing, fishing, and hiking are featured attractions.

Travel 4.4 miles north on NC 80 to:

2.   The Celo Community, a diverse group of craft workers and artisans living along NC 80. Stop at any of the studios to get information about the area.

Drive 4.4 miles north on NC 80 to NC 1186 at Micaville, then go 0.5 miles west on NC 1186 to US 19E. Travel 5 miles west on US 19E to:

Burnsville, North Carolina

Burnsville residents and visitors enjoy several festivals each year. Among these are the Spring Arts Festival in late May; the Yancey County Clogging/Arts and Crafts Show in mid-June; and the Mount Mitchell Crafts Fair in early August. All are held on the Burnsville town square — all feature arts, crafts, food, and entertainment.

3.   The Yancey County Chamber of Commerce is located at 106 West Main Street. 828-682-7413 or 800-948-1632.

4.   The Rush Wray Museum of Yancey County History, a North Carolina Regional Historic Site, is behind the Chamber of Commerce.   Artifacts and other Yancey County historical information is on display.

5.   The Parkway Playhouse, northeast of downtown Burnsville on Green Mountain Drive, presents musical and theatrical performances by the **Burnsville Little Theater** and other groups.

6.   The Toecane Ranger District Office, USDA Forest Service, is located on US 19E BYPASS, about 0.25 miles east of Main Street. Get information here about facilities available in the Pisgah National Forest. 828-682-6146.

Drive 5.6 miles west on US 19E to US 19W, then go about 18 miles north to:

7.   The Waterfall on Big Creek. This exciting waterfall can be viewed on the southwest side of US 19W.

Drive about 5 miles west on US 19W to the Tennessee State Line, then continue about 2.4 miles west on US 19W to:

8. Spivey Falls, in the Chandler Cove Road area, which is also viewable from your car. Both Upper and Lower Spivey falls make up this fine natural attraction on Spivey Creek.

Travel 9 miles west, then north on US 19W to:

9.   Chestoa Recreation Area, a USDA Forest Service facility featuring picnicking, restrooms, and access to the famous Nolichucky River.

Travel 3 miles northeast on US 19W to:

Erwin, Tennessee

The Apple Festival, held in early October, features arts and crafts displayed by more than 300 vendors. More than 60,000 people visit for gospel singing, a show and sale for collectors of Blue Ridge Pottery, square dancing, apple orchard tours, apple cooking contests, and many other kinds of delicious food.

10.   The Unicoi County Chamber of Commerce is located at 100 South Main Avenue. 423-743-0942.

Drive 2 miles northeast on TN 107 to:

18-1 Depot hack in front of 1913 courthouse —
Photo courtesy of the Town of Jonesborough

11. The Unaka District Ranger's Office, USDA Forest Service, at 1205 North Main (TN 107). Pick up information here on Cherokee National Forest campgrounds, recreational sites, and other services.

Travel 0.6 miles northeast on TN 107 to:

12. The Erwin National Fish Hatchery. This hatchery, operated by the USDI Fish and Wildlife Service, produces 14 million rainbow trout eggs annually that are sent to other hatcheries, to research laboratories, and to other countries. A picnic pavilion is provided for visitors.

13. The Unicoi County Heritage Museum was once the house provided for superintendents of the National Fish Hatchery. Built in 1903 and renovated in the 1980's, this grand old house now contains exhibits of antique furniture, clothing from the early 1900's, locally manufactured pottery, arts and crafts, railroad memorabilia, a replica of Erwin's Main Street shops, an old school house, an amphitheater, a nature trail, and much more.

Return to Erwin on TN 107, then drive 15.5 miles north on TN 81 to:

Jonesborough, Tennessee

Early October is celebrated in grand fashion at the National Storytelling Festival, a three-day extravaganza of stories, anecdotes, legends, myths, tall tales, folklore, and other performances by some of America's greatest storytellers.

14. The Historic Jonesborough Visitors Center, at 117 Boone Street, is the place to make reservations for Jonesborough's award winning **Times and Tales Tours,** which are guided visits to two historic homes and one historic church. As the first town in

Tennessee (1779-1780), Jonesborough contains many very old buildings. The Times and Tales Tours explore this heritage with visits and "tales" about the houses and churches. Also ask about **Escorted Walking Tours of Jonesborough,** featuring a slide presentation and a walking tour of downtown Jonesborough. This intriguing town was the first in Tennessee to be listed on the National Register of Historic Places. 423-753-1010 or 800-400-4221.

15. The Jonesborough - Washington County History Museum, located at the Visitors Center, offers displays, changing exhibits, an antique hand-powered water pumper, and many other artifacts from Tennessee's oldest town.

16. The Wetlands Water Park - Persimmon Ridge Park, located on the west side of Jonesborough, features a 200-foot waterslide, a natural wetlands area with a boardwalk access, picnicking, hiking, and camping on a 120-acre site.

From downtown Jonesborough, drive 10 miles southwest on US 11/US 321 to TN 75 (Opie Arnold Road), then go 1 mile south on TN 75 to Limestone, Tennessee. Travel about 3 miles southwest on Davy Crockett Park Road to:

17. Davy Crockett Birthplace State Park. This park on the bank of the Nolichucky River is a memorial to Davy Crockett, a famous frontiersman, known as a bear hunter, war hero, and backwoods statesman. A restored cabin, built in part from logs in Crockett's birthplace home, is featured along with a campground (with hookups), a bath house, a picnic area, a gift shop, a swimming pool, fishing, canoe access, hiking trails, a museum, and a visitors center.

Drive 8 miles southwest on US 11/US 321 to Doak Drive, then continue 1 mile southwest on Doak Drive to:

18. Tusculum College, the oldest college west of the Allegheny Mountains, which was founded by the Presbyterian Church in 1794. Eight campus buildings and the stone archway at the entrance are listed by the National Trust for Historic Preservation as the Tusculum College Historic District.

19. The President Andrew Johnson Museum and Library at Tusculum College presents the story of President Johnson before and after his term as president.

20. The Doak-Johnson Heritage Museum, also at Tusculum College, presents the special aspects of American frontier classical education. Reverend Samuel Doak, a Presbyterian minister, was the first president of Tusculum College.

Travel 5 miles west on TN 107/US 321 to:

Greeneville, Tennessee

Visit Greeneville in late May for the Iris Festival.

21. The Greene County Partnership, located at 115 Academy Street, provides information on Greeneville and Greene County. Ask about guided walking tours of the **Historic District** — a part of Tennessee's second oldest town. More than 25 structures on the National Register of Historic Places are visited. 423-638-4111.

22. The Nolichucky Ranger District Office, USDA Forest Service, is located at 124 Austin Street, Suite 3. Get information here about Cherokee National Forest campgrounds, recreation areas, and other services.

18-2 Andrew Johnson Home — Photo courtesy of the Greene County Partnership

23.   The Andrew Johnson National Historic Site, located at College and Depot Streets, features a visitors center, President Andrew Johnson's tailor shop, two homes originally owned by Johnson — one furnished with Johnson's possessions — and the National Cemetery.

24.   The Nathaniel Greene Museum, at 101 West McKee Street, presents the history and culture of Greeneville/Greene County during its first American century beginning in the late 1700's

25.   The Dickson-Williams Mansion, located at 114 West Church Street, served both Union and Confederate armies as headquarters in the Civil War.

26.   Kinser Park, a service of Greeneville and Greene County, is about 4 miles southeast of downtown Greeneville on Kinser Park Road overlooking the Nolichucky River.   This extensive park offers a large campground with full

hookups, a golf course and driving range, picnic tables, fireplaces, tennis courts, a playground, a swimming pool, a water slide, two bathhouses, horseshoe pits, a boat ramp, and more.   Ask at the Greene County Partnership office for specific directions to the site.

From downtown Greeneville, drive about 17 miles southwest on US 321/US 411 to:

27. The Swaggerty Blockhouse. Listed on the National Register of Historic Places, this 200-year old house was built by James Swaggerty for protection from Indian attacks.

Continue about 2 miles southwest on US 321/US 411 to:

Parrottsville, Tennessee

This third oldest town in Tennessee is home to several very old buildings, two natural bridges over Oven Creek (ask a local person for directions to the sites), and to the Parrottsville Heritage Days Festival, held in mid-October.

Drive about 7 miles southwest on US 321/US 411 to:

Newport, Tennessee

Visit downtown Newport in early October for the Harvest Street Festival. This event celebrates country life with quality arts and crafts, delicious food, and several kinds of entertainment.

28. The Newport/Cocke County Tourism Council is located at 360 East Main Street, Suite 141, Courthouse Annex. 423-625-9675.

29. The Newport/Cocke County Chamber of Commerce is at 423-B Prospect Avenue. 423-623-7201.

30. The Newport/Cocke County Museum, located at 433 Prospect Avenue, offers Indian artifacts, wildlife displays, and historic room exhibits. This museum is open by appointment only except during special exhibits. Ask at the Tourism Council or Chamber of Commerce for more information.

Drive 11 miles southeast on US 25/US 70 to TN 107, then go 1 mile south on TN 107 to:

Del Rio, Tennessee

This picturesque town hosts a two-day festival in late October called Del Rio Days. Special features include buggy rides, music, country food, arts and crafts, river raft rides, storytelling, and more.

Return to US 25/US 70, then go about 2 miles east to:

31. The French Broad Recreation Area, a USDA Forest Service facility on the spectacular French Broad River. Canoe access, fishing, and restrooms are available to visitors.

Continue for about 11 miles east on US 25/US 70 to:

Hot Springs, North Carolina

The Hot Springs Trail Fest offers arts and crafts, food, and entertainment in late April.

32. The Hot Springs Visitors Center Caboose, on US 25/US 70, provides information about the area. 828-622-7611.

33. The French Broad Ranger District Office, USDA Forest Service, on US 25/US 70 next to the Visitors Center, is the place to get information about facilities in the Pisgah National Forest. 828-622-3202.

34. The Paint Creek Side Trip. Drive across the US 25/US 70 bridge over the French Broad River, read the Paint Rock Historical Marker, then turn northwest on Paint Rock Road (NC 1304). Go about 4 miles northwest on Paint Rock Road to the **Murray Branch Recreation Area,** a USDA Forest Service facility featuring picnicking, hiking, canoeing access, fishing, and restrooms. Continue 2 miles northwest on NC 1304 to Paint Creek, where there are several more places to picnic and swim.

Return to US 25/US 70, then go 16 miles southeast on US 25/US 70 to Marshall and NC 213. Travel 8 miles east on NC 213 to:

Mars Hill, North Carolina

The Madison County Heritage Celebration and Lunsford Festival, held in early October, is an important regional event featuring top-notch musicians and crafters along with great country food and other entertainment.

35. The Madison County Chamber of Commerce Visitors Center, at the corner of Main Street and NC 213, is a great place to get information about activities at Mars Hill College and to pick up the brochure, *Madison County Driving Tours*. This brochure includes a description of **Driving Tour Loop #2** which is an attraction listed below. 828-689-9351.

36. Mars Hill College is the home of a number of cultural, historical, recreational, and educational activities and places. Included are the Rural Life Museum, the Orchard Hill Folk Art Collection, the Weizenblatt Art Gallery, the Heritage Log Cabin, the W. Otis Duck Fitness Trail, and the Southern Appalachian Repertory Theater. Get directions and performance schedules at the Chamber of Commerce Visitors Center.

37. Driving Tour Loop #2 is an alternate route to Marshall, North Carolina, the next town listed for Route 18. A winding mountain journey through spectacular mountain scenery, this trip is described in great detail in the brochure available at the Chamber of Commerce Visitors Center. If you choose not to make this tour, proceed as follows:

Return (on NC 213) to US 25/US 70 BYPASS, then go 2 miles west to US 25 BUS/US 70 BUS. Drive 1.6 miles south on US 25 BUS/US 70 BUS to:

Marshall, North Carolina

38. The Madison County Courthouse, built in 1907, features an unusual cupola and is on the National Register of Historic Places.

Drive 2.6 miles southeast on US 25 BUS/US 70 BUS to NC 251, then go about 5.5 miles southwest to:

39. The Walnut Island Park, a place to picnic and enjoy the French Broad River flowing nearby.

Continue about 2.7 miles southeast on NC 251 to NC 1727 (Monticello Road), then go 2.7 miles northeast on NC 1727 to US 25/US 70. Travel 1 mile east to:

Weaverville, North Carolina

Visit Weaverville and the Zebulon B. Vance Birthplace Historic Site in mid-April and mid-September for Pioneer Living Days. These festivals present life on the Vance farmstead during the latter part of the nineteenth century. Some of these events feature costumed history buffs who portray soldiers, camp at the site, and reenact famous battles.

From Downtown Weaverville, drive 1.4 miles south on US 19 BUS/US 23 BUS to NC 1003 (Reems Creek Road), then go 5.3 miles east to:

40. The Zebulon B. Vance Birthplace State Historic Site, located at 911 Reems Creek Road. This restored former home of a distinguished United States senator and North Carolina governor now serves as a living history museum of his life and times during the period from 1790 to 1840

Return to US 19 BUS/US 23 BUS, then drive 0.8 miles south to NC 1740 (Newstock Road) and US 19 BYPASS/US 23 BYPASS. Go 6 miles south on US 19/US 23 to I - 240, then 0.4 miles east on I-240 to Exit 4-C to:

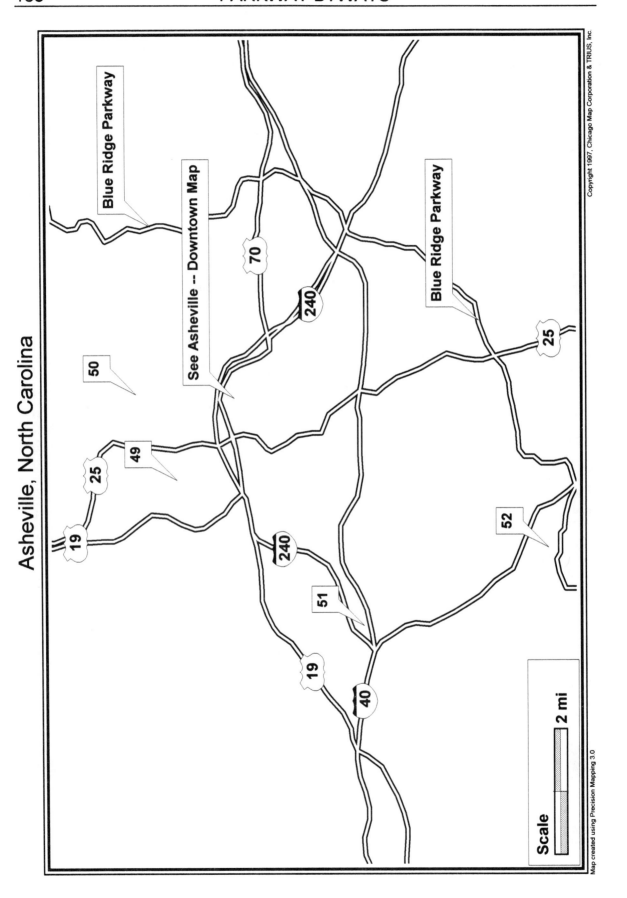

Asheville, North Carolina

Blue Ridge Parkway

Blue Ridge Parkway

See Asheville -- Downtown Map

Scale

2 mi

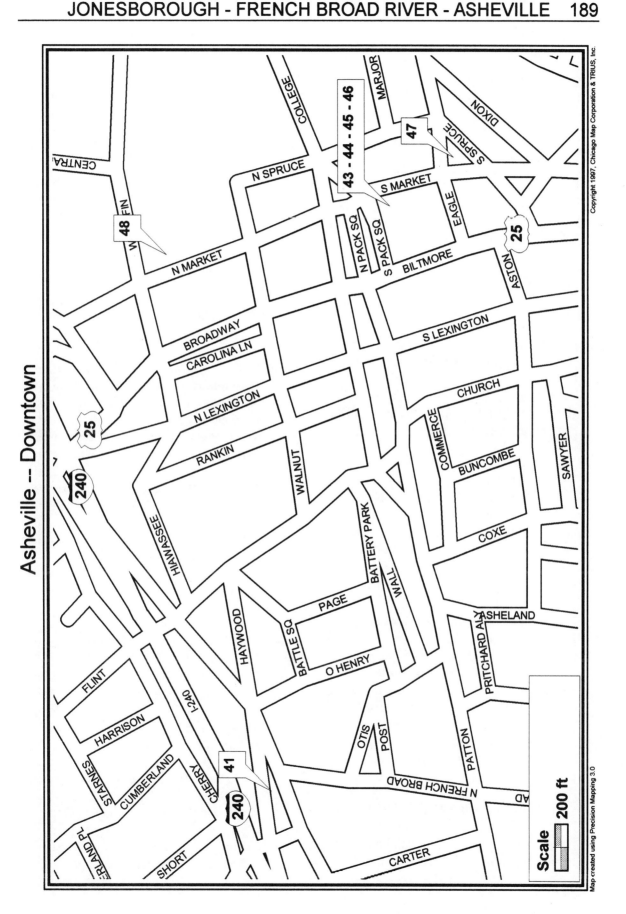

Asheville, North Carolina

Asheville holds about 150 festivals annually, appealing to every conceivable taste and interest. Call or write the Asheville Convention and Visitors Bureau for their brochure, *Mountain Festivals and Events* to get a detailed list. The address and phone numbers are listed below. Here are five of the most popular:

Shindig-on-the-Green "happens" every Saturday night during the summer. Celebrated by thousands over its long history, this tribute to all kinds of mountain music and dancing takes place at Asheville's City/County Plaza just east of Pack Square.

The Mountain Dance and Folk Festival is held in early July at the City/County Plaza and Diana Wortham Theater.

Bele Chere, an exciting downtown street festival, is celebrated in late July. This is one of Asheville's major festival events.

Craft Fairs, sponsored by the Southern Highlands Craft Guild, are held at the Asheville Civic Center in min-July and mid-October.

From I-240, drive south to Haywood Street, then east to:

41. The Asheville Convention and Visitors Bureau - Asheville Area Chamber of Commerce. This treasury of travel information is located at 151 Haywood Street, P. O. Box 1010, Asheville, NC 28802. 828-258-6109 or 800-257-1300.

42. The Asheville Urban Trail winds through Asheville's distinctive and historic downtown district. The buildings, built primarily in the period from 1880 to 1930,

present a bold statement on architectural diversity. Explanatory plaques are located along the trail; more information is available at the Asheville Convention and Visitors Bureau.

The Pack Place Education, Arts, and Science Center includes the five following attractions:

43. The Asheville Art Museum, at 2 South Pack Square, features exhibits of twentieth-century art by national and local American artists and crafts relating to the Southern Appalachians. Educational programs for children and adults are also provided.

44. The Coburn Gem and Mineral Museum, at 2 South Pack Square, presents permanent and traveling exhibits of gems and minerals from North Carolina and the world. Hands-on involvement with minerals is available at some of the exhibits.

45. The Diana Wortham Theater, at 2 South Pack Square, presents a variety of musical, theatrical, and educational performances in a 500-seat auditorium. Plays, poetry, jazz, symphony music, ballet, modern dance, lectures, and many other kinds of performing arts are featured regularly.

46. The Health Adventure, at 2 South Pack Square, is a museum devoted to physical health and applied science. Hands-on learning opportunities are available for children of all ages. Examples of exhibit names are Body Works, Miracle of Life, and Brain Storm.

47. The YMI Cultural Center, located at the corner of Market and Eagle Streets (southeast across the street from the attractions listed above), features permanent and traveling exhibits relating to the history and culture of African-Americans.

48. The Thomas Wolfe Memorial State Historic Site, located at 52 Market Street, is the former home of the famous author. Originally known as "Old Kentucky Home," Wolfe called the rambling old boarding house, "Dixieland," and used it as the setting for his classic novel, *Look Homeward, Angel.* This attraction is a North Carolina Historic Site and is maintained by the Division of Archives and History, Department of Cultural Resources.

49. The Botanical Gardens, located at 151 W. T. Weaver Boulevard, are a part of the University of North Carolina - Asheville. Ten acres of gardens feature native plants in natural settings, walking trails, a visitors center, and a gift shop. This delightful place offers a beautiful and restful environment — the perfect site for a break on a busy day.

50. North Carolina Homespun Museum, at 111 Grovewood Road, presents the history of Biltmore Industries. The art of handweaving is portrayed with artifacts and demonstrations. An antique automobile museum, displaying old cars and a fire engine, is located at the same address.

If you have a few extra minutes, visit the **Grove Park Inn,** located near the Homespun Museum. Although a commercial establishment and not included as an attraction in this book, the Grove Park Inn is a spectacular example of hotel architecture. Built in 1913 out of enormous boulders, this unusual building is an Asheville landmark. The lobby is especially impressive.

From downtown Asheville, drive 0.7 miles west on Patton Avenue to I - 240, then go 3.3 miles southwest on I - 240 to NC 191 (Brevard Road). Drive 0.7 miles south on NC 191 to:

51. The Western North Carolina Farmers Market, at 570 Brevard Road, is

18-3 North Carolina Arboretum — Photo courtesy of the
Asheville Convention and Visitors Bureau

owned and operated by the State of North Carolina. This 36-acre facility provides farmers, growers, and artisans with a place to market their produce, flowers, jams and jellies, plants, and handmade crafts. A restaurant and a garden center are also available.

Travel 5 miles south on NC 191 to the Blue Ridge Parkway, then drive west on the Parkway to Fredrick Law Olmsted Way, entrance to:

52. The North Carolina Arboretum. A facility of the University of North Carolina, this multi-faceted complex features gardens, nature trails, horticultural exhibits, greenhouses, and the National Native Azalea Repository. The site covers more than 400 acres in the Bent Creek Research and Demonstration Forest — USDA Pisgah National Forest.

Return to the Blue Ridge Parkway.

CHAPTER 19 - ROUTE 19

Franklin, NC
Helen, GA
Cherohala Skyway, TN/NC

ROUTE 19

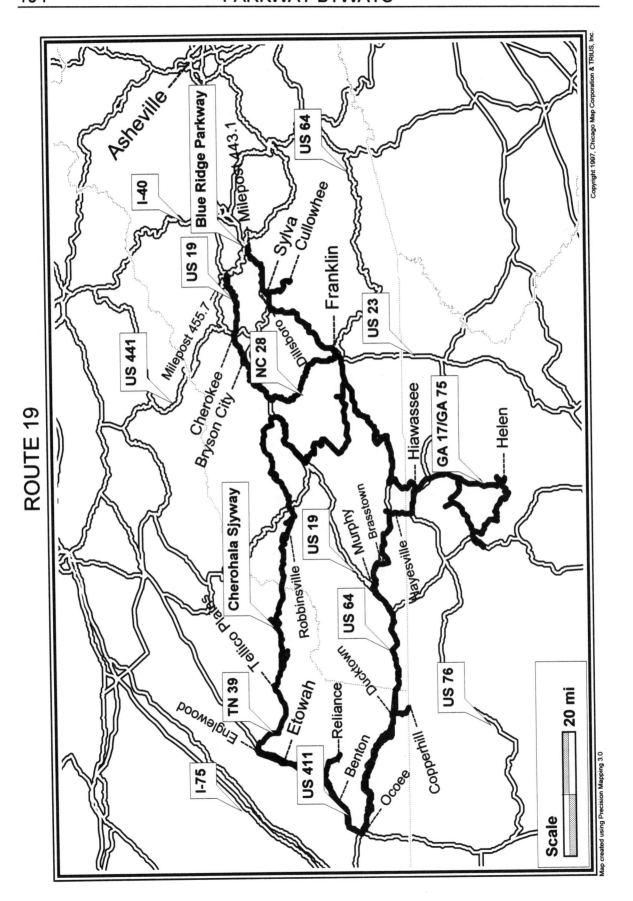

Asheville

Blue Ridge Parkway

Milepost 443.1

I-40

US 64

US 19

Sylva

Cullowhee

Franklin

US 441

Milepost 455.7

Cherokee

Bryson City

Dillsboro

NC 28

US 23

GA 17/GA 75

Hiawassee

Helen

Cherohala Sjyway

US 19

Murphy

Brasstown

Tellico Plains

Robbinsville

US 64

Ducktown

Wayesville

TN 39

Etowah

Reliance

Englewood

I-75

US 411

Benton

Copperhill

Ocoee

US 76

Scale

20 mi

Copyright 1997, Chicago Map Corporation & TRIUS, Inc.

Map created using Precision Mapping 3.0

T he Franklin - Helen - Cherohala Skyway Route tours the North Carolina counties of Jackson, Macon, Clay, Cherokee, Graham, Swain, the Georgia county of White, and the Tennessee counties of Polk and Monroe. It is about 480 miles long and will require two to four days to travel, depending on the number of attractions you visit; there are more than 70. Although the byways are quite different, the attractions listed for Franklin, Dillsboro, Sylva, and Cullowhee can also be visited on Route 17 and the attractions listed for Robbinsville, Bryson City, and Cherokee can also be visited on Route 20. This trip starts at Milepost 443.1 on the Blue Ridge Parkway at Balsam Gap and continues in a clockwise direction to Milepost 455.7 at Soco Gap.

THE BYWAYS —

Almost 500 miles long, Route 19 offers something for every interest, including state and national scenic byways in three states.

First, drive again on the North Carolina Waterfall Byway (US 64), from Franklin to NC 175 north of Hiawassee, passing along ridges of the Chunky Gal Mountains.

A side trip to Helen, Georgia, offers some interesting scenery along GA 17/GA 75 followed by a trip on Georgia's Richard B. Russell/Brasstown National Scenic Byway. This awesome road winds through tall mountains to the summit of Brasstown Bald, the highest mountain in Georgia. Panoramic views in every direction are featured from an elaborate visitors center on top of this great mountain.

From the sublime to the sublime, continue your trip on US 64 along the astounding Ocoee River, site of the Olympic Whitewater Slalom Canoe/Kayak Competition in July 1996. Spectacular by any standard, this stretch of river is not only the nation's first National Forest Scenic Byway but a Tennessee Scenic Parkway as well.

Your scenic experience is about to explode now, with a trip on the majestic Cherohala Skyway. Costing more than one hundred million dollars, this 45-mile Skyway — so very reminiscent of the Blue Ridge Parkway — is an engineering masterpiece. Starting in Tellico Plains, Tennessee, it climbs from less than 1,000 to more than 5,000 feet at the North Carolina line before descending to Robbinsville. Frequent overlooks add to the pleasure of the trip.

Last, but certainly not least, is a trip through the Nantahala Gorge on US 19/US 74. Part of the NC Nantahala Byway and a favorite destination of whitewater fans, this extraordinary river is host to more than 250,000 of them every year. Millions more drive through on the scenic highway. This trip continues along the Nantahala river on NC 1310, past still another waterfall, then on to the summit of Wayah Bald. This 5,000-foot high vantage point offers a birds-eye view of the terrain explored on Route 19.

19-1 Race channel on the Ocoee River created for the 1996 Olympics —
Photo courtesy of the Tennessee Overhill Heritage Association

THE TOWNS —

Sylva, Franklin, Hayesville, Murphy, Benton, Robbinsville, and Bryson City are comfortable county seat towns, where the emphasis is on county government, retail trade, business, industry and tourism.

Activities in Dillsboro, Hiawassee, Ocoee, Etowah, Englewood, and Tellico Plains relate mainly to retail trade, tourism, and business.

Ducktown and Copper Hill are in a historic copper mining district that now focuses on tourism and retail trade. Reliance is interested in its history and in visitors to the beautiful Hiwassee River.

Helen and Cherokee are places to shop, dine, and enjoy a wide variety of commercial attractions. Cherokee also presents many facets of Indian history and culture.

Cullowhee is essentially Western Carolina University plus supporting businesses and services.

All of the towns on Route 19 portray the rich cultural heritage of this mountain region in North Carolina, Georgia, and Tennessee. Early settlers, Indians, and modern residents are all represented in these fine towns.

THE ATTRACTIONS —

From the Blue Ridge Parkway, drive to:

1. The Balsam Welcome Center, located on US 23/US 74. 828-452-7307.

Travel 10.5 miles southwest on US 23/US 74/US 23 BUS to NC 107, then go 5 miles south on NC 107 to:

Cullowhee, North Carolina

Mountain Heritage Day, rated among the top 200 art events in the United States, is held on the fourth Saturday in September at Western Carolina University. Among many exciting activities, dancing, singing, playing music, story telling, demonstrating crafts, and eating American/Indian foods, are featured. Annual attendance is more than 35,000.

2. The Mountain Heritage Center, at Western Carolina University, offers displays of historical information and artifacts relating to the area's culture and society. A permanent exhibit describes settlement of the area by Scotch/Irish people in the eighteenth century. Other exhibits portray handcrafts, farming, and family life. This fine center is a major resource for anyone interested in the history and culture of North Carolina mountain people.

Return to US 23 BUS, then drive west to downtown:

Sylva, North Carolina

Greening Up the Mountains, an Earth Day celebration, is held in Sylva in late April.

3. The Jackson County Chamber of Commerce and the Jackson County Tourism Development Authority are located at 116 Central Street. Ask for a map of beautiful **Downtown Sylva,** a great place to walk and look at old buildings, especially the **Historic Jackson County Courthouse.** Call the Chamber or Tourism Development Authority at 828-586-2155 or 800-962-1911.

Drive 2 miles west on US 23 BUS/NC 107 to:

Dillsboro, North Carolina

Visit Dillsboro in mid-June for the Heritage Day Festival. Arts and crafts are the featured attraction, but you will also enjoy great food, fiddling and banjo pickin'.

4. The Jackson County Visitor Information Center, located at the corner of Front and Depot Streets, is the place to pick up a brochure describing **Downtown Dillsboro.** This area is a fascinating place to walk, look at the unique buildings, shop, and eat.

Drive 17.5 miles southwest on US 23/US 441 to:

Franklin, North Carolina

Visit downtown Franklin on any Saturday night from June through October for Pickin' on the Square.

Franklin is renowned for minerals and gems. The Macon County Gemboree in late July and the Annual Leaf Lookers Gemboree in early October celebrate this interesting activity.

Franklin's Foot Stompin' Festival, held in mid-October, features clogging competitions and exhibitions.

5. The Franklin Area Chamber of Commerce is located at 425 Porter Street. 828-524-3161 or 800-336-7829

6. The Smoky Mountain Host, at 4437 Georgia Road (US 23/US 441), provides information about several counties in western North Carolina and about the Great Smoky Mountains. 828-369-9606 or 800-432-4678

7. The Franklin Gem and Mineral Museum, located at 25 Phillips Street in the former county jail, exhibits unusual gems, mineral specimens, and a rock collection, plus educational displays, books on gems and minerals, and a wide variety of other materials.

8. The Macon County Historical Society Museum, at 36 West Main Street, displays historical memorabilia including documents, artifacts, and photographs.

9. The Scottish Tartans Museum and Heritage Center, located at 95 East Main Street, offers exhibits, a library, and other materials relating to tartan dress, the kilt, and weaving.

10. The Macon County Arts Association, at 6 East Main Street, features a variety of art works in their gallery, and works to encourage interest in the arts in Macon County.

From downtown Franklin drive about 3 miles southwest on US 23/US 441, then /US 64 to NC 1153 (Sloan Road). Go south on NC 1153 to:

11. The Wayah Ranger District Office at 90 Sloan Road. This USDA Forest Service office will provide you with information about camping and other facilities available in the Nantahala National Forest. 828-524-6441.

Return to US 64, then drive about 11 miles southwest to NC 1448 (Old US 64). Follow signs east on NC 1448 to Forest Service Road 67, then go south to:

12. The Standing Indian Recreation Area and Campground, a USDA Forest Service facility. Among the many features are a campground with tent and trailer spaces, picnic areas, restrooms, showers, fishing, many hiking trails, and an amphitheater for interpretive programs. You may also want to visit Big Laurel Falls and Mooney Falls. Both of these delightful waterfalls are in the Standing Indian area.

Return to US 64, then drive about 16 miles southwest on US 64 to NC 175. Travel 3.3 miles south on NC 175 to NC 1156, then go northwest on NC 1156 to:

13. The Jackrabbit Mountain Campground, a USDA Forest Service campground on Chatuge Lake.. Services include tent and trailer camping, a trailer dump station, picnic tables, restrooms, showers, a boat ramp, swimming, fishing, hiking, and an amphitheater where evening interpretive programs are presented in season.

Return to NC 175, then drive 5 miles south on NC 175/GA 175, then US 76 to:

Hiawassee, Georgia

The Annual Rhododendron Festival, held at the Georgia Mountain Fairground, west of Hiawassee on US 76, takes place on successive weekends in mid-May. This six-day celebration features country bands, clogging, singing, arts and crafts, and religious services.

Early August brings the twelve-day Georgia Mountain Fair, offering arts and crafts, regional food, living exhibits; country, gospel, and bluegrass music; a parade, a carnival, and much more.

The Fall Festival, also held at the Georgia Mountain Fairground, is scheduled for early October. In addition to arts, crafts, and food, this festival includes the Official Georgia State Old Time Fiddlers' Convention, Georgia's oldest and only convention of fiddlers.

14. The Towns County Chamber of Commerce Welcome Center is located at 1411 Fuller Circle in Young Harris, Georgia. (West of Hiawassee on US 76 — look for signs). 706-896-4966 or 800-984-1543.

15. The Fred Hamilton Rhododendron Garden, located at the Georgia Mountain Fairground, is the largest rhododendron garden in Georgia with 400 varieties and 2,000 plants. Many other kinds of flowering plants are also on display, insuring beautiful bloom from spring through fall. The garden is open year round and is the perfect place to walk, enjoy the flowers, and commune with nature.

From downtown Hiawassee, drive 14.5 miles south on US 76/GA 17/GA 75 to:

16. Andrews Cove, a USDA Forest Service facility, featuring camping, hiking, and fishing along a beautiful mountain stream.

Continue 5.5 miles south of GA 17/GA 75 to GA 356, then go east on GA 356 to:

17. The Unicoi State Park and Lodge. This fine park offers a 100-room lodge, a restaurant, cottages, a large campground, tennis courts, swimming, boating, hiking, a craft shop, picnicking, and much more. For reservations, call 800-864-7275.

18. The Anna Ruby Falls, located 3.6 miles north of Unicoi State Park , is a USDA Forest Service attraction. Features in the area, in addition to two spectacular waterfall, include a visitor center, a gift shop, places to picnic, snack and drink machines, restrooms, and public phones.

Return to GA 17/GA 75, then drive 1 mile south to:

Helen, Georgia

Visit Helen in early June for the Annual Helen-Atlantic Hot Air Balloon Race and Festival.

Mid-September brings — would you believe — Octoberfest? Actually, this celebration only starts in September, continues through October, and ends in early November.

19. The Helen-White County Convention and Visitors Bureau is located at 726 Bruckenstrasse. 706-878-2181 or 800-858-8027.

Drive 1.4 miles northwest on GA 17/GA 75 to GA 75-A, then go 2.4 miles southwest on GA 75-A to GA 348. Continue south on GA 75-A to:

20. The Smithgall Woods - Dukes Creek Conservation Area, a facility of the Georgia Department of Natural Resources. This 5,000-acre area features a visitor center, nature trails, wildlife viewing stands, trout fishing, hiking, hunting,, bicycling, photography, picnicking, guided tours, and educational programs. All visitors must register at the welcome center.

Return to GA 348, which is the start of:

21. The Richard B. Russell/Brasstown National Scenic Byway. This route (on GA 348 and GA 180), described as the most scenic in Georgia, provides spectacular views of the mountains and the lower land to the south toward Atlanta. Interpretive signs and scenic overlooks will add interest to your trip.

Drive 2 miles northwest on GA 348 to:

22. The Dukes Creek Falls Recreation Area, where a 0.8-mile trail leads to 300-foot Duke Creek Falls.

Continue 0.8 miles northwest on GA 348 to:

23. The Raven Cliff Falls, an unusual waterfall that flows through an opening in a solid rock outcropping before falling 100 feet to the ground below. There are no facilities at this attraction.

Travel 11 miles northwest on GA 348 to GA 180, then go 1 mile west on GA 180 to US 19/US 129. Drive 3 miles south on US 19/US 129 to:

24. Vogel State Park. This park offers cottages, a campground with tent, trailer, and RV pull-through sites, camping supplies, picnic tables, a lake, pedal boats, swimming fishing, nature trails, and interpretive exhibits.

Return to GA 180 (east), then go 7.4 miles northeast to GA 180 SPUR. Drive 3 miles north on GA 180 SPUR to the parking lot for:

25. Brasstown Bald, Georgia's highest mountain at 4,784 feet. An impressive building on top of the mountain is accessible by a steep half-mile hike or on a concessionaire bus for a fee. Features at the summit include a 360-degree panoramic view, a fire tower, historical and cultural exhibits, and a mountain top theater offering interpretive programs. Picnic tables, snack foods and drinks, a bookstore, and hiking trails are available at the parking lot.

Return to GA 180, then drive 5.5 miles east to GA 17/GA 75. Travel 15 miles northwest on GA 17/US 76 to the North Carolina state line, then continue about 4.6 miles north on NC 69 to:

Hayesville, North Carolina

Hayesville celebrates in mid-July with the Festival on the Square, sponsored by the Historical and Arts Council. Enjoy arts and crafts, good food, and Appalachian music at the Clay County Courthouse. Thousands of residents and visitors attend this two-day event every year.

26. The Clay County Chamber of Commerce is located on US 64 BUS. 828-389-3704.

27. The Clay County Courthouse, listed on the National Register of Historic Places, is a distinctive building built in 1888/1889.

28. The Chatuge Dam, a Tennessee Valley Authority structure, is located about 3 miles southeast of Hayesville on the Hiwassee River. Picnic tables, fishing, and a launch site for canoes and tubes are provided at a site north of the dam. Ask for exact directions to the dam at the Chamber of Commerce.

29. The Old County Jail has been converted into a museum by the Clay County Historical and Arts Council. Indian artifacts, early telephone equipment, photographs, a moonshine still, and old farm equipment are among the many items displayed.

30. The Peacock Playhouse presents a variety of musical, theatrical, and educational programs throughout the year. The Licklog Players and the Brasstown Concert Association are featured performers.

Drive 8 miles west on US 64 to NC 1135, then go 2 miles southwest on NC 1135 to:

Brasstown, North Carolina

Celebrations of folk music, dancing and storytelling are held frequently at the John C. Campbell Folk School. A Fall Festival, with crafts, food, music, dance, and children's activities is held in early October.

31. The John C. Campbell Folk School, internationally known for its expertise in teaching artisans and crafters, operates from a beautiful 365-acre campus designated as a Historical District by the National Register of Historic places. More than four dozen crafts are taught, from basketry to woodcarving. Handcrafted items produced by more than 200 mountain craftspeople are displayed and sold at the The Craft Shop, located on the school grounds.

Return to US 64 on NC 1100, then NC 1548. Drive 5.5 miles west on US 64 to:

Murphy, North Carolina

Visit Murphy in early May for the Spring Festival. Arts and crafts, food and entertainment are all on the agenda.

Mid-October brings the Cherokee County Chile Cook-off, a festival dedicated to good eating.

32. The Cherokee County Chamber of Commerce Welcome Center is located at 805 US 64 West. 828-837-2242.

19-2 View of Murphy, North Carolina — Photo courtesy of the Cherokee County Chamber of Commerce

33.   The Tusquitee Ranger District Office, USDA Forest Service, at 123 Woodland Drive (off US 64), is the place to stop for information about facilities in the Nantahala National Forest. 828-837-5152.

34.   The Cherokee County Historical Museum, at 205 Peachtree Street, is next to the Cherokee County Courthouse in the former Carnegie Library building.   The museum collections display artifacts relating to the Cherokee Indians before their removal to Oklahoma along the infamous "Trail of Tears" and to the white settlers that came after the Indians departed. A replica of Fort Butler, where the some of the Indians were assembled for removal, is also on display along with an extensive doll collection..

35. The Cherokee County Courthouse is a unique structure, distinguished by its great architecture and regal blue color resulting from the use of blue marble building stone from the nearby community named Marble.

From downtown Murphy, drive 8 miles southwest on US 19/US 64/US 74 to NC 294, then go 10 miles northwest on NC 294 to:

36. The Fields of the Wood, an elaborate religious theme park, operated by the Church of God. A giant display of the Ten Commandments covering a hillside is a major feature. Other exhibits include depictions of Golgotha, Joseph's Tomb, a Prayer Mountain, and the All Nations Cross, where flags from the countries where the Church of God is established are flown.

Return about 1 mile southeast on NC 294 to NC 1314, then go 5 miles northeast to:

37. Hiwassee Dam, a Tennessee Valley Authority project. In addition to great views of the dam and lake, a boat ramp and a basic (no hookups) campground are provided.

Return to US 64/US 74, then drive 16 miles southwest (crossing the Tennessee state line) to TN 68. Drive 0.5 miles north on TN 68 to:

Ducktown, Tennessee

38. The Copper Basin Area Chamber of Commerce is located at 134 Main Street. 423-496-9000.

39. The Ducktown Basin Museum offers exhibits that portray the unique history and unusual scenery of this extensive copper mining area. The museum is on the famous Burra Burra Mine which was placed on the National Register of Historic Places in 1983 as the Burra Burra Mine Historic District.

Travel 4 miles south on TN 68 to:

Copperhill, Tennessee

40.   The Copper Basin Information Center, located off TN 68 near the Georgia state line, offers a brochure describing a walking tour through this unusual town. Many of the buildings are listed on the National Register of Historic Places. A self-guided driving tour of the area is also available.

Return to US 64/US 74, then drive about 7 miles northwest to:

41.   The Ocoee Whitewater Center, headquarters for the 1996 Olympic Slalom Canoe/Kayak Competition, and now a spacious welcome and information center.

Continue about 9 miles west on US 64/US 74 to TN 30, then go northeast to:

42. The Parksville Lake Recreation Area. Facilities include a campground with flush toilets, warm water showers, drinking water, picnic tables, and grills; boating, fishing, hiking, and bicycling.

Return to US 64/US 74, then drive about 0.6 west miles to:

43. The Mac Point Swimming Area, which offers a beach, picnic sites, drinking water, and flush toilets on Lake Ocoee (Parksville Lake).

Travel about 1.5 miles west on US 64/US 74 to:

44. The Ocoee Ranger District Office, USDA Forest Service. The Cherokee National Forest offers many opportunities for camping and other forms of recreation. In particular, ask about the many neat places along Forest Service Road 77, part of the Ocoee Scenic Byway, which runs north from the District Office. 423-338-5201.

Drive about 7 miles west on US 64/US 74 to:

Ocoee, Tennessee

Travel about 4 miles northeast on US 411 to:

45. The Nancy Ward Grave, the final resting place of a Overhill Cherokee Indian princess and her son, Five Killer.

Continue about 2 miles northeast on US 411 to:

Benton, Tennessee

Visit Benton in late August for the Benton Lions Club Antique Car Show.

46. The Polk County Chamber of Commerce is located on US 411 at Town Plaza. 423-338-5040 or 800-633-7655.

47. Fort Marr, once used to protect Cherokee Indians in their war against the Creek Indians, later was used as a place to collect Cherokee Indians for deportation to Oklahoma. A log blockhouse remains at the site.

Drive 6 miles northeast on US 411 to TN 30, then go 6 miles southeast on TN 30 along the beautiful Hiwassee River to:

Reliance, Tennessee

48. The Historic District of Reliance, listed on the National Register of Historic Places, includes the L&N Watchman's House, Vaughn-Webb Homeplace, Hiwassee Union Church/Masonic Lodge, Higdon Hotel, and the Webb Brothers General Store. These buildings were built 1880 to 1910.

Return to US 411, then travel 7 miles north to:

Etowah, Tennessee

Celebrate the Fourth of July at the restored L&N Depot in Etowah and stay for the Annual Arts and Crafts Exhibit, presented by the Etowah Arts Commission, during the rest of July.

Return in early October for the Arts and Crafts Fall Fest, also at the L&N Depot.

49. The L&N Depot, is home to the **L&N Depot Railroad Museum,** the **Etowah Arts Commission Gallery,** a restored L&N

19-3 L&N Depot and Museum — Photo courtesy of the
Tennessee Overhill Heritage Association

caboose, a forestry exhibit, the **Etowah Area Chamber of Commerce** (423-263-2228), and the **Tennessee Overhill Heritage Association** (423-263-7232). This great old building is listed on the National Register of Historic Places.

50. The Gem Theater, located across the street (US 411) from the L&N Depot, presents a variety of theatrical and musical programs throughout the year. Built as a movie house in 1927, the building has been renovated and converted to a live performance theater.

51. The Hiwassee Ranger District Office, USDA Forest Service, is located at 274 TN 310. Ask here about facilities and services in the Cherokee National Forest. 423-263-5486.

Travel 8 miles north on US 411 to:

Englewood, Tennessee

52. The Englewood Textile Museum - Women: Then and Now examines and explains the role of women in the textile industry. This museum was a recent winner of the Tennessee Association of Museums' Award of Excellence.

Drive 16 miles southeast on TN 39 to:

Tellico Plains, Tennessee

The Annual Square Dance, held in early July at the Tellico Plains Town Square, is a special treat for residents and visitors alike.

Drive 5 miles southeast on TN 360/TN 165, (the first section of the Cherohala Skyway) to Tellico River Road (Forest Service Road 210), then go 0.8 miles southeast to:

53. The Tellico Ranger District Office, USDA Forest Service. This district office is in the center of a vast system of campgrounds, hiking trails, waterfalls, horse trails, hunting areas, fishing spots, and much more. The friendly staff will be happy to tell you about the area and answer any questions you may have. 423-253-2520.

Drive about 5 miles southeast on the Tellico River Road to:

54. The Bald River Falls. Of all the attractions in the area, this is one you don't want to miss. This beautiful waterfall is easily accessible and the experience will make your day.

Return to TN 165 and get ready for a fantastic driving adventure.

55. The Cherohala Skyway, a world-class recreational highway nearly equals the scenic grandeur of the Blue Ridge Parkway. Check the Byways section at the beginning of this chapter for more details.

Drive about 19 miles east on this spectacular highway to the North Carolina state line, then continue on the Skyway for about 21 miles to NC 1127. Drive about 4 miles northwest on NC 1127 to Joyce Kilmer Road, then go southwest to:

56. The Joyce Kilmer Memorial Forest, a magnificent virgin forest of enormous trees, some over 100 feet tall, some more than 20 feet in circumference, and some more than 400 years old. Miles of trails wind through 3,800 acres of these natural giants, affording a close-up experience you will never forget. Picnic tables and restrooms are provided at the trailhead parking area.

Return to NC 1127/NC 1134, then go north on NC 1134 to:

57. Horse Cove Campground, USDA Forest Service, offering tent and trailer camping, restrooms, fishing, and hiking.

Return to NC 1127, then drive 12 miles southeast to:

Robbinsville, North Carolina

The Robbinsville Rescue Squad invites you to visit in late April for the Ramp Festival, centered around eating ramps, a bitter herb stronger than either onions or garlic.

The Heritage Festival, held in early July on the courthouse lawn, pays tribute to war veterans, followed by a parade, a duck race, and other festivities.

58. The Graham County Chamber of Commerce is located at 72 Main Street. A sales gallery for local craftspeople is a special feature at this office. 828-479-3790 or 800-470-3790.

59. The Grave of Chief Junaluska, a prominent Cherokee chief credited with saving the life of Andrew Jackson, is located in Robbinsville (follow signs in front of the courthouse). Junaluska was exiled to Oklahoma in 1838, but walked all the way back to Graham County, where he was given a farm and made a citizen of North Carolina.

60. The Cheoah Ranger District Office, USDA Forest Service, near US 129 on NC 1116, north of Robbinsville, provides information on many Forest Service facilities in the Nantahala National Forest. This office also offers hiking trails, picnicking, boating, and a fitness/jogging trail. 828-479-6431.

Drive 10 miles northeast on NC 143 to NC 28, then go 5.5 miles east on NC 28 to

Forest Service Road 521. Go 1.5 miles north on FSR 521 to:

61. The Tsali Recreation Area, a USDA Forest Service facility, featuring camping spaces for tents and trailers, showers, restrooms, drinking water, a boat ramp, fishing, hiking, horse trails, and a bike trail.

Return to NC 28, then drive 5.5 miles east to US 19/US 74 and the start of:

62. The Nantahala Gorge. This gorgeous stretch of highway runs parallel to the famous Nantahala River as it winds its way down through the mountains. More than 250,000 whitewater enthusiasts come to this spectacular place every year to engage in rafting, canoeing, kayaking, fishing, hiking, horseback riding, and much more.

Travel about 8 miles southwest on US 19/US 74 through the Nantahala Gorge to:

63. The Ferebee Memorial Recreation Area, offering picnic tables with grills, restrooms, and a launching area for canoes, rafts, and kayaks.

Continue for about 4 miles southwest on US 19/US 74 to NC 1310 at the **Nantahala River Launch Site.** Drive 2.9 miles southeast on NC 1310 to:

64. Camp Branch Falls. Located near NC 1310, the combination of this waterfall and the Nantahala River is an inspiring sight.

Drive 16 miles southeast on NC 1310 to Forest Service Road 69. **Note: this is a steep gravel road that may not be suitable for some vehicles.** Travel about 1.4 miles north to:

65. The Wilson Lick Historic Site, the first ranger station built in the Nantahala National Forest in 1916. Historical displays are featured.

19-4 Rafters in the Nantahala Gorge — Photo Courtesy of the
Swain County Tourist Development Authority

Continue northeast on Forest Service Road 69 for about 3 miles to:

66. Wayah Bald, at 5342 feet, quite a spectacular place to view an area from Tennessee to South Carolina and Georgia. This mountain top is especially beautiful in June when azaleas bloom in wild profusion. Features include the historic **Wayah Bald Fire Tower,** circa 1930's, and places to picnic.

Return to NC 1310, then travel 9 miles east to Old Murphy Road (NC 1442). Go 0.3 miles south on NC 1442 to US 64, then go 5 miles east on US 64, then US 23/US 441 to downtown Franklin and NC 28. Drive 20 miles northwest on NC 28 to US 19 at Lauada. Go 6 miles northeast of US 19 to:

Bryson City, North Carolina

Visit Bryson City in late May for Riverfest, held at Riverfront Park. River raft rides and races, arts and crafts, good food, and live entertainment are features.

Freedom Fest, held at the town square on the Fourth of July, offers a 5K race, food, and entertainment.

Firemen's Day, in early September, features mountain music, other entertainment, barbeque meals, arts and crafts, and much more.

67.   The Swain County Chamber of Commerce and Visitors' Centre is located at 16 Everette Street. 828-488-3681 or 800-867-9246.

68. The Bryson City Island Park, reached by a swinging bridge across the Tuckasegee River, is a winner of the Park of the Year award by the State of North Carolina. Drive north on Everette Street across the river to Island Street, then go east on Island Street to

Bryson Street and the parking lot for the park. Features include a hiking trail, picnic facilities, and a place to launch canoes or kayaks.

Drive 10 miles northeast on US 19 to:

Cherokee, North Carolina

The Fourth of July Pow Wow and Fireworks Display is held annually at the Cherokee Ceremonial Grounds.

Visit Cherokee in early October for the Cherokee Indian Fair, a five-day celebration at the Cherokee Ceremonial Grounds.

69. The Cherokee Visitor Center, on US 19/US 441 BUS, provides information about the large variety of activities and attractions available in the Cherokee area. 828-497-9195 or 800-438-1601.

70. The Museum of the Cherokee Indian, on US 441 at Drama Road, is a major repository of artifacts, books, and other materials relating to Cherokee history and culture. Extensive exhibits, described as the finest and most diverse in the United States, and a large gift shop are noteworthy features.

71. The Qualla Arts and Crafts Mutual, across the street from the Museum, is a Native American owned and operated arts and crafts cooperative.   More than 300 Cherokee craftspeople are represented. Demonstrations of basket weaving, beadwork, and wood carving are featured.

72. The Oconaluftee Indian Village, on Drama Road, is a re-creation of a 1790's Cherokee community, where guides explain pottery making, basket weaving, and other native skills and crafts.

19-5 Mingo Falls — Photo courtesy of the
Cherokee Tribal Travel and
Promotion Office

73. The Outdoor Drama, *Unto These Hills,* is presented during the summer season at the Mountainside Theater on Drama Road. The history of the Cherokee people from the time of Hernando deSoto (1540s) through the exile in 1838 is portrayed. Ask at the Welcome Center for show dates and times.

From the Visitors Center, drive about 2 miles north on Acquoni Road, then Big Cove Road to:

74. The Cherokee Heritage Museum and Gallery. This museum features displays of Cherokee art and cultural items and maintains a gallery of Indian crafts and art.

Continue about 5 miles northeast on Big Cove Road to:

75. Mingo Falls. Falling more than 150 feet, this magnificent waterfall is one of the most beautiful in North Carolina.

Return to Cherokee, then go 12 miles east on US 19 to the Blue Ridge Parkway, Milepost 455.7 at Soco Gap.

Smoky Mountains NC/TN
Fontana Lake, NC
Cherokee, NC

ROUTE 20

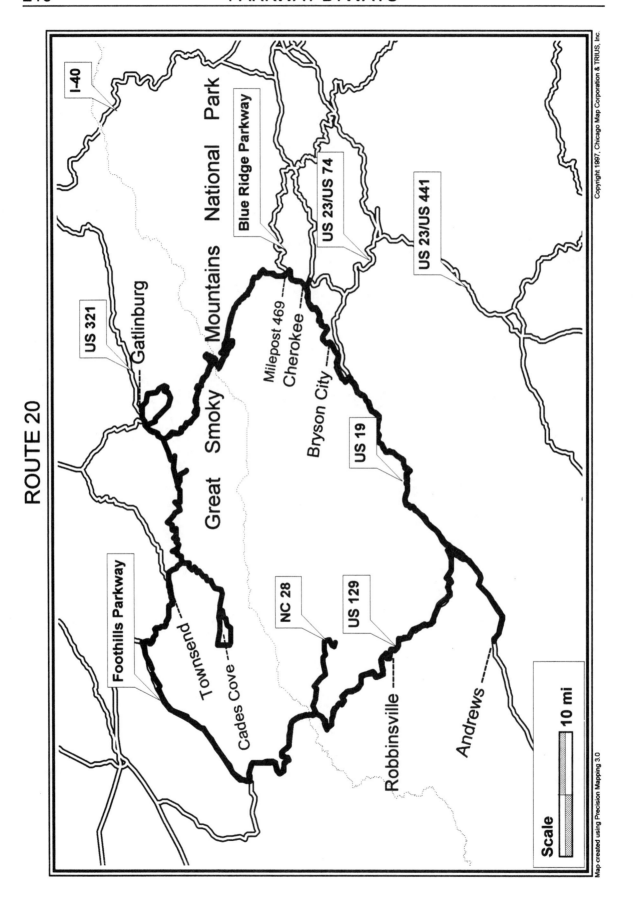

Great Smoky Mountains National Park

Blue Ridge Parkway

I-40

US 23/US 74

US 23/US 441

US 321

Gatlinburg

Milepost 469

Cherokee

Bryson City

US 19

Foothills Parkway

Townsend

Cades Cove

NC 28

US 129

Robbinsville

Andrews

Scale

10 mi

The **Smoky Mountains - Fontana Lake - Cherokee Route** tours the North Carolina counties of Swain and Graham and the Tennessee counties of Sevier and Blount. It is about 250 miles long. Although the byways are quite different, the attractions listed for Robbinsville, Bryson City, and Cherokee can also be visited on Route 19. This trip starts and ends at Milepost 469 on the Blue Ridge Parkway near Cherokee, North Carolina.

THE BYWAYS —

Route 20 starts with one of the most frequently traveled recreational highways in the United States, US 441 from Cherokee, North Carolina, to Gatlinburg, Tennessee. This great trip bisects the Great Smoky Mountains National Park, reaching more than 6,000 feet in elevation in the process. The views in every direction are breathtaking, and deserve your undivided attention. For this reason and because the highway is so popular, weekends and holidays should be avoided if possible. Also be sure to allow plenty of time, whatever day you do travel; you're sure to have a lot of company, including many cars, people, and probably a few bears.

Route 20 continues with an idyllic passage along the fabulous Little River, then around the valley of Cades Cove. Also heavily traveled, this is an inspiring trip, showcasing some of the most attractive natural environments you will ever see. The contrast between the grand panoramic vistas along US 441 and the intimate experiences along the river and in the valley is remarkable.

Getting back to panoramic vistas, the next part of your trip is on the Foothills Parkway. Still another highway

dedicated to recreational driving, the Parkway runs along a ridge north of and paralleling the western part of the Smokies, thus affording a southern grandstand view of the towering mountains. Views of the Tennessee Valley to the northwest are quite different but equally interesting.

NC 28 toward Fontana Dam and US 129 toward Robbinsville are part of the NC Indian Lakes Scenic Byway. Beautiful lakes, streams, and rivers with mountain backdrops are the focus of attention along these highways.

The last section of Route 20 features a trip through the Nantahala Gorge on US 19/US 74. Part of the NC Nantahala Byway, and a favorite destination of whitewater fans, this extraordinary river is host to more than 250,000 of them every year. Millions more drive through on the scenic highway.

THE TOWNS —

Cherokee and Gatlinburg and, to a lesser extent, Bryson City and Townsend, offer the attractions of commercial tourism in a big way, catering to the millions of people who visit the Great Smoky Mountains National Park. Motels, restaurants, gift shops, arts and crafts stores, and many kinds of entertainment are available in great profusion. Cherokee also presents Indian history and culture in several well-run museums.

Robbinsville and Andrews are much quieter towns, relying on tourism to some extent, but also interested in the business affairs of their area. Robbinsville is the county seat of Graham County.

THE ATTRACTIONS —

From the end of the Parkway, drive north on US 441 to:

1. The Oconaluftee Visitors Center and the Pioneer Farm Museum. The Visitors Center is the North Carolina source of information about the Great Smoky Mountains National Park. Stop here to learn about activities, accommodations, campgrounds, and regulations, and to get maps, brochures, and books. The Mountain Farm Museum features demonstrations of what a local mountain farm would have been like a century ago.

Drive about 0.5 miles north on US 441 to:

2. The Mingus Mill, where you can see costumed attendants grind corn and wheat into cornmeal and flour.

Continue for about 3 miles north on US 441 to:

3. Smokemont Campground. Features include sites for tents, trailers, and RV's: a disposal station, picnic tables, drinking water, fireplaces, restrooms, wood for sale, naturalist programs, fishing, and horses for rent. There are no showers or trailer/RV hookups.

20-1 Pioneer Farm Museum — Photo courtesy of the
Cherokee Tribal Travel and Promotion Office

Drive about 12 miles northwest on US 441 to Clingman's Dome Road, then go about 7 miles west to:

4. Clingman's Dome. You are on top of the world here, at 6643 feet elevation. A half-mile trail leads to the **Clingman's Dome Observation Tower,** where the magnificent views are unsurpassed in every direction.

Return to US 441, then drive about 13 miles northwest to:

5. The Sugarlands Visitor Center, the park's most complete and comprehensive information and merchandise center. Official information is available here on backcountry permits, ranger programs, wildflowers, and waterfalls. You can also obtain park newspapers, hiking maps, videos, camera film, books, mountain music tapes, and much, much more. Check out the exhibits of animals in native habitats.

Travel 3 miles northeast on US 441 to:

Gatlinburg, Tennessee

The Annual Spring Wildflower Pilgrimage, held in late April and the Scottish Festival of Games, celebrated in mid-May, are two of Gatlinburg's favorite festivals. Ask about others at the Chamber of Commerce on the Parkway.

6.   The Gatlinburg Department of Tourism maintains two welcome centers in downtown Gatlinburg, one at 234 Airport Road (traffic light #8) and another at 520 Parkway (traffic light #3). Friendly attendants at either of these centers will tell you about Gatlinburg's many commercial attractions, restaurants, and places to stay. For telephone information, call 423-436-2892 or 800-267-7088.

7.   The Roaring Fork Motor Nature Trail. Follow Airport Road (traffic light #8) to the Cherokee Orchard entrance to the park, then continue on Cherokee Orchard Road to the Rainbow Falls trailhead. Turn here onto the one-way Motor Nature Trail. A paved road winds for six miles through forests, waterfalls, and mountain streams, ending on US 321 in Gatlinburg. Busses, travel trailers, and motor homes are not allowed on this road.

Return to the Sugarlands Visitor Center on US 441, then drive about 5 miles southwest on Little River Road (TN 73) to Elkmont. Go southeast on Elkmont road to:

8.   Elkmont Campground. Facilities include tent, trailer, and RV sites; drinking water, fireplaces, picnic tables, and restrooms; places to fish and naturalist programs.   There are no showers or trailer/RV hookups.

Return to Little River Road, then drive about 12 miles west to Cades Cove Road. Travel about 8 miles southwest on Cades Cove to:

9. Cades Cove Loop Road, a picturesque eleven-mile loop road through one of the most beautiful places in the park. This road circles a large open valley of fields and meadows tucked in among the towering mountains. An auto tour booklet, published by the Great Smoky Mountains Natural History Association, and available at the start of the loop road, provides a lot of information about the area. Several buildings once used by the residents have been preserved and now stand as mute testimony of the heritage of this unusual area. Visit the **Cable Mill,** a water-powered grist mill, which demonstrates how cornmeal was made. A Visitors Center at the mill site offers information and restrooms.

20-2 Little River Railroad and Lumber Company Museum —
Photo courtesy of the Smoky Mountain Visitors Bureau

10. The Cades Cove Campground features sites for tents, trailers, and RV's; drinking water, fireplaces, picnic tables, and flush toilets; a sewage disposal station, groceries, horses and bicycles for rent, places to fish, and wood for sale. There are no showers or hookups.

Return to TN 73, then go about 4 miles northwest to:

Townsend, Tennessee

The Townsend in the Smokies Spring Festival and Old Timers Day, a nine-day celebration held in late April and early May is a special occasion for residents and visitors alike.

Late September brings the Townsend Heritage Festival and Old Timers Day along with Autumn Leaves Arts and Craft Show.

11. The Smoky Mountain Visitor's Bureau is located at 7906 East Lamar Alexander Parkway (US 321). 423-448-6134 or 800-525-6834.

12. The Little River Railroad and Lumber Company Museum, located on US 321, features a restored locomotive, a railroad depot, a steam sawmill, and a collection of railroad/lumber company artifacts and memorabilia.

Drive 6.4 miles northwest on US 321 to:

13. The Foothills Parkway, providing a series of fabulous views of the Smoky Mountains to the southeast and of the Tennessee Valley, northwest toward Maryville and Knoxville. This recreational highway runs along a ridge that is elevated above the surrounding countryside and which opens up the dramatic views.

Drive about 17 miles southwest on the Foothill Parkway to US 129 at Chilhowee Lake. Travel 14 miles southeast on US 129 (crossing into North Carolina) to NC 28, then go 11 miles east on NC 28 to NC 1245. Drive 1.4 miles north on NC 1245 to:

14.   The Fontana Dam and Visitors Center. This 480-foot high dam, the highest dam east of the Rockies, was built to provide electricity for military production at Oak Ridge, Tennessee. It was started on January 1, 1942, only 24 days after Pearl Harbor. Views of the lake and river below from the Visitors Center are quite impressive. A special feature is a tram railroad car that travels to the base of the dam providing a totally different perspective of the giant structure.

Return to US 129 on NC 28, then go about 11 miles southeast on US 129 to NC 1146. Drive south to:

15.   Cheoah Point Recreation Area, a USDA Forest Service facility offering tent and trailer camping, picnic tables, restrooms, a boat ramp, fishing, and hiking trails. While in the area, visit **Santeetlah Dam,** operated by Tapoco, Inc.

Return to US 129, then travel 6 miles southeast to NC 1116. Go southwest on NC 1116 to:

16.   The Cheoah Ranger District Office, USDA Forest Service, which provides information on the many facilities and services in the Nantahala National Forest. This office also offers hiking trails, picnicking, boating, and a fitness/jogging trail. 828-479-9706.

Return to US 129, then drive south to:

Robbinsville, North Carolina

The Robbinsville Rescue Squad invites you to visit in late April for the Ramp Festival, centered around eating ramps, a bitter herb stronger than either onions or garlic.

The Heritage Festival, held in early July on the courthouse lawn, pays tribute to war veterans, followed by a parade, a duck race, and other festivities.

17.   The Graham County Chamber of Commerce is located at 72 Main Street. A sales gallery for local craftspeople is a special feature at this office. 828-479-3790 or 800-470-3790.

18.   The Grave of Chief Junaluska, a prominent Cherokee chief credited with saving the life of Andrew Jackson, is located in Robbinsville (follow signs in front of the courthouse). Junaluska was exiled to Oklahoma in 1838, but walked all the way back to Graham County, where he was given a farm and made a citizen of North Carolina.

Drive 12 miles northwest on NC 1127 to Joyce Kilmer Road, then go southwest to:

19. The Joyce Kilmer Memorial Forest, a magnificent virgin forest of enormous trees, some over 100 feet tall, some more than 20 feet in circumference, and some more than 400 years old. Miles of trails wind through 3,800 acres of these natural giants, affording a close-up experience you will never forget. Picnic tables and restrooms are provided at the trailhead parking area.

Return to NC 1127/NC 1134, then go north on NC 1134 to:

20. Horse Cove Campground, USDA Forest Service, offering tent and trailer camping, restrooms, fishing, and hiking.

Return to NC 1127, then drive 12 miles southeast to Robbinsville. Travel 11 miles southeast on US 129 to US 19/US 74, then go 9 miles southwest of US 19/US 74 to:

Andrews, North Carolina

The Valley River Festival, held in early July, features family, community, and class reunions, along with church homecomings. These events share excitement with the Andrews Summer Celebration, which offers live musical entertainment and a gigantic fireworks display.

21. The Andrews Chamber of Commerce is at the corner of First and Locust Streets in the Andrews Depot. 828-321-3584

Drive 11 miles northeast on US 19/US 74 to:

22. The Nantahala Gorge. This gorgeous stretch of highway runs parallel to the famous Nantahala River as it winds its way down through the mountains. More than 250,000 whitewater enthusiasts come to this spectacular place every year to engage in rafting, canoeing, kayaking, fishing, hiking, horseback riding, and much more. The **Nantahala River Launch Site** is located at the beginning of the gorge on NC 1310.

Drive about 4 miles northeast on US 19/US 74 to:

23. The Ferebee Memorial Recreation Area, offering picnic tables with grills, restrooms, and a launching area for canoes, rafts, and kayaks.

Travel about 17 miles northeast on US 19/US 74 to:

Bryson City, North Carolina

Visit Bryson City in late May for Riverfest, held at Riverfront Park. River raft rides and races, arts and crafts, good food, and live entertainment are features.

Freedom Fest, held at the town square on the Fourth of July, offers a 5K race, food, and entertainment.

Firemen's Day, in early September, features mountain music, other entertainment, barbeque meals, arts and crafts, and much more.

24. The Swain County Chamber of Commerce and Visitors' Centre is located at 16 Everette Street. 828-488-3681 or 800-867-9246.

25. The Bryson City Island Park, reached by a swinging bridge across the Tuckasegee River, is a winner of the Park of the Year award by the State of North Carolina. Drive north on Everette Street across the river to Island Street, then go east on Island Street to Bryson Street and the parking lot for the park. Features include a hiking trail, picnic facilities, and a place to launch canoes or kayaks.

Drive 10 miles northeast on US 19 to:

Cherokee, North Carolina

The Fourth of July Pow Wow and Fireworks Display is held annually at the Cherokee Ceremonial Grounds.

Visit Cherokee in early October for the Cherokee Indian Fair, a five-day celebration at the Cherokee Ceremonial Grounds.

26. The Cherokee Visitor Center, on US 19/US 441 BUS, provides information about the large variety of activities and attractions available in the Cherokee area. 828-497-9195 or 800-438-1601.

27. The Museum of the Cherokee Indian, on US 441 at Drama Road, is a major repository of artifacts, books, and other materials relating to Cherokee history and culture. Extensive exhibits, described as the finest and most diverse in the United States, and a large gift shop are noteworthy features.

20-3 Statue of Sequoyah, inventor of the Cherokee alphabet. The statue is located in front of the Museum of the Cherokee Indian — Photo courtesy of the Cherokee Tribal Travel and Promotion Office.

28. The Qualla Arts and Crafts Mutual, across the street from the Museum, is an Indian owned and operated arts and crafts cooperative. More than 300 Cherokee craftspeople are represented. Demonstrations of basket weaving, beadwork, and wood carving are featured.

29. The Oconaluftee Indian Village, on Drama Road, is a re-creation of a 1790s Cherokee community, where guides explain pottery making, basket weaving, and other native skills and crafts.

30. The Outdoor Drama, *Unto These Hills,* is presented during the summer season at the Mountainside Theater on Drama Road. The history of the Cherokee people from the time of Hernando deSoto (1540's) through the exile in 1838 is portrayed. Ask at the Welcome Center for show dates and times.

From the Visitors Center, drive about 2 miles north on Acquoni Road, then Big Cove Road to:

31. The Cherokee Heritage Museum and Gallery. This museum features displays of Cherokee art and cultural items and maintains a gallery of Native American crafts and art.

Continue about 5 miles northeast on Big Cove Road to:

32. Mingo Falls. Falling more than 150 feet, this magnificent waterfall is one of the most beautiful in Western North Carolina.

Return on Big Cove Road past the Parkway to the next road to the right. Cross the bridge over the Oconaluftee River to US 441, then drive north to the Parkway, Milepost 469.

Adams, Kevin. *North Carolina Waterfalls - Where to Find Them - How to Photograph Them.* John F. Blair, 1994.

Adkins, Leonard M. *Walking the Blue Ridge.* University of North Carolina Press, 1994.

American Automobile Association. *Georgia, North Carolina, South Carolina, 1996.*

American Automobile Association. *Mid-Atlantic, 1977.*

Bannon, James. *North Carolina - A Guide to Backcountry Travel and Adventure.* Out There Press, 1996.

Bledsoe, Jerry. *Blue Horizons.* Down Home Press, 1993.

Chaff, Lin and Jones, Wendy Price. *The Insiders Guide to Virginia's Blue Ridge.* Richmond Times Dispatch and The Insiders' Guides, Inc., 1996.

Fields, Jay and Campbell, Brad. *The Craft Heritage Trails of Western North Carolina.* Handmade in America, Inc., 1996.

Houck, Peter W., Editor. *Tour Lynchburg.* Warwick House Publishing, 1994.

Johnson, Randy. *Hiking North Carolina.* Falcon Press, 1996.

Johnson, Randy. *Hiking Virginia.* Falcon Press, 1996.

Lord, William G. *Blue Ridge Parkway Guide.* 2 Volumes. Menasha, 1981.

North Carolina Department of Transportation. *North Carolina Scenic Byways, 1997*

Pacher, Sara and McDaniel, Lynda. *The Insiders' Guide to North Carolina's Mountains.* Knight Publishing Company, Inc. and The Insiders' Guides, Inc., 1996.

Reader's Digest Association, Inc. *The Most Scenic Drives in America, 1997*

Skinner, Elizabeth and Charlie. *Bicycling the Blue Ridge.* Menasha, 1990.

If you had a secret, would you tell?

The author of *Parkway Byways*, Jim Hinkel, has driven more than 200,000 miles over the less-traveled winding roads along the Blue Ridge Parkway. This book shares his favorite "secret places" -- picturesque towns, historic sites, parks, museums, galleries, etc. -- along 5,000 miles of the most scenic back roads in America.

There are a number of guidebooks which tell about things to see and do *on* the Parkway. This book is different; it tells the visitor about interesting attractions *off* the Parkway, describing 19 "loop trips" extending into the countryside. Attractions featured are non-commercial, free or low-cost, and are family oriented. The emphasis is on entertaining, educational, and economical visits to beautiful mountain towns and landscapes. Discover leisurely drives, breathtaking waterfalls and covered bridges. Have fun!

Whether you are a visitor in search of the perfect secluded camping or picnic spot, a busy professional seeking weekend tranquility, or a weary traveler just passing through, Jim's *Parkway Byways* will show you a world most of us thought was gone forever. Enjoy every mile and every minute!

Use this coupon and we will waive shipping charges!